# WOMEN

## THE RISE AND FALL *of*

# MONEY

## ECONOMIC EQUALITY

# POWER

Josie Cox

ABRAMS PRESS, NEW YORK

To Livi

I ask no favors for my sex. I surrender not our claim to equality. All I ask of our brethren is, that they will take their feet from off our necks.

—Sarah Grimké

Neither working for someone nor paying someone's wages ought to give you power over them.

—Mary Parker Follett

The principle which regulates the existing social relations between the two sexes—the legal subordination of one sex to the other—is wrong in itself, and now one of the chief hindrances to human improvement; and . . . it ought to be replaced by a principle of perfect equality, admitting no power or privilege on the one side, nor disability on the other.

—John Stuart Mill

# Contents

# PROLOGUE

*Some Women Just Don't Want To*

In early February 2021, I spoke to one of the most powerful men in America. Throughout my career, I'd put in several requests to interview him. Most had been ignored; none had been granted. So I didn't push back when the CEO of this Fortune 500 company agreed to the conversation with me and a small handful of other journalists but stipulated that he would only do so on the condition of strict anonymity: We could ask him anything we wanted, but our exchange was to go no further.

Since we were confined to our homes because of COVID-19, our heads popped up on-screen at the agreed-upon time, he with his all-smiles spokesperson in tow. We introduced ourselves and exchanged easy pleasantries about the state of pandemic-ridden America and the recent end to the tumultuous Trump era. He offered an unsolicited interpretation of something peculiar that had happened in stock markets that day, to which I responded with feigned interest and a polite laugh. Then, with the mood established—convivial but not overly familiar, amicable but certainly professional—I deemed the moment appropriate to launch into the questions I'd waited a long time to ask.

"Congratulations on your initiative to hire more women," I began, consulting my imaginary notes to calm my nerves. He nodded graciously, perhaps excited by the prospect of an opportunity to impress his colleague from the public relations department with a pitch about diversity. "But I do have one concern."

The truth was that I'd been ruminating on this concern for years. Despite high-profile efforts by some of the world's biggest corporations to create equal opportunities and equal representation for different genders within the workplace, businesses globally—and especially those in sectors such as finance—remained stubbornly skewed, predominantly led by white men and blighted by an undeniable pay gap that, in the majority of cases, was not diminishing. In the worst examples, a culture of toxic masculinity prevailed.

The company run by this particular CEO was no exception. Despite purported attempts at closing a considerable gender pay gap—defined as the difference in the average annual compensation of male and female employees—progress had been sluggish at best. Unlike the United States, the United Kingdom has since 2017 required by law all businesses employing at least 250 people to publicly disclose their gender pay gaps. This CEO's company was headquartered in the United States but had British operations, so I had combed through its most recent state-mandated gender pay gap reports in preparation for our conversation.

"It doesn't look great," I now understatedly informed him, referring to the fact that his business's overall double-digit pay gap in the United Kingdom had not contracted by even a single percentage point over the last couple of years. In vain, I tried to keep anger from seeping into my now slightly quavering voice. "I'm assuming this is a decent proxy for what's going on elsewhere in your company. Can you explain why you're not doing better?"

This CEO is profoundly intelligent. No one makes it to the highest echelons of corporate America without a vast knowledge base. He's tremendously well-educated and possesses an ability to negotiate astutely and make brilliant decisions under formidable pressure. But on that Tuesday afternoon as we sat—pixelated face to pixelated face—he revealed an ignorance, authentic or not, that stunned me to the core.

"The gender pay gap has many causes, Josie," he began, as if preparing to walk me through the peculiarities of a complex financial product. Most important, he assured me, his company always paid women and men the same amount of money for the same work.

I interjected. Doing otherwise, I explained, would—under the Equal Pay Act of 1963—quite simply be illegal.

But he continued without acknowledging my remark. "And the other thing you have to understand, Josie," he charged on, now a little more pointedly, "is that sometimes, when a woman temporarily leaves the workforce to have a baby, she doesn't *want* to be promoted when she comes back. Some women just don't want to." In the seconds of silence that followed I glanced to the other side of my computer screen to see his PR rep frantically taking notes. The CEO was looking at me anticipatorily.

Academically, of course I know all about the attitudes and preconceptions that people foster about gender in the workplace. I've written and reported on the subject intently and for years. But whenever it's presented to me in situ and in the grotesque and undeniable detail that it was on that day, it hits me afresh. Undoubtedly, there's some truth to what the CEO said. Sometimes a woman's priorities really do shift singularly after she has a child. Indeed, my own personal experience substantiates this. I quit my newsroom staff job in 2018 after my daughter was born. My employer was not able—or willing—to offer me the flexibility that I wanted and that made sense financially, considering the cost of childcare. But it was astonishing that, as my interlocutor cast around for a quick explanation for why the gender pay gap was so cavernous within his firm, the first thing he landed on was women's choice. It was as if he was trying to absolve himself of any responsibility in the matter.

In the weeks that followed, this exchange, and particularly the CEO's comment in response to my question about pay, preoccupied me. Over the last century, plenty of legislation has been passed that ostensibly affords women equal status in American society: The Equal Pay Act of 1963, the Civil Rights Act the following year, and Title IX in 1972 represent perhaps the most obvious examples. Yet inequity between genders is rampant. And that's even before accounting for factors like race. The long-established infrastructures, parameters, norms, and ideals that we live by inhibit the power of the law to an extent that few of us can even appreciate, because it's what we've always known. The CEO's beliefs about what women want were a prime example of that.

And so, a few weeks after that exchange, I set out to begin a journey back in time. Think of this book as a travelog through the rise and fall of gender equality in America. Through the lives of famous trailblazers but also of unsung heroes—women who dedicated their lives to female economic empowerment but who largely don't feature in history books or on school syllabuses—I wanted to understand how we got here. I wanted to establish who effected meaningful change, how they overcame challenges and setbacks, and what ultimately went wrong; why, fifty and sixty years ago, progress seemed abundant with promise and why now, in 2024, it appears to have stalled so dramatically. Chronologically, we've moved forward, but in many ways we've stumbled backward. The answers that I found are complex and inconvenient; they're both concrete and abstract, logical but also, in some cases, wildly counterintuitive.

Starting with the women who broke with social norms by joining the paid labor market during World War II, this book will chronicle the most influential cultural, political, and legal developments of the twentieth century as they relate to women's efforts to secure the opportunities they deserved to make money and to exercise power over their own lives and decisions. It will tell the stories of women's fight for birth control, for employment rights, and for acceptance in every realm of society. It will document how women broke into the finance industry, an elite bastion of swashbuckling masculinity that, to this day, remains a breeding ground for discrimination and sexism. And then it will examine why, in the 1990s, after decades of progress, momentum began to slow and, by some measures, stop altogether. The gender pay gap, one of the most intractable examples of a lack of economic parity between genders, has hardly budged for years.

Money and, by extension, power, remain stubbornly gendered. The blame for that lies everywhere, and the effects of it are everywhere too. It's easy to look away from the most uncomfortable truths, to ignore them or to gloss over them with explanations—like the CEO's—that don't pass muster. But we all have a duty to resist that impulse. To that end, this book is an attempt—from my particular vantage point—to make sense of it all, to shed light on the mistakes we've made in the past so that they are not repeated in future. There's simply too much at stake.

A short note on the scope of this book and its limitations. It would be impossible to write a single coherent and comprehensive book on the vast topic of systemic economic inequality in America, even solely through the lens of gender. There are simply too many ways in which inequality becomes manifest. It would be impossible to accurately document the headwinds faced by every single person who is disadvantaged or victimized by the mechanism and trappings of this country's economic system. For one thing, there's a lack of research on the lived experiences of certain demographic groups—individuals who are not white and cisgender, for example. That is both a cause and a consequence of inequalities that shape this nation.

Although it is critical that we understand the challenges faced by America's most marginalized, this book could never do that adequately. I have neither the resources nor the knowledge nor the experience nor the cultural and social perspective to take on the responsibility of doing that all-important work. As such, this book is inherently limited to making generalizations that speak, in large part, to the experience of a particular section of society. Nonetheless, my hope is that it will form part of an eventually extensive body of work that, when taken together, can begin to paint a true picture of the devastating scale and scope of economic inequality in the United States. This book is my contribution, to the best of my ability and judgement. So much more still has to be done.

## CHAPTER 1

### *Was Rosie the Riveter Robbed?*

Keeps a sharp lookout for sabotage,
Sitting up there on the fuselage.
That little girl will do more than a male will do.
——"Rosie the Riveter," by Redd Evans and John Jacob Loeb, 1942

"Isn't memory maddening?" says Anna Mae Krier on an unseasonably warm afternoon in late October 2021 as she struggles to decipher the numbers strewn across a pay stub that's dated April 1945, making it much older than the town in which she lives.

Krier lives alone in Levittown, Pennsylvania, a planned community in Bucks County northeast of Philadelphia where each house resembles the next, save for a varying array of political flags and garden gnomes that flank the front doors and porches. Krier can call to mind with visceral clarity the potent mix of fear and shock she felt the first time she ever saw her father cry, for example—it was 1941, and her brother had just boarded a train for the Second World War—but she can't for the life of her remember whether or not she bought Coca-Cola at the grocery store yesterday. Or what she did with that letter she once received from Barack Obama commending her on the work she's doing to get women's wartime efforts recognized more widely. "I'm walking history," she says as she stretches out a stiff hip that's been aching since she mowed the lawn the previous day. "But I'm also running out of time. I need to tell my story before it's too late."

Krier is ninety-five years old. Her life so far has spanned the terms of seventeen presidents, of whom Franklin Delano Roosevelt—she concludes after some consideration—was probably her favorite. She has eight great grandchildren and three great-great grandchildren. Norm, her husband of almost seven decades, died in 2014, and she frequently sits in the comfortable chair in the living room by the urn containing his ashes and asks for advice or just talks about her day. "He always was, and still is, a great listener."

In the morning, Krier usually drinks coffee in her garden—often two cups—and talks to whoever might be listening, even if it's just the nervous sparrows and the changing trees. She runs errands in her red Chevrolet pickup truck. Her grandkids laugh at the fact that the windows still need to be wound down manually. A few times a week, Krier tends to her yard and to her neighbors' yard when they're on vacation. Every day—twice on most days—her son Norm Jr. checks in. He lives just down the road, but at the age of seventy-four, he's starting to find even the short trip to his mother's house a little taxing.

If daily routines lay the tracks for Krier's life to keep moving forward, then it's her history, and specifically her determination for that history to be recognized, that provides the fuel. "When we Rosies entered the workforce—as riveters, like me, or as something else—we took a giant step for women of the day, but also for women of future generations," she says, now nibbling on a chicken salad sandwich. "We showed everyone what's possible, that women and men are equal and should be treated as such. But what did we get in return? Not that much," she sighs with a little shrug. "And that's what I'm going to change. That's what we all need to be fighting for."

\*\*\*

Anna Mae Burkett was born on March 21, 1926, in the tiny farming community of Dawson, North Dakota, just as the Midwest was thawing out after yet another punishing winter. She was the great granddaughter of Austrian immigrants who, four decades earlier, lured by the promise of amber waves of grain, had pioneered the Dakota Territory in covered wagons. Later, Mae—as she was only ever known—would joke that her ancestors never would have made the trip if they had known that they would "freeze their butts off."

Dewey Burkett, Mae's father, operated grain elevators, while her mother, Lyla, brought home a meager salary from the catering jobs she picked up around town when she wasn't looking after the children. Mae and her siblings worked hard at school and were popular. They were happy kids who lived for the evenings of spirited discussions around the family's dinner table, as well as the stories about the moon and stars that their father regaled them with as they huddled in front of the stove before bed.

But the image of familial harmony projected by the Burketts belied the struggles that most Dakotans at the time were facing. The state was in crisis. During World War I, prices for commodities like wheat and beef had soared considerably above the cost of production, yielding a windfall for landowners. As peace dawned, those prices fell rapidly. By 1930, farmers were pocketing just sixty cents for a bushel of wheat that cost seventy-seven cents to produce. In the late 1920s, a drought had also set in that severely limited crop and hay production. Across the Southern Plains, the era of the Dust Bowl dawned, a time of high winds and choking storms that swept from Texas to Canada. Farmers jostled to sell more goods to compensate for lower market prices, but they couldn't grow enough to balance the books. At the same time, counties were hiking taxes on property and farmland. A farm that was worth forty-one dollars per acre in 1920 was by 1940 worth just thirteen. Eventually, like dominoes falling, farmers started defaulting on loans en masse, forcing banks out of business. All the while, the drought endured, and incomes fell, driving thousands of households to quit the Midwest in search of more promising pastures and a more fulfilling version of that mythical American Dream.

When Mae was fifteen years old, the world shifted on its axis. On December 7, 1941, not long before 8:00 A.M, hundreds of Japanese aircraft launched a massive attack on a Hawaiian port, claiming the lives of some 2,400 Americans. Mae, a curious girl with a general interest in politics, had been following the developments of the hitherto faraway war. That afternoon, she had attended a matinee with her older sister, Lyola. When they arrived home, they found their parents speechless at the family's radio, their pale faces etched with expressions of alarm. She knew immediately that something was very wrong, but before that day, Mae had no idea what or where Pearl Harbor was.

Within weeks, North Dakota's depleted population, reeling from the plight of the previous decade, became even smaller. Thousands of young men enlisted almost immediately, including Mae's brother Duane, her uncle, and several cousins. The family was horrified by the palpable risk of losing loved ones to war, but they kept working hard. Mae's mother Lyla, whose brother had been a postal worker before enlisting, started delivering mail in his stead—something that Mae admired deeply, even at that time. Mae herself was determined to finish school; education, her parents had taught her, was the bedrock of a successful life.

In 1942, as the anniversary of America's involvement in the war loomed, the parents of Cathy Cooker, one of Mae's closest school friends, joined the throng of Dakotans leaving the region to pursue more promising professional opportunities outside the hobbled state. Cathy's father had been offered a job in Seattle at the headquarters of a corporation called Boeing, but Cathy, like Mae, had set her sights on graduating high school, so she moved in with Mae and her family.

Beyond their educational ambitions, however, the girls were also gripped by a juvenile appetite for adventure, tinged, perhaps, with the slightest sense of civic duty and a naivety common in teenagers. Their brothers, hardly older than they, had joined the global war. Many of their friends had left home to fight. So, in the summer after they graduated, Mae and Cathy, who were both just seventeen, and Lyola, who was just shy of nineteen, boarded a train to Seattle, intending to spend a few months working within the awe-inspiring edifice of the Boeing factory. It would be a lark, Mae thought, and then they'd head back to Dawson and the real world. They had no idea what the work would entail.

\*\*\*

Stories of women valiantly leaving their homes in the 1940s to perform the jobs of men are often framed as examples of victorious female
empowerment, a sign that women had secured agency over their own
lives and decisions and that, after centuries of oppression, they'd finally
found freedom. But at that time, even though women across much of
America had enjoyed two decades of suffrage, they were still, in almost
all respects, lesser citizens than men in the eyes of the law. In many
ways, women were treated as property—as being under the hand of first
their fathers and then their husbands. The custom of bestowing—or
asking for—the hand of a daughter in marriage is just one small but
obvious example. And many of the rights and freedoms that women
had technically obtained by the 1940s were also relatively recent developments. It frequently took decades for laws on paper to make a real
difference in the lived experiences of the individuals to whom they pertained. One prime example: the Nineteenth Amendment to the U.S.
Constitution. Passed in 1919 and ratified in 1920, it granted women the
right to vote, but for decades thereafter, narrow interpretations of the
amendment, as well as impediments and conditions—like literacy tests
and the poll tax—would prevent many poor women, particularly in the
Deep South, from exercising this right.

Well into the twentieth century, the vestiges of a legal practice
called coverture loomed. Based in English law, coverture held that no
female person had an independent legal identity. At birth, a girl was covered by her father's identity and, when she married, by her husband's.
The wedded couple became one identity, and that identity was that of
the man. To symbolize the subsumption, a woman took her husband's
last name—and she became not just Jane Doe but Mrs. John Doe.
"Married women owned nothing, not even the clothes on their backs,"
wrote Catherine Allgor, a former professor of history at the University of
California, Riverside, who later became president of the Massachusetts
Historical Society. "They had no rights to their children, so that if a
wife divorced or left a husband, she would not see her children again."

Under coverture, a woman also had no right to her own body,
which meant that any wages she generated through her own labor

legally belonged to her husband. He had absolute right to sexual access. Through marriage, her consent was implied, perpetually. "His total mastery of this fellow human being stopped short, but just short, of death," Allgor wrote. "Of course, a man wasn't allowed to beat his wife to death, but he could beat her."

Some women did work. In fact, in the 1830s, many mill towns offered enticing opportunities for women to work outside the home and earn some money, as did factories that were springing up in urban spots like New York City, but the conditions were grim and the hours long. Working while also raising a family was impossible for most. Dependable and affordable childcare simply wasn't available. In some areas, women who had children but needed to support themselves financially turned to prostitution. The business hours of a sex worker were shorter and the pay was frequently much better, but ultimately there was a major downside that couldn't be ignored: untreatable sexually transmitted diseases were frequently a death sentence. By one estimate, in the 1850s, a woman working in New York as a prostitute would only survive for an average of four years.

Little by little, throughout the second half of the nineteenth and into the twentieth century, the influence of coverture was eroded. In April 1848, New York passed the Married Women's Property Law, protecting a married woman's personal property and creating a blueprint for legislation in other states. Progress outside the home, however, took time to be replicated within the privacy of a home.

The daughter of abolitionist John Brown, Anne Brown Adams, wrote to a friend in the 1880s to lament that the "struggle for a married woman's right will be a longer and harder fought battle than any other that the world has ever known." She contended that "men have been taught that they are the absolute monarchs in their families." Women, on the other hand, she wrote, "are taught from infancy that to betray by look or word or even to mention to an intimate friend the secrets of their married life is worse than disgraceful." And she concluded that "therein lies the power of the man: He knows that no matter what he does, the woman will keep [as] silent as the grave."

Over the decades that followed, domestic arrangements and the balance of power within a marriage started to shift in accordance with the law. As they gained more individual rights, women also started working in greater numbers. Between 1880 and 1910, the number of women in paid employment across the country rose from about 2.6 million to 7.8 million. But even though women were starting to work in business and industry, the vast majority of better-paying positions still went to men. By the turn of the century, almost two-thirds of women earning money outside the home were employed as domestic servants, and many weren't married. And indeed—as would largely be the case for the next fifty years—society expected a woman to leave the paid workforce as soon as she got married or became pregnant.

In the 1910s and 1920s, and even after the ratification of that all-important Nineteenth Amendment, women remained decidedly inferior citizens. In 1919 a woman named Mira Edson Kohler penned an article in the *New-York Tribune* berating the inequity and specifically the fact that a woman was still treated as little more than an extension of her husband. "The man without a country has been held as one deserving of our sympathy," she wrote. "It is perhaps true of a woman, too—though no one seems to have thought of it."

In 1935, the senate of the state of Wisconsin issued a report arguing that it was unacceptable for a husband and wife both to work for the government. The report noted that unemployment levels were high and that there were, at that time, about six million married women working in the U.S. Of these, the report added, some four million had husbands who were "adequately gainfully employed." If these four million women's jobs were made available, it concluded, that "would bring employment to a normal trend."

Even by the late 1930s, less than a decade before women joined the wartime labor market, public opinion overwhelmingly did not favor female workforce participation. A national poll in 1936 reported that 82 percent of Americans believed wives should not work outside the home if their husbands did. A year later, a similar poll reported over half of Americans believed married women should never work.

To this day, the remnants of coverture still exist, and as Mae headed west, its influence was still glaringly apparent. It wasn't until the Civil Rights Act of 1957 that women were widely granted the responsibility to serve on federal juries. Ivy League schools didn't start admitting women until 1969. Until the Equal Credit Opportunity Act of 1974, a bank still had the legal right to refuse a woman a credit card based only on her sex. Credit institutions in many cases required women who were divorced, widowed, or single to have a male proxy, and credit card limits for women were generally much lower than for men. Until 1978, a woman could be fired from her job for getting pregnant. The Civil Rights Act of 1964 created the basis for discrimination cases in its Article VII, and it also established the Equal Employment Opportunity Commission, but it took another decade and a half—until 1980—before the EEOC issued guidelines explicitly determining that sexual harassment was a form of sex discrimination. It took another eight years after that—until 1988—for the Women's Business Ownership Act to pass, allowing women to finally obtain business financing without a male cosigner.

*** 

When Mae, Cathy, and Lyola arrived in Seattle, Boeing, an airplane company founded in 1916 by lumber industrialist William E. Boeing, was producing the B-17, a four-engined heavy bomber. Before too long, the young women understood that America's wartime success might well hinge on the country's ability to churn out enough of these mighty planes. It was extremely exciting—thrilling, even—not to mention wildly fun: the sense of freedom, the responsibility, and the sweet novelty of independence. No parents around to interrogate or nag. No chores. No schoolwork. So, when the summer was over and Cathy moved home and got married, Mae and Lyola extended their stay at a boardinghouse they'd moved into in the Georgetown neighborhood of Seattle, not far from the factory. They got accustomed to the idea of working—for their country, of course, but also for themselves.

Unwittingly, the Burkett sisters became part of a nationwide cohort of women who were doing something that just years—even months—earlier had been entirely unthinkable. In the wake of Pearl Harbor, hundreds of thousands of women sought paid employment outside the home. And it wasn't only white women like Cathy, Lyola, and Mae. An estimated 600,000 African American women left jobs that were frequently oppressive and demeaning—as domestics and sharecroppers, for example—to build airplanes, tanks, and ships, fueling America's "arsenal of democracy." Most labored in the service sector and in clerical jobs, positions that had already in some cases been filled by women for decades, but demand for people of any gender in the war industries was overwhelming.

Frequently donning their male counterparts' uniforms or coveralls, rolling up their literal sleeves and stuffing the toes of the man-sized boots to improve the fit, women trained and then labored to make the products and tools necessary to keep the country running during a period of dire need.

War material was produced by a huge array of manufacturers, including refrigerator, jukebox, and even typewriter companies. By 1944, some 70 percent of manufacturing in the United States was geared toward wartime production. In 1940, only 1.9 billion dollars had been spent on defense, but by the end of the war that figure had ballooned to 304.4 billion, mostly on account of munitions. By 1943, an estimated two million women were employed in war industries. In many areas, surging demand for workers in critical plants attracted virtually the entire female workforce into the war effort. In Fort Wayne, Indiana, for example, which at the time was home to several converted military-vehicle plants, more women were working in war production by the summer of 1944 than were employed in any job in 1940. Initially, managers in many businesses were skeptical—*a woman doing manual labor?*—but soon they noticed that women frequently excelled at the tasks they were handed, even the most unfamiliar ones. Eventually bosses started praising women for specific skills, such as their "nimble fingers" and ability to squeeze into tight spaces that were too narrow for a man's broad shoulders or long limbs.

At a conference of Allied leaders in Tehran in 1943, Joseph Stalin toasted American production, saying that, without it, "This war would have been lost." But it was women like Mae who constituted the mostly unacknowledged engine that made that herculean production possible. By 1944, women held one-third of all manufacturing jobs in the United States, and the number of women in the overall paid labor force increased by 49 percent between 1940 and 1944. For fourteen- to nineteen-year-olds, the increase was 130 percent, and for forty-five- to sixty-four-year-olds it was 65 percent. In fact, the 1940s saw the largest proportional rise in female labor of any decade of the twentieth century. Many of the women who joined the paid labor force were inspired by patriotism and fear of national defeat. Many appreciated that America's industrial might was essential to winning the war and that they had a responsibility to support that effort in whatever way would be most meaningful. Plenty were also driven by the simple prospect of avoiding financial hardship now that their breadwinning spouses had left home; for the most part wartime stipends were paltry.

But there were other advantages for women, too, advantages that in many cases were still shrouded in stigma. Women were proving to themselves and to anyone who cared to pay attention that the societal parameters that for centuries had determined which tasks should be assigned to men and which to women were almost entirely trivial. They developed a brand-new, liberating, and empowering sense of independence that fueled self-esteem and—in many cases, despite the suffering and turmoil of the war—exhilaration. Of course, the money helped too. Of the women working in the Willow Run manufacturing plant in Michigan, a majority earned more than three times any wages that they'd made prior to the war, something that was true of only 15 percent of men.

Women also found camaraderie with like-minded compatriots who had sacrificed their domestic routines to support their nation and their families. They were proud of being able to master new skills and tasks, and through this period of forced societal experimentation, they were able to demonstrate a previously invisible competence, an untapped proficiency. A transformational realization swept across America's female population—namely, that nothing, practically speaking, precluded a woman doing a man's work.

*** 

Mae loved Boeing and developed a great affection for her new hometown. Having tolerated years of relentless summertime droughts and the brutal cold of midwestern winters, she came to cherish Seattle's relatively temperate seasons and even its frequent drizzle.

In 1943, at only seventeen years old, she was one of the youngest new recruits, naive and wide-eyed but hungry to learn and tirelessly propelled by a youthful curiosity—a giddiness, even. After two weeks of training, she was appointed to the position of bucker, on account, she was told, of her slight frame. She would be the person who crawled, snakelike, into the wing of an aircraft and used a bucking bar against the stem end of a rivet to ensure that it was inserted in just the right way.

The work was arduous, physically taxing, but Mae was captivated by the grace and might of the "Flying Fortress" and by the idea of what it might be able to do with the machine guns and bombs buried deep in its cavernous belly. Clad like her fellow workers in a bandana and ill-fitting overalls, she worked as many hours and days as she was needed, sometimes not even resting for weekends but always finding fleeting moments to marvel at the extraordinary machinery that she was helping to assemble.

Between Pearl Harbor and May 1944, the workers in Mae's factory rolled five thousand B-17s onto the tarmac. The five thousandth bore the name of everyone who had worked on it—including Mae—and a raucous cheer sounded as it was pushed out, victoriously, to champagne toasts and vivacious applause. It was these instances that the sisters from North Dakota lived for. The glow of accomplishment seeped deeply into Mae's weary body. She felt as if she was about to burst with pride.

Women riveters at the Boeing plant in Seattle in the early 1940s.

In the evenings, Mae would dash home to the boardinghouse, shrug off her dusty work clothes in favor of something lighter, and rush to a local bar, where she'd dance late into the night, the fatigue of manual labor forgotten. On days when she wasn't at the factory, she would wander through Seattle's vast parks or go ice skating at the Civic Center, but she never resented her work. Being able to serve, she felt, was a privilege as much as it was a duty. Yes, even at eighty-three cents an hour (equivalent to about fourteen dollars today), which was half of a male counterpart's wage.

It was on one of those Seattle dance floors, while jitterbugging in late 1944, that Mae locked eyes with Norm Krier, a Navy officer and a particularly jaunty dancer. The two struck up a conversation and a rapport that blossomed into a friendship and then a heartwarming romance that gathered pace as the year drew to a close.

As Mae's life appeared to be on the cusp of seismic change, America, too, seemed headed toward an inflection point. On the afternoon of April 12, 1945, Franklin Delano Roosevelt—who days earlier had travelled from Washington, D.C, to Warm Springs, Georgia, to recover from fatigue—suffered a massive cerebral hemorrhage and collapsed while sitting for a portrait by the artist Elizabeth Shoumatoff. Just over an hour later, the thirty-second president of the United States was pronounced dead.

As the *New York Times* reported that day, "The armies and fleets under [his] direction as Commander in Chief were at the gates of Berlin and the shores of Japan's home islands." And as he died, "The cause he represented and led was nearing the conclusive phase of success." No president of the country, journalist Arthur Krock wrote, "has died in circumstances so triumphant and yet so grave."

The United States, within touching distance of victory, was suddenly without the man who had led the country for twelve years. Mae and Norm, like so many others of their generation, knew nothing of vice president Harry S. Truman's credentials to lead a nation across the finish line of a bloody conflict. They were fearful of what this eleventh-hour presidential switchover might mean, but the man from Independence, Missouri, rose to the challenge of shepherding a nation that was both mourning and sincerely optimistic. Eight days after Roosevelt's demise, Mae and Norm married.

About four months later, at 7:00 P.M. on August 14, 1945, Truman announced to reporters gathered at the White House the unconditional surrender of Japan, ending a war that had ravaged the globe. The relief and exaltation spread like wildfire, but Mae Krier couldn't ignore a lingering feeling in the pit of her stomach that restrained her when everyone else was celebrating. Men were returning to their hometowns as heroes—as saviors—to parades and flying flags. Women were coming back with pink unemployment slips and a sensation of loss that couldn't, and wasn't allowed to be, put into words. Attempting to do so would have been considered uncouth. Just as swiftly as women had rearranged their lives to join the war effort on the home front, they'd been cast aside when men filtered back into the factories and offices. Like a stubborn elastic band, society's norms were snapping back into their old form, unquestioned and challenged only on rare occasions and in hushed tones.

Norm resumed work at The Westinghouse Electric Corporation in Trenton, New Jersey, where he'd worked prior to joining the Navy, and the newlywed couple relocated to his hometown of Morrisville, Pennsylvania, just across the Delaware River. By then Krier was entirely consumed with preparations for the birth of her first child—a daughter who would be named Anita—but a quiet resentment simmered within her. The sacrifices that women had made in those four years of conflict were undeniable, Krier thought. Almost every day she reflected that if it weren't for the efforts of American women—their selflessness, their grit—things might well have turned out very differently for the United States.

***

On May 29, 1943, Memorial Day, the *Saturday Evening Post* appeared on millions of newsstands and doorsteps across the country, graced with a cover that caught the attention of a nation, precisely as intended.

Designed and painted by Norman Rockwell, it showed a brawny woman, clad in a collared work shirt and wide-legged pants, perched on some sort of stool, with a rivet gun in her lap and a lunchbox, labelled "Rosie," below her arm. An uneaten sandwich sits in her hand. Her loafer-clad feet rest on a copy of Adolf Hitler's manifesto, *Mein Kampf.* Her face is tilted away, her nose slightly upturned, and her eyes are almost closed, evoking an unapologetic confidence and an almost androgynous strength that was entirely unconventional for the portrayal of any female person at that time.

Rockwell's image, reportedly based on a nineteen-year-old telephone operator from Vermont, Mary Doyle Keefe, who was paid ten dollars for her time, would evolve to eventually go down in history as one of the most popular depictions of America's working women. Indeed, the original was even lent to the U.S. Treasury Department for several years to assist in war bond drives. But Rockwell can't be credited with inventing the character of Rosie the Riveter who became an unmistakable symbol of working women's courage and grit.

In late 1942, Redd Evans and John Jacob Loeb penned the song "Rosie the Riveter," the protagonist of which was reportedly inspired by Rosalind Palmer Walter, a wealthy Long Island heiress who during the war went from high school to building fighter airplanes. "All the day long, whether rain or shine, she's a part of the assembly line," the lyrics went. "She's making history, working for victory, Rosie the Riveter!"

Rockwell's Rosie was undoubtedly inspired by Evans and Loeb's merry tune, but despite its extreme prominence at the time of its publication, the image's popularity didn't last. J. Howard Miller, a graphic artist who had been painting posters throughout the war, was commissioned by the same Westinghouse company where Norm Krier had worked, to create a series of posters sponsored by the company's War Production Coordinating Committee. Purportedly inspired by the photograph of a woman named Geraldine Hoff Doyle, who had been working at Westinghouse, he created a poster in 1943 showing a female worker with a speech bubble caption reading: WE CAN DO IT! Ironically, Doyle reportedly only worked at the factory for a couple of weeks. As an avid cellist, she feared the heavy machinery might mangle her hands.

At the time of its production, Miller's artwork garnered little attention, not least because it wasn't displayed outside of the Westinghouse premises. However, in the 1980s it was rediscovered. Since then, the bold-colored image of a clear-eyed Doyle—staring confrontationally straight ahead, biceps flexed, lips ever so slightly pursed, and cheekbones delicately rouged—has become the quintessential and timeless symbol of the mettlesome wartime working woman. It elegantly blended the grace of a middle-class woman with the fearlessness of blue-collar brawn in a way that had never been mastered before. Still today, Miller's poster is commonly referred to as "Rosie the Riveter." And though the artist apparently didn't explicitly intend for her to be named Rosie when he first put pen to paper, the mythical alliterative

The iconic poster produced by Westinghouse during World War II for the
War Production Coordinating Committee.

character has, over time, become the sobriquet for any woman—like
Mae Burkett Krier, Mary Doyle Keefe, Rosalind Palmer Walter, or Geraldine Hoff Doyle—who labored for wartime America on the home front,
not only as a riveter but in any job that was previously reserved for men.

Countless women have claimed to be the original inspiration for the
"real" Rosie. Some historians argue that Rosie was actually Ronnie, or
Veronica Foster, a young woman from Toronto who in 1941 was scouted
by the Canadian National Film Board and chosen as the star of their
publicity campaign: "Ronnie the Bren Gun Girl." Foster, who had three
brothers, all of whom were off at war, was cast in an advertisement that
proclaimed that "factory work is usually no more difficult than housework." Then there was Rose Bonavita, of New York, who, shortly after
Rockwell's illustration was published, set a production record with her
partner in the factory where she was working of drilling 900 lap joint

holes and completing more than 3,300 rivets in a Grumman Avenger torpedo bomber during a six-hour shift. President Roosevelt reportedly sent her a personal thank-you note.

But while it's likely that no single Rosie—if, indeed, any of them—can lay decisive claim to being the inspiration for the "Rosie the Riveter" song that would end up breathing life into a cultural icon, they can all legitimately assert that they were part of a movement that changed the role of women in the workplace forever.

\*\*\*

After the war, Mae Burkett Krier didn't work in paid employment for over a decade. She gave birth to Anita in June 1946 and to a son, Norman Jr., two years later. She was the homemaker who—prewar—she had always expected to become. All around her, female labor-market participation declined precipitously as America reacquainted itself with peace, and as men resumed work in the factories and offices that had briefly served as the domain of their wives, sisters, and even mothers.

Women were leaving the workforce for several reasons. Some companies scaling back wartime production were striking people off the payroll regardless of gender, simply because their services were no longer needed. But according to Evan K. Rose, assistant professor in the department of economics at the University of Chicago, women were also, in many cases, being unceremoniously replaced by men, particularly in industries that were traditionally considered to be male.

Citing records from the U.S. Employment Services (USES), Rose explains that a sharp drop in female job placements coincided precisely with war veterans beginning to rejoin the civilian workforce. Many of those veterans, he says, were not only heroized by society, but also had a legal right to their old jobs, or they received priority for a new job because of what were known as "veterans' preference" rules. Referencing a 1946 report from the War Manpower Commission, the U.S. agency tasked with balancing the labor needs of agriculture, industry, and the armed forces, Rose says that between July 1944 and the beginning of 1946, 120,000 veterans had returned to jobs in the federal government under reemployment rights. The female share of federal jobs, meanwhile, fell from a wartime high of 38 percent to just 28 percent by the end of 1946, and then to 22 percent by 1950. In 1940, it had been hovering around 19 percent, according to statistics from the U.S. Department of Labor.

Even in sectors that tended to employ women before the war, the increase in women working during the war was, in many cases, reversed entirely. In the hosiery industry, for example, where two-thirds of employees were female, many of the women hired during the war to knit and to fix machines were simply "bumped" as veterans returned, Rose says.

An arguably palatable explanation, and one that many researchers historically made, is that women left voluntarily: They wanted to go back to being full-time housewives and mothers, and they chose to effectively hand over their work to those returning from battle. Indeed, despite the resentment that Mae Krier admits to having felt, she did give up her paid work of her own volition to move to Pennsylvania with Norm because "that was just what was done at the time." But Evan Rose doesn't buy the theory that female labor force participation slumped so dramatically at the time simply because of a choice that women were making. A huge proportion were still applying for work, he explains. Data from the USES show that it received more than 660,000 new applications from women to work in the first quarter of 1946 alone. In that year, a survey conducted by the Women's Bureau, an agency within the Department of Labor, showed that some 57 percent of housewives who had entered the labor force wished to continue working after the war ended.

Separately, a special study done by the USES and Bureau of Employment Security examined unemployment compensation claims in three cities during the autumn of 1945, immediately after the war ended. Across Atlanta, Georgia; Trenton, New Jersey; and Columbus, Ohio, women comprised 60 percent, 69 percent, and 77 percent of total unemployment compensation claims. A woman was only eligible to make such a claim if she did not leave her job voluntarily and if she was actively looking for work while claiming.

Many of those who registered as unemployed and filed a compensation claim, though, knew that it was mostly futile. According to Rose, up to 80 percent of jobs posted in USES offices in these cities specified that the employer was recruiting "men only."

Those women who did manage to secure any of the scant and coveted paid positions in the labor market almost always had to stomach a steep wage cut from what they had been receiving during the war. Rose's research shows that fewer than 1 percent of all women in Atlanta were offered a job paying ninety cents an hour immediately after the war. During the war, 68 percent had earned that much. In Columbus, just 1 percent of jobs for women offered wages of eighty cents an hour or more. About 77 percent of claimants had previously earned that.

Reflecting on all of this, Rose says that although the employment opportunities that women experienced during the war were remarkable—not only for their "breadth" but also their "rewards and novelty"—the experience of being such a substantial part of the labor market was for them a "short-lived exception to prevailing norms." It "was only made possible by the extreme circumstances of war and was abruptly ended by the arrival of peace," he says.

Krier's brief spell of earning money and developing new skills left her wanting. After she left Boeing, she felt the buzz of bottled-up energy in her body yearning to be let out. Even as her days became consumed with raising two young children, often single-handedly, she craved being challenged intellectually and stimulated cognitively. Like others of her generation—and particularly other Rosies—she was preoccupied with the realization that she had been able to work just as hard and well as any man. She understood that, for the time being, her place was in the home, but in the years to come she would once again seek paying work. Eventually, Krier would become a bookkeeper, a job that she held for thirty years until her retirement.

\*\*\*

In 1993, Nancy A. Nichols, at the time a senior editor at *Harvard Business Review*, published an article under the headline WHATEVER HAPPENED TO ROSIE THE RIVETER? In it, drawing on extensive research into female labor market participation, Nichols concluded that Rosie had been robbed.

Citing a study from academics at the University of Michigan, Nichols explained that, for example, prior to the war, there were never more than forty-five women working at Ford's huge River Rouge plant in Dearborn, Michigan. At the height of the war, though, women accounted for a comparatively staggering 12 percent of the 93,000-person-strong workforce; thus, well over 11,000 of them. By the end of the war, the female proportion was back to 1 percent.

The researchers explained that to justify laying off so many women and hiring male replacements, Ford managers claimed that the production process had changed so much after the war that the occupations in which women had proved themselves no longer existed. Bombers, the bosses ventured, had to be riveted, but cars, on the other hand, really had to be welded. Therefore, it was possible for Ford managers to make a not-exactly-convincing argument that women were no longer qualified. More fundamentally, Nichols concluded, the managers' behavior demonstrated that the brief time that women had spent in these jobs was not enough to expand the cultural perception of factory work from "men's" work to include "women's" work.

"Rosie was done in not by the men who came home from the front, nor by the men who ran the plant," Nichols wrote. Instead, she continued, "Rosie was a victim of the power of definition, a demon that managerial women still struggle with today." She continued: "For deeply embedded in our definition of what it means to be a manager is the belief that the manager will be male. In fact, being male and being a manager have been synonymous since the inception of the managerial class in the early 1900s."

Of course, Nichols's argument stands. Rosie *was* undermined. Rosie *was* pushed out of the work that she should have had the right and opportunity to pursue. Rosie did deserve better. But none of these things should distract from Rosie's worth as a role model—and not just the iconic, stylized Rosie with the bulked-up biceps who today adorns tote bags and bumper stickers, or even the petulant, slightly brutish-looking Rosie resting her feet on a copy of *Mein Kampf.*

Many Rosies, like Krier, didn't only embody a "can do" spirit during the war, but also—however subtly and in however small a social circle—demonstrated beyond doubt that a woman's work capacity extended far beyond the domestic tasks of a homemaker. (And that's not to say that those homemakers' tasks were in any way easy.) While many of Krier's peers might hesitate to think of themselves as role models, their stories of riveting, drilling, and welding have chipped away at calcified stereotypes and erroneous beliefs every time they've been told, firsthand or not, over the years.

Maria Ingrid Teresa Olsson, an associate professor at the Inland Norway University of Applied Sciences, is an expert in the importance of role models and identities in the workplace. Her research has demonstrated that gender-counter-stereotypical role models, or individuals who engage in roles that are antithetical to gender stereotypes, can be immensely powerful in influencing aspirations and career choices of subsequent generations. Stereotypes, of course, may change over time, but in the 1940s, when Mae Burkett first crawled inside the wing of an aircraft to assist the riveters, she was perhaps the epitome of a gender-counter-stereotypical role model.

Just three decades earlier, in the *Muller v. Oregon* case of 1908, the U.S. Supreme Court had upheld the constitutionality of laws restricting women's work hours and working conditions. The decision was largely based on a legal brief by Louis Brandeis, who would later go on to serve as associate justice on the Supreme Court, which asserted that "overwork" was medically bad for women and specifically for their ability to bear children. "As healthy mothers are essential to vigorous offspring, the physical wellbeing of woman is an object of public interest," the opinion read. "While the general liberty to contract in regard to one's business and the sale of one's labor is protected by the Fourteenth Amendment, that liberty is subject to proper restrictions under the police power of the State," it added.

In 1938, President Roosevelt had signed the Fair Labor Standards Act into effect, banning oppressive child labor and setting the minimum hourly wage at twenty-five cents and the maximum workweek at forty-four hours, but it wouldn't be until 1963 that Congress would pass the Equal Pay Act, making it illegal for employers to pay women lower wages than men for equal work on jobs requiring the same skill, effort, and responsibility.

The backdrop against which Mae Burkett and her fellow Rosies joined the workforce was deeply, systemically discriminatory against women. Rules and laws purportedly intended to protect them and their reproductive function were pervasive. Some jobs, these rules prescribed, were simply too strenuous for a woman's delicate physique, and barring women from doing them was considered a protective act rather than a discriminatory one. The actual science behind these claims was, seemingly, irrelevant.

It's impossible to objectively measure or quantify the exact impact that Rosies had on women's earning power, or on the norms that determined what was acceptable "female behavior," in the years and decades that followed. But it's undeniable that they did have an effect, even if that didn't become patently clear until more than a decade later. What complicates an assessment of the role of gender in the workplace immediately after the war is the intense anti-feminist backlash that occurred in the 1950s, when it became evident that America's safety was no longer dependent on women working. The Cold War was now the country's collective focus. And although women were needed in the fight against Communism, economist Elizabeth Cook-Stuntz wrote in a paper in 2015 that they were only needed "as mothers and wives."

As the postwar economy recovered and then boomed, America witnessed the dawn of technological innovations like the microwave oven and the automatic washing machine. "A burgeoning economy needed women as consumers," according to Cook-Stuntz. "No longer constrained by a war, the advertising industry released its pent-up energy convincing women how easy their lives would be with some new product." It seemed that a country that only a decade earlier had championed Rosie the Riveter as the savior of a nation—thanks to her awesome combination of brawn and brain—was now recasting her in a role that was much more familiar, far less intimidating, warmly maternal, and even a little quaint: Rosie the Housewife, a model of citizenship and responsibility and the perfect mate for a hardworking veteran of war who'd served the nation so gallantly.

The seed had been planted, though. World War II had not led to an instant and permanent upheaval in work patterns and gender roles, but the notion of a new role for women in society had endured, no matter how subtly. Maureen Honey, a professor of English and Women's Studies at the University of Nebraska, in a book she published in 1984, characterized the Rosie the Riveter campaign and associated promotional material as "the most comprehensive, well-organized effort this society has made toward ending prejudice against women in male occupations and toward legitimizing the notion that women belong in the paid workforce." Almost four decades on, her statement may well still stand.

Despite being silenced by a return to social norms and expectations in the immediate aftermath of the war, many of the women who became mothers to the baby boomers born after 1945, having enjoyed what was possible, actively encouraged their daughters to seek education and employment, enabling them to pursue full-fledged careers.

Cook-Stuntz observed that baby boomers were the first generation in which a significant proportion of women began planning for careers and not just jobs. "Unlike their mothers, female baby boomers chose their careers as a piece of their own identity," she explained, "something they often developed before they married and subsequently gained an identity as a wife." And it wasn't just the baby boomers who proudly joined the labor market. Many of the women who had worked during the war—indeed, women like Mae Krier—went back to paid employment later in life, often once their children had left home to seek their own educational or professional opportunities.

Other academics have also produced research attempting to demonstrate the lasting impact of Rosies in the workforce on the professional ambitions of the women who followed in their footsteps. In a paper published in 2004, although academics Raquel Fernández, Alessandra Fogli, and Claudia Olivetti found no correlation between a woman's chance of working in paid employment and her own mother's work history, they did find one between a woman's labor force participation and her mother-in-law's work history. Those authors conclude that boys who grew up in homes with working mothers were less likely to object to their wives working outside the home. They also reason that boys who grew up with working mothers may have been able to perform domestic tasks and household chores, which would have provided more time for a wife to work.

A separate study, and one that Cook-Stuntz favors, was published by Melinda Sandler Morrill and her husband, Thayer, in 2014. The pair conducted a fairly complex statistical analysis on reams of labor market data relating to mothers, daughters, wives, and sons, but the upshot is simple: If a woman decides she wants to work outside the home, she's more likely to be attracted to a male partner who accepts—even supports—the idea of his wife working and is prepared to pick up some of the domestic chores that traditionally would have fallen to the woman in the household.

So, is it fair to conclude that the female babies born to women who took on paid employment outside the home during World War II were more likely to pursue their own careers when they became adults? Not categorically. But women born in the 1940s were certainly more likely to pursue education beyond high school than any generation that came before them. And there's compelling anecdotal evidence that the daughters of Rosies were fired up to claim their own spot in the labor market because of how fondly their mothers spoke of their time in the factories, offices, and stores across the country. But it's impossible to determine all the drivers of the broader demographic trend. Social expectations and norms were evolving. Tectonic shifts were occurring. Economic forces were controlling the ebbs and flows of supply and demand, and political and ideological landscapes were morphing in unpredictable ways.

And then in April 1956, a scientist and a doctor from the Boston area started distributing a tiny innocuous-looking pill, about the size of a garden pea, initially to a few dozen women. It was research that, at first, looked like it was going nowhere. Almost no one suspected the silent and controversial revolution that was about to unfurl.

\*\*\*

By that time, Mae Krier had decided that she wanted to do much more to get Rosie the Riveter recognized with the same zeal as the veterans who'd fought on the front line. She was as convinced then, as she is today, that her generation, the Silent Generation, staked out a path for those who followed. She's never shown any interest in the economic reports that suggest otherwise.

In the late 1990s, Krier started making white-polka-dotted red bandanas, which she distributed as emblems of the underappreciated and sometime forgotten efforts of her female peers in the wartime workplace, and she spent her days writing letters to politicians—to any who would listen—demanding attention, recognition, and a little respect.

In 2020, when the COVID-19 pandemic started ricocheting around the world, destroying lives and livelihoods, Krier hunkered down in her living room in Levittown and began making cotton face masks for nurses and others who might need them. Hunched over her small Singer sewing machine, silver curls piled high upon her head, the nonagenarian would trace each fold and each seam of the fabric, squinting through thick-rimmed glasses to make sure the red and white polka-dot pattern was aligned just right. Every finished mask would be folded carefully inside a custom-made envelope, embellished in the bottom right-hand corner with the J. Howard Miller image, in the top left-hand corner, Krier's home address.

But by the time Krier reached her personal milestone of five thousand masks sewn and mailed out to nurses, care home workers, and anyone else who wanted one, she had another achievement to celebrate. On December 3, 2020, Senator Bob Casey Jr.'s bipartisan Rosie the Riveter Congressional Gold Medal Act was signed into law, honoring American women who had joined the workforce in support of the war effort during World War II.

Senator Casey of Pennsylvania had led the effort to get the bill passed, along with Senator Susan Collins of Maine and Representatives Jackie Speier of California and Brian Fitzpatrick of Pennsylvania. Seventy-six senators cosponsored the bill, including every woman senator.

The politicians cited Mae Krier by name and her advocacy as the reason the act was passed; her grit, her "can do" spirit, and Krier—emotional, charming, and a little perplexed—reveled in the festivities, proudly speaking to local media but maintaining, too, that the fight wasn't over. In her soft but authoritative voice, tinged with that enduring North Dakotan twang, Krier explained that she wanted a Rosie statue at the World War II Memorial in Washington, D.C—"Is that too much to ask?"—and, generally, a broader acknowledgment that working women not only helped win the war for America but also sowed the seeds of economic empowerment for their daughters, their daughters' daughters, and many of the daughters still to come.

On that warm afternoon in October 2021, sitting in a large armchair beside her sewing machine—"my replacement riveting gun"—dressed in a white short-sleeved, button-down shirt and slacks, with her trademark bandana around her neck, Krier thumbed through a file of old press clippings about Rosies, interspersed with sepia photographs ragged around the edges and that pay stub from 1945. "America's still the beautiful," she said with a small nod. "It always will be. But it definitely needs a little fixing."

## CHAPTER 2

*Wonderful Things in Small Packets*

So here's to my tiny daily dose of freedom, and also estrogen and pro-gesterone. A combination of the three, really.

—Samantha Bee in November 2010, at the fiftieth birthday party of
the contraceptive pill

In May 1946, exactly nine months after the end of World War II, "the cry of the baby was heard across the land," as Landon Jones wrote in his 1981 book *Great Expectations*. In that month, more than 233,000 children were born in the United States, a surge from the February low of just over 206,000. By the end of the year, the government had recorded more than 3.4 million births, a staggering 20 percent increase over the previous year's figures. It was the beginning of the "Baby Boom," Jones wrote, or the "birth quake," in the words of economist Diane J. Macunovich. Over the following year—1947—births numbered 3.8 million, and at least 4 million babies were born during every year that spanned the decade from 1954 to 1964.

After what felt like a lifetime of the punishing Great Depression and war, many Americans, it seemed, were starting to feel confident that the rebounding economy, combined with G.I. Bill of Rights benefits that guaranteed access to stable work and affordable housing for most, would enable them to support larger, happier families. It's worth noting here, however, that these benefits didn't extend to all. Black veterans were frequently unable to get bank loans for mortgages in Black neighborhoods, and they faced prejudice and discrimination that overwhelmingly excluded them from buying homes in suburban neighborhoods that were predominantly white.

Many couples who had been separated by war were making up for lost time, getting married at a younger age. By 1950, the median age of marriage for a woman was just 20.3, down from 21.5 a decade before. Almost 2.3 million couples wed in 1946, marking a record that wouldn't be broken until the 1970s, when the country's population was considerably larger, and many young couples were conceiving earlier than previous generations had. By 1960, the average number of children a couple in the United States was having was above 3.5, up from just 2.2 in 1940.

Women who were marrying at age twenty often had two or three children by the time they were twenty-five. By age thirty, many knew that they didn't want any more offspring, but contraception wasn't easy to come by, leaving them feeling helpless and unable to wield control over their own reproductive choices, which limited any options they might have had to embark on a career. Female workforce participation had risen from 27 percent in 1940 to 37 percent just four years later, powered by the Rosies of World War II. But then in peacetime it had promptly returned to only slightly above prewar levels. By 1950 it had clawed its way back up somewhat, but many women felt stuck in a life in which any element of choice completely eluded them and making babies had automatically become their socially assigned priority.

The two-parent family was idealized, and large families of three, four, or even five and six children were profiled in popular culture as aspirational. But some women, particularly those like Mae Krier, who had worked outside the home during the war, were starting to feel shortchanged. The economic independence they'd tasted had proven short-lived. And the baby boom was also throwing into sharp relief how cumbersome it generally still was to obtain contraception, and the extent to which women lacked control over their own bodies and their own lives.

In the 1840s, Charles Goodyear had started vulcanizing rubber, making condoms cheaper to produce and easier to come by. Around the same time, ill-fitting cervical caps—precursors to diaphragms—started appearing, but, like the latter, tended to be messy to use. In March 1873, Congress had passed an act that banned the trade in and circulation of "obscene literature and articles of immoral use." What became known as the Comstock Act made it illegal and punishable by fines, imprisonment, or both, to send six types of material through the mail: erotica, contraceptive medications or devices, abortifacients (substances that induce abortion), sexual implements (such as those used in masturbation, which today we'd refer to as sex toys), contraceptive information, and advertisements for contraception, abortion, or sexual implements. So-called little Comstock laws followed, which outlawed the sale of these items, and Anthony Comstock, a dry goods merchant who was the law's chief proponent and namesake, personally served as a special agent for the U.S. Postal Service to help ensure enforcement.

In 1933, physician and reproductive rights advocate Hannah Mayer Stone imported pessaries—a new type of diaphragm—from Japan for use in the New York clinic she managed. The U.S. government sued her for violating the Tariff Act of 1930, which had incorporated some of the provisions of the Comstock Act. A lower court ruled in favor of Stone and against the government, and when the government appealed, the appellate court affirmed the ruling.

Judge Augustus Noble Hand, who presided over the case, wrote in his decision that although the Comstock Act was designed to ban contraception in cases where the sole purpose was to stop a healthy woman from giving birth to a healthy baby, it was not designed to ban contraception if that was not the case. If, for example, Judge Hand reasoned, a pregnancy was likely to have to result in an abortion, then contraception should be permissible so that the need for a termination could be avoided. "It seems unreasonable," Hand concluded, "to suppose that the national scheme of legislation involves such inconsistencies and requires the complete suppression of articles, the use of which in many cases is advocated by such a weight of authority in the medical world."

In the 1936 ruling, the Comstock Act's birth control provisions were therefore deemed to violate the U.S. Constitution. Although this marked a victory for birth control advocates, it changed little for the average American woman. For most, reliable and safe birth control remained hard to come by. Getting a diaphragm required a prescription, and many women didn't even have access to a physician. In light of Jim Crow laws, women of color in particular were frequently afraid of and didn't trust doctors. Many women were too scared or embarrassed to undergo an internal examination. Over-the-counter contraceptive products such as vaginal jellies and foaming tablets were available but not reliable. Douching was cheap and accessible, too, but it was dangerous. The most popular brand of douche was Lysol—an antiseptic soap that, up until 1953, contained cresol, a compound that was reported in some cases to cause inflammation, burning, and even death.

By 1946, the baby boom was being hailed as a joyous sign of America's economic revival, but not all pregnancies were wanted or even the result of consensual sex, and for all expectant mothers, pregnancy imposed strict limits on the opportunities they had to work outside the home. Employers could legally fire pregnant women and replace them with men. They could refuse to hire pregnant women on account of the pregnancy or because of prejudices that coworkers, clients, or customers might have about the pregnancy or about a pregnant woman. In fact, until the mid-1960s, the de facto expectation was that a female employee would resign of her own accord upon conceiving—the timing of which was frequently entirely beyond a sexually active woman's control.

*** 

In the late afternoon of January 19, 1947, Stanley McCormick, a seventy-two-year-old multimillionaire living in Montecito, California, drew his last tremulous breath and closed his eyes on the world for good.

Stanley's death made headlines across America. Professionally, he'd done very little since his health had started to fade considerably in 1906, but his family was extremely wealthy and prominent in the business community. His father, Cyrus McCormick, had in 1834 patented the mechanical reaper and had subsequently grown the McCormick business into a major agricultural enterprise that revolutionized the grain trade. Stanley, his youngest son, was born in November 1874, raised in Chicago, and graduated with highest honors from Princeton, where he played football and tennis; he then attended Northwestern's law school. Degree in hand, Stanley joined the family business as comptroller, later proving instrumental in arranging the merger of the McCormicks' company with that of other manufacturers to form International Harvester, a corporation that would go on to dominate the American tractor market. Other branches of the sprawling family had incorporated the financial firm William Blair & Company and published and edited the *Chicago Tribune*.

But as much as Stanley's life was gilded, it was marred by misfortune. In the fall of 1904 he married Katharine Dexter, a beautiful and erudite socialite with deep-set, haunting eyes and a sonorous voice that unnerved men and forced them to instantly forgive her when she railed—as she so often did—against the patriarchy. A descendant of Samuel Dexter, a land baron and statesman who served in the U.S. Congress and in the presidential cabinets of John Adams and Thomas Jefferson, Katharine was born in August 1875 in Michigan and raised in Chicago. In May 1890, her father suffered a sudden and severe heart attack and died before his fourteen-year-old daughter's eyes. Just four years later, Katharine's only brother, Samuel, a recent graduate of Harvard Law School who was seven years older than her, succumbed to meningitis. Devastated, Katharine vowed to pursue a career in medicine, and, propelled by boundless ambition and a healthy portion of idealism inherited from her late father, she set her sights on the Massachusetts Institute of Technology (MIT). Shortly after her brother's funeral, Katharine wrote to Samuel's grieving lover, Elsie Clews, who would later become a dear friend: "I have concluded that justice seemed better served to those who took control of their lives."

In 1896, after an eighteen-month tour of Europe with her mother, designed to help process their grief, Katharine started the prerequisite work for passing MIT's arduous entrance exam. It would take her three years, but in September 1899, at the age of twenty-four, she sailed through the exam, forcing the school's staid governing body to welcome—albeit reluctantly—what was still an extreme rarity at the time: a female student.

Katharine Dexter McCormick, who married Stanley McCormick in 1904.

In September 1903, a year before she graduated from MIT, Katharine, who had previously shown little interest in men, crossed paths with Stanley, a handsome thirty-year-old bachelor, while on a brief vacation at the exclusive oceanfront resort of Beverly Farms, just north of Boston. The two had shared acquaintances in Chicago; in fact, they'd met sixteen years earlier during a dance class. In Beverly Farms, they quickly rekindled their friendship, bonding over a common history and their families' respective fabulous fortunes. Identifying in her a perfect mate who was smart, mature, ambitious, and wealthy—not to mention extremely attractive—Stanley showered her with gifts and dinners. But their courtship was stormy on account of his frequent and manic mood swings and spells of poor health. When she first accepted his marriage proposal, Katharine broke it off months later, saying that she was too busy with school and unable to tolerate his erratic behavior. Katharine found Stanley's persistence and charm disarming, though, and eventually she acknowledged that they probably were destined for each other.

The nuptials took place at and around the bride's family's eighteenth-century castle, the Château de Prangins, a recent gift from her mother, in the Swiss town of Nyon on the northwestern bank of Lake Geneva. In a photograph taken on the day—Katharine, clad in pearls and layers of luxurious French muslin, Stanley in tails and a white tie—the couple might be mistaken for members of a European royal family. But what would have passed as a blissful start to married life, or at least a peaceful conclusion to a tumultuous initial courtship, was in fact the final period of relative calm before decades of pain and heartache.

In the lead-up to the wedding, Stanley's mood swings had escalated into serious bouts of unstable mental health. Katharine had chalked this up to the effects of his overbearing family—particularly his dominating mother, Nettie—but after a fraught honeymoon and a move from Chicago to Boston, it quickly became clear that his condition was not about to improve. Over the course of 1905, Stanley started showing signs of seriously impaired cognition. He became pugnacious and panicked, even violently at times, on one occasion physically attacking his dentist. In 1906, Stanley officially resigned from his position in the family business. Shortly thereafter he was admitted to the McLean Hospital for the Insane in a suburb of Boston.

Katharine McCormick, who sought explanations in the textbooks and notebooks she'd retained from her years at MIT, was convinced that her husband was suffering from a hormonal imbalance or a malfunctioning adrenal gland, but his doctors disagreed. They insisted on treating Stanley with psychotherapy, and his condition deteriorated steadily. A spiritless suicide attempt saw him try to hang himself with the drawstrings of his pajamas, and eventually he was diagnosed with "dementia praecox of the catatonic type," now known as schizophrenia. Stanley endured violent outbursts and hallucinations, interspersed with periods of relative clarity and apathy, which provided some hope to his loved ones—later abruptly dashed—that he might be healing.

According to one medical report, he largely subsisted on eggnog, malted milk, and oyster stew. His regular treatment, based on doctors' orders, consisted mostly of cold baths and sedation.

In 1908, the family decided to relocate Stanley to the McCormick family estate, Riven Rock, in Santa Barbara, California. Surrounded by beautiful oak trees, this was where Stanley's older sister, Mary Virginia, who at the age of nineteen had also been diagnosed with schizophrenia, had stayed before she was admitted to a sanatorium. As befit an extremely rich family, no expense was spared to try to ensure the young man's comfort. A nine-hole golf course was constructed on the estate, around which beautiful azaleas and rhododendrons bloomed from early spring until well into fall. A musical director was hired. A theater was built, and a large art collection was amassed with the goal of igniting some pleasure in the ailing resident. From time to time, Stanley stepped out onto the stone terrace and took in the breathtaking vista of the Channel Islands and the Santa Barbara Mountains. Every once in a while, he was bundled into a Rolls-Royce and driven to the family's beach cottage at Sandyland. But nothing at all seemed to be able to remedy or even stabilize his dire condition.

In the months after he arrived at Riven Rock, Stanley seemed to become extremely angry and even more violent, particularly to and around women. His all-male medical staff had by this time restricted visits from any women, including Stanley's own mother, sister, and wife. Katharine McCormick would nonetheless frequent Riven Rock often, sometimes crouching in a patch of begonias with binoculars and witnessing from afar as her husband, once a strapping college athlete brimming with professional potential, slowly regressed to cognitive infancy.

Relatives and even medical staff urged McCormick to divorce him. Her mother had always pined for grandchildren and hoped that her only daughter would end her marriage so that she could find another husband with whom to start a family. But even though McCormick felt more helpless by the day, she was intent on not giving up hope or abandoning the love of her life. Relentlessly, she implored the attending doctors to examine alternative treatment methods beyond psychotherapy and those icy baths, but these appeals largely fell on deaf ears: Why should they heed the advice of a young woman—even a young woman of her lineage and with a Bachelor of Science degree from MIT—when they were members of the country's respected medical elite?

To distract herself from the dire situation, McCormick turned her attention to issues that gave her a sense of purpose and that she could control. She approved funding to build a primate laboratory, because her husband's doctors had mentioned that studying apes might help them develop a cure for the obsessive sexual behavior that Stanley, who had now been declared legally insane, had started to display. And she also channeled money into research that was being done into schizophrenia at Worcester State Hospital in Massachusetts and at Harvard.

But there was another cause that gave McCormick strength and the will to get out of bed in the morning. As a young girl, she'd discovered that her mother had secretly (doing so publicly would have led to criticism by her well-to-do peers) supported the women's suffrage movement. Ever since then, women's rights—or, more specifically, the lack thereof—had intrigued McCormick, and now she began dedicating more and more time to fighting for them.

In 1909 she joined the women's suffrage movement, speaking at rallies, handing out leaflets, and helping to organize protests. She coveted the chance to be vocal, to be heard, and it gave her an ardor for life that had been missing during the entirety of her tragic marriage. While she was at MIT, it had occurred to her just how senseless so many of the enduring gendered societal norms were. Tending to Stanley, she'd become almost unbearably angry at the doctors' dismissive attitude toward her. While studying, she had seen firsthand the potential she had to effect change, when she successfully campaigned for MIT's chemistry department to alter a rule requiring female students to wear hats in science labs, because such attire created an easily avoidable fire hazard. But far more fundamental inequities remained and bothered her deeply. It was ludicrous that so many more men than women should be granted the nation's best educational opportunities. It was absurd that men and not women should be able to cast their votes on matters that would, in the end, impact everyone's life. And it was completely preposterous that women were still treated as an accessory by much of society, mostly valued for their ability to reproduce.

With no children to raise, a husband who was drifting further away by the day, and with vast financial resources, McCormick decided to devote her time to the National American Woman Suffrage Association, of which she eventually became treasurer and then vice president. In August 1920, following the ratification of the Nineteenth Amendment to the U.S. Constitution, which granted women the right to vote, McCormick also served as first vice president of the League of Women Voters. But it was a speech in 1917 by Margaret Sanger that ignited a determination in McCormick so fierce that it shaped the entire remainder of her life.

Sanger, whose legacy would later be blighted by her racist and eugenicist influences, was, at the time, considered the U.S.'s best-known birth control advocate, and McCormick heard her speak in Boston about women bearing "the brunt of unwilling motherhood." "The world is full of undesired babies, and every undesired baby represents a terrible infringement of the personal rights of a mother," Sanger declared. "Women do not desire to spend the whole of their adult lives in bringing children into the world."

McCormick latched on to every single one of Sanger's words, growing more frustrated and passionate with each. She agreed vehemently that contraception was the key to women's freedom, and by the time Sanger stopped speaking, the socialite knew with unparalleled clarity what she wanted to fight for.

\*\*\*

Margaret Sanger hailed from Corning in the southern part of the Finger Lakes region of New York State. Of Irish descent and one of eleven children, she worked as a schoolteacher and then trained as a nurse after caring for her own mother, who had suffered from tuberculosis. Through her work, Sanger witnessed many tragic scenes of mothers, babies, or both perishing because of complications during childbirth,

Margaret Sanger, who at one time was the U.S.' best-known
birth control advocate.

and she subsequently decided that she wanted to use her healthcare
training to educate women on ways to avoid getting pregnant. She
became an organizer for the labor union the Industrial Workers of the
World, and then a journalist who dedicated most of her work to the pre-
dicaments of working-class mothers.

From the moment Katharine McCormick first encountered Margaret Sanger, she felt deep admiration for the New Yorker's bravery and
certitude, her altruism and fearlessness. The mother of three was also
something of a captivating, exotic creature to McCormick, a complete
rarity: a woman who unapologetically and vocally spurned convention
and proudly championed the feminist cause without sparing a thought
for social codes of conduct.

In 1914, Sanger fled to England to avoid prosecution for distributing a pamphlet, called *Family Limitation*, describing six different contraceptive methods, but back in the States in October 1916, she joined

People with baby carriages sitting in front of Margaret Sanger's clinic at
46 Amboy Street in Brownsville, Brooklyn.

forces with her sister and a friend to open the first birth control clinic in
the country—the Brownsville Clinic in a working-class neighborhood
of Brooklyn.

The clinic was shut down just ten days after opening because it
blatantly violated the Comstock Act. Nonetheless, it was successful at
educating women about contraception simply on account of the media
storm that its closure prompted, as well as its popularity during the
short time that its doors were open. On the first day of operation, clinic
staff reportedly saw 150 patients, who had learned about it thanks to
subtle advertisements in local newspapers and on posters. By the tenth
day, the Brownsville Clinic had met with 450 women, helping them to
understand that becoming pregnant didn't necessarily have to be part
of womanhood.

When the clinic was shuttered, Sanger was arrested. She appealed
her case, and although the presiding judge upheld the Comstock Act, he

did determine that a doctor's responsibility was to prevent ill health: If contraception prevented diseases, he reasoned, then contraception might well be the best recommendation to keep a sexually active woman healthy.

In 1921, Sanger founded the American Birth Control League, a precursor to Planned Parenthood. It had three governing principles; namely, that children should be "conceived in love," "born of the mother's conscious desire," and "only begotten under conditions which render possible the heritage of health." Sanger reached out to physicians to organize and run birth control clinics under the direction of the League, and she also started to enjoy a surge of support from wealthy suffrage leaders who, up until 1920, had squarely focused their efforts on women's right to vote. Among them, most notably, was Katharine McCormick, who had been following Sanger's work with keen interest and who was desperately eager to become a full-fledged collaborator.

In 1921, McCormick reached out to Sanger and requested a private meeting, during which the two women recognized their contrasting and complementary backgrounds, personalities, and strengths. McCormick, with her beguiling charm and the clout of both the Dexter and McCormick names, had access to the highest echelons of society, not to mention a lot of cash. Sanger, for her part, was wildly charismatic, with an infectious energy and vast experience organizing and campaigning for the feminist cause.

The women immediately started working together with an enthusiasm that was palpable. McCormick obtained funds to pay for Sanger's national lecture tour, and in 1922, Sanger incorporated the American Birth Control League, immediately making McCormick an integral member.

In January 1923, Sanger opened the doors to the Clinical Research Bureau in New York, the first legal birth control clinic in the United States. It was officially classified as a research institution, and, thus, any woman who turned up as a patient was legally considered a research subject, which marked a huge step in Sanger's broader mission. She could now theoretically distribute contraceptives to women seeking reproductive freedom.

Only there simply weren't enough contraceptives to accommodate the staggering demand. It seemed that every woman in the city wanted a diaphragm. McCormick, resourceful by nature, had an idea. While on an annual trip to Geneva that summer, she planned several forays to other European cities, including Rome and Paris, prime destinations for wealthy women wishing to indulge in shopping sprees and also—and not coincidentally—home to some of the Continent's largest diaphragm manufacturers.

Relying on her linguistic skills—a product of her privileged upbringing—and the technical knowledge that came with having earned her degree at MIT, she posed as a French and then a German scientist, placing orders for hundreds of diaphragms, which were still mostly illegal in America. Back in Switzerland, the grand rooms of the Château de Prangins filled up not just with beautiful garments and coats from the world's metropolitan fashion capitals, but also with dozens of boxes jam-packed with birth control devices. Next, McCormick hired a fleet of local seamstresses to delicately remove the linings from the coats and gowns and carefully place the diaphragms inside the linings before sewing up the seams again. Tightly packed, everything filled eight steamer trunks.

No one thought to question the aristocratic lady or her unusually voluminous luggage as she journeyed to the French coast. But as she boarded her ship to America, French customs officials asked her how on earth a single woman could possibly need so much luggage. Using the power of flattery and self-deprecation, she responded that American women just couldn't help themselves—they simply adored French fashion.

Stateside, with her copious luggage in tow and unscathed, McCormick was ushered through U.S. Customs as a member of the social elite who had typically indulged herself during her time abroad. Her trunks were then loaded onto trucks and promptly delivered to Sanger's clinic. McCormick's experiment had proved successful, and a repeat mission was scheduled for the following year.

Only this time, she was even braver. Diaphragms—numbering far more than the previous year—were wrapped up in festive paper and disguised as continental Christmas gifts for friends and family back home. Diaphragms were hidden in cosmetics cases, and some— because it had worked so nicely the first time—in the linings of coats and dresses. Aware that the volume of her contraband might well look suspicious this time, McCormick convinced the captain of her returning ship to drop off some of her haul at a port in Canada. From there, liquor smugglers transported it across the U.S border and safely into a warehouse controlled by Noah Slee, Sanger's second husband.

The following year proved more challenging. McCormick came down with an aggressive case of strep throat and couldn't travel as widely, meaning that her contraceptive haul was only half as big as it had been the previous year. And the next year she had to call off her clandestine sojourn entirely. At dawn on June 29, 1925, a powerful earthquake rocked Santa Barbara, leaving much of the city, including Riven Rock, destroyed or heavily damaged. McCormick managed a quick trip to Europe in the fall, but by the winter of that year, Stanley's deteriorating health was demanding more of her time. Desperate to keep supporting the mission, however, she offered Sanger the Château de Prangins as a location to host the world's first international summit on birth control in 1927, even though there was no way she herself would be able to attend. She'd become embroiled in a legal battle with Stanley's siblings over his care, which she would eventually win, and she was also busy overseeing the reconstruction of Riven Rock, parts of which had been reduced to rubble by the quake. Her short-lived career as a diaphragm smuggler had ended. Her deep-seated determination to keep working for women's contraceptive rights, though, was burgeoning.

***

The January afternoon in 1947 when Stanley slipped away was, for McCormick, filled with both a profound feeling of loss and a sobering sense of closure. Whether she knew it or not, though, that Sunday also marked the beginning of a new chapter in her quest to make birth control universally available. As Stanley's sole beneficiary, McCormick, who by now was seventy-two years old, inherited an estate worth almost 40 million dollars, the equivalent of about 570 million dollars today. Combined with the millions of dollars she'd already inherited a decade earlier from her mother, McCormick's fortune was immense. She knew that if she spent intelligently, she now had the resources to effect immense change.

Even during the years that McCormick was preoccupied with affairs at Riven Rock, she had maintained a close relationship with Margaret Sanger and donated generously to the American Birth Control League and Planned Parenthood, as it became known in 1942. The two women's shared conviction that science was key to the emancipation of women and their economic and social empowerment had bonded them powerfully despite their obvious socioeconomic differences.

America also seemed to be catching up with them—hesitantly, at least. The Rosies of World War II had challenged the social norms and standards that good American women were expected to abide by. Earning money had helped women shape their own identity and, in cases like Mae Krier's, liberated them from their childhood homes earlier than if war hadn't erupted. Sexuality was being reexamined, too. Women were dating and having sex with men even if they had no intention of committing to a life of holy matrimony.

Around the time that Stanley was nearing death, Margaret Sanger had been touring the country for research purposes and had concluded that the diaphragm was not an adequate form of birth control. It was messy, complicated, and in most cases women could only get one with a doctor's prescription. Instead, she had decided to pin her hopes on what she started calling a "magic pill," something that relied on the potency of chemistry. A woman could swallow one every morning, surreptitiously if needed and without consent of the man she was sleeping with or of anyone else, for that matter. The greatest hurdle, Sanger realized, was that neither pharmaceutical companies nor the federal government wanted to invest in contraceptive research—or even be associated with it. Even though the relevant sections of the Comstock Act had effectively been invalidated in 1936, many states continued to enforce laws that restricted the advertisement, sale, and use of contraceptives. It was seen a disreputable area of study, shrouded in stigma, and perhaps the only man in America at the time who was as troubled by this as Sanger was, was Gregory Goodwin Pincus.

***

One night in 1950, Margaret Sanger had met Pincus—or Goody, as his close friends and colleagues called him—at a Manhattan dinner hosted by Abraham Stone, the medical director and vice president of Planned Parenthood. Of Russian descent, Pincus was one of the world's leading experts on mammalian reproduction and had been a professor at Harvard. In 1930 he had become the first person to fertilize a rabbit's ova in a test tube, a technique that paved the way for in vitro fertilization for humans. Although his achievement was recognized as historic, Pincus was considered morally outrageous and ethically radical. The press, in articles about his "fatherless" test tube rabbits, likened Pincus to Mary Shelley's Victor Frankenstein, a comparison that was made that much more effective by his bristly mustache, thick eyebrows, and wild hair. By some accounts because of his radical experiments, and by others because of a wave of anti-Semitism that was sweeping through parts of the United States at that time, Harvard denied Pincus tenure in 1936, ruining his chances of being tapped by any other reputable university.

Uncowed, he continued to conduct research. He moved to Worcester, about fifty miles west of Boston, where a former Harvard colleague had offered him a job at Clark University, a small private research institute. There he met Hudson Hoagland, a neuroscientist who would later serve as president of the American Academy of Arts and Sciences, and the two men decided to strike out on their own by launching an independent scientific research center.

In 1944, the Worcester Foundation for Experimental Biology opened its doors, operating on a shoestring budget and out of an old residential property. On most days, Pincus personally cleaned the animal cages of their research subjects while Hoagland mowed the lawn.

The pair relied almost entirely on generous donations and grants to keep the lights on, literally, but at last they could dream big without the rules and norms of academic institutions looming over them.

Sanger, who was seventy-one years old by the time she met Pincus, had heard about all of this and suspected that he might just be the key to making her magic pill a reality. He was unequivocally smart, fearlessly ambitious, unafraid of allowing scientific discovery to challenge accepted convention, and his gender might just give him the credibility and access that she had so frequently failed to secure.

After some introductory chatter, she took her chance and got right to the point, describing the contraceptive pill as she envisioned it: simple, reliable, and entirely nonintrusive. "Do you think that it would be possible?" she asked Pincus. "I think so," he responded, a little cautiously at first. "Well," Sanger countered, "let's start right away."

By this time Pincus was experimenting with synthetic progesterone, hopeful of being able to uncover a cure for infertility. He was collaborating closely with a Chinese researcher, who had previously worked in the United Kingdom, named Min-Chueh Chang, and it was Chang to whom Pincus first spoke after returning from New York that winter. With a zeal Chang had become accustomed to seeing in his colleague, Pincus relayed the conversation, placing particular emphasis on the fact that the "magic pill" had to be a pill and not some sort of jelly, injection, or a mechanical device. The research would have to be extensive and the science entirely unprecedented, but there was one other massive hurdle, they both knew, a hurdle that might scupper the whole damn idea before it even had a chance to become fully formed. That hurdle was money.

Work started tentatively. Planned Parenthood provided some funding, but the organization's leaders, and particularly its national director, William Vogt, weren't completely convinced about the viability of Pincus's plans. Sure, the idea was brilliant, and some of the research was promising, but this was extremely ambitious not to mention risky. Would enough people buy into it to help it reach point of completion? Vogt had yet to be convinced.

Katharine McCormick had already, through Sanger, channeled some cash into Pincus's coffers, too, but by early 1952 it was clear that money was burning up at an unsustainable rate. McCormick wrote a letter to her friend and confidante explaining that Planned Parenthood evidently hadn't bought into Pincus's research so far. It was time, she suggested, that they do something to really get the ball rolling.

A few months later, McCormick took a trip to Worcester, where she met with Hoagland and Chang. Pincus was out of town, but she scrutinized the work being done and took time to pepper the researchers with pointed questions that bore evidence of the knowledge she'd gained both as an MIT student and through years of poring over medical journals in search of a cure for Stanley. She was impressed by what she saw and heard, but that only served to stoke her frustration that Pincus and his team were not getting more support from both inside the medical community and beyond.

The facilities were basic, to say the least: one small building with a handful of lab areas and a very limited staff. Chang lived in the lab. And McCormick was outraged when she learned that Planned Parenthood had recently refused to grant Pincus a $3,600 stipend on the basis that they just weren't "sold" on his work.

"It's pretty trying not to be able to push it!" McCormick wrote to Sanger in a later letter. To this her friend suggested that, perhaps in a few months, they should pay Pincus a visit personally and see how they might be able to help. Her thinly veiled hope, of course, was that McCormick would commit to the massive silver bullet that nobody else was rich and courageous enough to fire.

On June 8, 1953, that's exactly what the two women did. After an extensive tour of the utilitarian facilities of the Worcester Foundation for Experimental Biology, McCormick put it to Pincus straight: "How much do you need?" she asked him. Pincus had recently secured a 17,500-dollar grant from Planned Parenthood to cover the cost of a year of clinical trials on humans. Planned Parenthood, in turn, had already approached McCormick for help with that grant, and she'd agreed to foot half the bill. But everyone who was there that day knew that 17,500 dollars was a fraction of what would be required in the long run to see this project to completion. *How much would the entire program set the foundation back?* McCormick wanted to know. *How much cash to make the "magic pill" real?* The answer, Pincus finally admitted, was 125,000 dollars. McCormick nodded coolly, got back into the car, and returned to Boston, where she was now living. Later that night she wrote to Pincus. She'd been impressed by the tour and by meeting him, she said, and she was willing to write a 10,000-dollar check immediately. More cash, she promised, would be on its way soon.

And Katharine McCormick stuck to her word. Over the years that followed she would end up contributing around 2 million dollars—or about 20.5 million dollars in today's money—to Pincus's work. Author Jonathan Eig wrote in his book *The Birth of the Pill* that Gregory Pincus was a remarkable scientific visionary who understood that the contraceptive pill "might not only change women's lives but also help tame the world's population growth." But, Eig writes, Pincus was not a true evangelist for the cause. Instead, he was a scientist busy chasing leads and pitching for grant money. "If it had not been for the persistence and extraordinary beneficence of Katharine McCormick, the birth control project might have gone nowhere."

\*\*\*

Pincus started with rabbits and rats. He established that female ovulation could be stopped by administering synthetic progesterone. After crossing paths with him at a scientific conference in 1952, he'd also started working with John Charles Rock, whom he initially got to know back in the 1930s. Rock was not only a renowned obstetrician-gynecologist at Harvard University Medical School but was also heavily involved in the Catholic Church. He was interested in the social implications of science. Across America, but particularly in Massachusetts, laws still constrained research into anything relating to human contraception.

Rock, despite the opinion of the Catholic Church on the subject, was a fierce proponent of contraception, but not necessarily because he cared about women's rights. He did care about his patient's health but he was also intent on curbing population growth—specifically the growth of populations that he considered to be primitive, people he considered to be inferior. Throughout his career, this particular goal would become one way he'd attempt to reconcile his commitment to contraception with his staunch Catholicism. And it was also precisely because of his faith that he was uniquely positioned to convince other Catholics—committed to the notion that human life starts and must be protected at the point of conception—of the benefits of birth control. Coincidentally, just as McCormick and Pincus were drawing up the terms of an agreement to work together, Rock was experimenting with progesterone injections designed to regulate women's menstrual cycles and help them conceive.

Pincus and Rock's initial trials were held at the Free Hospital for Women under the guise of research into fertility issues, but the two physicians soon realized that they would have to think bigger to make real headway. They considered going to a different state, where contraception was less legally restricted, but that option was soon dismissed. After World War II, American women of reproductive age had become highly mobile. To be able to collect usable data over a years-long period, it was important that a trial cohort stay in the same place for the duration.

Japan, Hawaii, India, and Mexico were all considered, but in the end, Rock and Pincus settled on the U.S. unincorporated territory of Puerto Rico. The island had no laws banning contraception; it also had a well-established network of birth control clinics (many of them funded by eugenicists) and was close enough to the United States for the research team to easily be able to travel back and forth. A significant number of the medical professionals in Puerto Rico had also been trained in the States, and Pincus already knew and trusted many of them. As an island, Puerto Rico had a relatively stable population—few people moved to or from the territory—that could be depended upon for the full length of the trials, however long they might take. And finally—and tragically—the island already had explicitly eugenicist legislation in place. In 1937, the United States had imposed Law 116, legalizing sterilization, onto Puerto Rico, motivated by the belief that Puerto Rico was too overpopulated to have a stable economy and that the only way to curb unemployment was to decrease the population density.

In Puerto Rico, Pincus teamed up with Celso-Ramón García, another experienced obstetrician-gynecologist who also spoke English, and later Edris Rice-Wray, an American-trained physician with a graduate degree in public health and who was the medical director of Puerto Rico's Family Planning Association, the latter to oversee day-to-day operations.

Research resumed apace. Rock began working out of a medical facility provided by Harvard on the grounds of the Free Hospital, which he called the Rock Reproductive Study Center. His idea was that by physically working at the intersection between the hospital and the university, he would be able to balance his patient care with the studies he and Pincus were doing; and Katharine McCormick and Margaret Sanger—whose attention had never drifted far from the work the men were doing—applauded the ambition.

McCormick was covering a sizable chunk of the cost of making the research possible, regularly channeling tens of thousands of dollars into refurbishments to the building that housed the Rock Reproductive Study Center. She had started calling it "the hovel," only somewhat in jest, and made no secret of her disgust at the conditions under which Harvard and the Free Hospital were making their brightest doctors work. She wanted the pill to become a widely available option for every woman in the country. If the chance of that happening might be enhanced even in the slightest by making a few research labs more aesthetically appealing, then she was willing to give it a try.

\*\*\*

In 1956, relatively early in the trials, Pincus and Rock selected a particular combination of chemical compounds that would produce the fewest side effects and be the most reliable as a contraceptive. The carefully calibrated mixture of noretynodrel, a chemical compound first synthesized in 1952 by American chemist Frank Colton of pharmaceutical business G. D. Searle & Company, headquartered in Skokie, Illinois, and mestranol, an estrogen compound, was given the proprietary name Enovid.

In June 1957, the U.S. Food and Drug Administration (FDA) approved the use of the pill to regulate menstruation, and by 1959, some half a million women were using it, ostensibly to regulate their periods while also benefiting from one particularly serendipitous side effect. Every package of Enovid contained a warning label about the drug's contraceptive activity. For a year or two the true reason many women opted for Enovid might have been America's worst-kept secret.

On July 23, 1959, Searle filed an application with the FDA to license Enovid for use as an oral contraceptive. Though today they would likely be deemed inadequate for a whole host of reasons spanning from ethics to safety, the trials for Enovid constituted the most extensive ever done for a drug examined by the FDA. The data submitted was for 897 women who had taken 10,427 cycles of Enovid with no side effects that the doctors who had examined the report considered to be harmful. Later, there would be reports of Enovid causing blood clots, but at the time, the FDA had already reviewed potential safety issues when it approved Enovid as a menstrual regulator, so Searle assumed the application would pass swiftly.

It didn't. For weeks, the FDA said nothing. Their concern, it seemed, was less tangible. This was the first drug designed not explicitly to cure or improve a medical condition, but instead for healthy women to take over a long period of time and for a purpose that could be interpreted as primarily social. This was uncharted territory, and the FDA was not entirely comfortable with how ethics, morality, and beliefs should or should not shape its decision.

Rock requested a meeting with the FDA, which was granted, and in late December 1959, he and Searle's medical director, Irwin Winter, took a train to Washington, D.C., to discuss the matter. For ninety minutes, the two men were kept waiting before finally being escorted into a conference room, where a hearing officer received them. Rock flinched. Pasquale DeFelice, the hearing officer tasked with determining the fate of Enovid and, therefore, of Rock's professional success and destiny, was in his mid-thirties, barely out of medical school, and not a board-certified physician but a devout Catholic. DeFelice would later go on to father ten children and have an illustrious medical career, but on that day and in that moment, Rock couldn't see anything other than an unqualified juvenile naively standing between him and the fulfillment of his lifelong ambition.

DeFelice opened the meeting by underscoring his worries relating to a possible link between Enovid and cancer. And then there were the religious and moral concerns, of course. Rock's blood boiled. Winter later recalled how Rock at one point even refused to refer to DeFelice by name, calling him "young man" instead. He vehemently criticized DeFelice's lack of experience, at which the latter said that he intended to send the trial data to several more consultants before making a final decision. Then he promptly declared the conversation over and left the room.

Christmas came and went, and the year 1960 began with no further word from the FDA. Eventually, on April 22, DeFelice wrote to Searle and said that the pill had been approved conditionally. Short-term usage of Enovid for therapeutic purposes was acceptable, he wrote, but the agency continued to be anxious about the drug's extended use as a contraceptive.

Finally, on May 9, 1960, the FDA approved Enovid explicitly as a means of preventing pregnancy, but for no more than two years at a time. It would be years before it could legally be prescribed in every state and regardless of marital status; nevertheless, Rock, Pincus, Garcia, and others in the medical community rejoiced. Champagne flowed liberally. Margaret Sanger, in her late seventies by then, and McCormick, who was well into her eighties, had reached the end of a road that so frequently had looked too treacherous and challenging to travel. The "magic pill" was real. The gamble had paid off. Katharine Dexter McCormick's fortune really had achieved something remarkable.

\*\*\*

On August 22, 1967, Gregory Goodwin Pincus died at Boston's Peter Bent Brigham Hospital. He'd been suffering from a blood disease called myeloid metaplasia and was sixty-four years old. The *New York Times*'s obituary ran well over a thousand words and opened by praising him as one of the three "fathers" of the birth control pill, the others being John Rock and Min-Chueh Chang. The article described his research journey in detail, his experiments with "'fatherless' rabbits," and how he had "interested local businessmen and professionals in raising funds" to support his foundation in Worcester. No mention was made of either Margaret Sanger or Katharine McCormick.

Later that year, in the early hours of December 28, Katharine McCormick suffered a massive stroke while sleeping and died. She was ninety-two. Before she died—as an octogenarian—she'd managed to get a prescription for the contraceptive pill from her doctor and had gone to the drugstore to get it; not because she needed it, but because she could. Her body was buried in the Dexter family plot, next to her brother Samuel. Few of the major newspapers carried more than a brief mention of her death. Most didn't even make space for that. The few obituaries that did appear focused on her studies at MIT, her tragic marriage to a mad millionaire, or the money that she left to the Art Institute of Chicago and the Santa Barbara Museum of Art. The fact that she funded the development of the first contraceptive pill was mostly limited to a subclause or short sentence, a rhetorical afterthought. McCormick left five million dollars to the Planned Parenthood Federation and one million dollars to the Worcester Foundation for Experimental Biology.

Margaret Sanger had passed away the previous year at the age of eighty-seven, having developed dementia. She died in a sanatorium. In her lengthy *New York Times* obituary—also featuring no mention of McCormick—she was recognized as the "best-known" advocate of birth control who sought to free women from sexual servitude.

Around that time, a darker side of Sanger's story was also coming to the fore: her indisputable ties to the eugenics movement, which sought to "improve" the human race through planned breeding based on genetic traits. Aside from the birth control advocacy work for which she was, and still is, best known, Sanger also supported the sterilization of some people with mental illnesses.

Years later, Esther Katz, a retired associate professor of history at New York University and founder of the Margaret Sanger Papers Project, which aims to collate and edit Sanger's historical papers and letters, told the *Washington Post* that Sanger also believed that if a woman gave birth to a large number of children, the younger children would be weaker. To advance the birth control movement, Katz explained, she even spoke with the Ku Klux Klan. In 2020, Planned Parenthood of Greater New York announced that it would remove Sanger's name from one of its Manhattan clinics in an attempt to reckon with her complicated legacy.

In the decades since John Rock and Gregory Pincus conducted their trials, both in the Boston suburbs and in Puerto Rico, the horrifying nature of the way they frequently treated their research subjects—not to mention the racist nature of their overarching motive for the work they were doing—has come to light too.

It was a mostly unregulated period in U.S. scientific history—a time when research subjects were frequently thought of as expendable commodities. In 1947, the Nuremberg Code established the importance of informed consent, but it was not a legally binding document. The Kefauver–Harris Drug Amendments to the federal Food, Drug and Cosmetic Act, requiring proof of the safety and efficacy of medications, were only passed by Congress in 1962, and the Belmont Report, which required proof of drug safety and "respect, beneficence, and justice" throughout all human trials, was only published in 1979. Some have compared the trials Rock and Pincus organized in Puerto Rico to the Tuskegee Syphilis Study, in which the government conducted research, without their consent, on African American men suffering from the disease in Alabama from 1932 until 1972.

In a biography of Rock published in 2008, authors Margaret Marsh and Wanda Ronner describe the Puerto Rico trial in grim detail. "Within weeks of the trial's start," they write, "*El Imparcial*, a popular newspaper, accused the project's sponsors of conducting a 'neomalthusian campaign,' and local doctors told their patients that the pill was dangerous." Three women reportedly died in those trials. Autopsies were never conducted.

Katharine McCormick's legacy—though necessarily complicated by her association with known racists and eugenicists—lives on, thanks to the lasting impact of her activism and philanthropy. But compared to Sanger, Pincus, Rock, and even Chang, her name is relatively unfamiliar even in the world of medical history. Often, she's simply referred to as Mrs. Stanley McCormick. At best she's commended for being one of the first women to earn a biology degree from MIT.

According to the Centers for Disease Control and Prevention, the CDC, almost all women in the United States today will at some point in their lives use birth control. Data from the 2017 to 2019 National Survey of Family Growth shows that more than six in every ten women between the ages of fifteen and forty-nine in America use contraception, of which about 14 percent use "the pill." The simplicity of its common, monosyllabic nickname is testament to the revolutionary effect it has had, not only on women but on communities, countries, cultural standards, and undoubtedly even entire economies. As early as the 1930s, scientists had been experimenting with ways to arrest female ovulation and prevent pregnancy. The invention of the "magic pill" was, therefore, always a possibility, but McCormick was the person who enabled it to be pushed out into the world much sooner than it otherwise might have been. And unlike that of so many of the people who shared her goal— Rock, Pincus, and Sanger, to name but three—McCormick's driving force was not eugenics or racism, but a desire for women to be able to enjoy fulfilling, independent lives.

As Armond Fields notes in one of the only biographies ever to be written about McCormick, "At the beginning of the last century, the acknowledged achievement of a woman did not assure her acceptance as a self-determining equal, because a male-dominated society refused to recognize women as self-determining citizens. In response to this societal mind-set, Katharine became a dedicated advocate for women's rights." He added: "Her determination and commitment, while clashing with fierce opponents and overcoming sizeable barriers, contrived to make things happen and carried her efforts to successful conclusion." Loretta McLaughlin, in her book on the development of the birth control pill, candidly describes her as "a woman more strange and powerful than fiction could ever invent." Without her vigor, steely principles, and passion for empowerment, decades might have passed before women would have been able to take control of their bodies, careers, and lives. Had it not been for Katharine McCormick, Gregory Pincus, though obviously a genius, might have remained a footnote in the annals of medical history, praised in obituaries as a brave visionary but perhaps primarily as the father of fatherless rabbits.

***

The approval of the pill was dubbed a socioeconomic revolution, by media outlets, and a revolution was, indeed, simmering. By 1965—likely encouraged by a considerable price cut, from about ten dollars a month (or eighty dollars today) to about four—one out of every four married women in America under the age of forty-five had used the contraceptive pill. Two years later, nearly thirteen million women in the world were relying on it, and that number ballooned to somewhere between fifty and eighty million by 1984. In the space of just a few years, family planning had evolved from being a stigmatized concept to an accepted and openly acknowledged cultural norm—a societal necessity, even. Years later, *The Economist* crowned the birth control pill one of the Seven Wonders of the Modern World. "When the history of the twentieth century is written, [the approval of the pill] may be seen as the first [time] when men and women were truly partners," the magazine declared. "Wonderful things can come in small packets."

Up until this point, unwanted pregnancies had not only constrained a woman's access to paid work and education, they had also made social outcasts of the unmarried. They had ruined lives. A new era of sexual and personal liberation was dawning. The mores of society were being recalibrated, biological laws rewritten. For the first time,

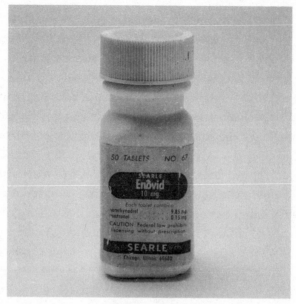

A bottle of Enovid oral contraceptive. Courtesy Science History Institute.

sex and reproduction were properly distinguishable, and the former could be enjoyed without fear of committing to decades of parenting on account of the latter.

Just like the Rosies, the birth control pill's eventual economic impact on America and the world is impossible to quantify objectively, particularly because the ensuing massive political, legislative, and cultural changes that occurred in short order shifted women's status and enhanced their opportunities significantly. But while it's impossible to decouple any single development during that period from the others to assess its specific impact, it is possible to assert that the effect of the pill was stupendous.

In 2011, Kevin Stange, an economist and associate professor of public policy at the University of Michigan, published a paper in which, based on a representative sample of high school seniors from 1992, he found that almost all young women who planned to delay motherhood until their late twenties or beyond also expected to obtain a college degree or a graduate or professional degree. Conversely, women who planned to have children while they were younger were less likely to aspire to a bachelor's degree. In other words, the ability and choice to delay childbirth enabled women to increase their personal investment in education and their careers. In 1960, there were 1.60 men for every woman graduating from a U.S. four-year college, according to data from the Department of Education, but over the decades that followed, female college enrollment and graduation rates surged to the point that female enrollment overtook male enrollment in the early 1980s. Young women no longer anticipated that they would, by default, follow in the footsteps of their mothers, who never, or only temporarily, worked outside the home. Women also started taking more math and science courses in high school and electing college majors that more closely resembled those of their male peers, challenging the "Mrs. degree" label that had condescendingly been applied to women accused of attending university with the primary goal of finding an eligible spouse.

A resurgence in feminism was certainly one of the driving forces as to why so many women sought out higher education, as were government guarantees in the form of those laws that protected women from discrimination in education and employment. But the birth control pill was the engine. Everything else played ancillary roles.

And then there was the labor market. In a 2002 paper, professors Claudia Goldin and Lawrence F. Katz, both of Harvard, tracked wage growth for college-educated women in each state and concluded that the legality and availability of the pill did indeed determine earnings potential later on.

In 2005, Amalia Rebecca Miller, a professor of economics at the University of Virginia, took a closer look at what she calls the "postponement premium" and found that delaying motherhood leads to a substantial increase in career earnings of 10 percent per year of delay. A few years later, in 2012, Miller teamed up with two other academics, Martha J. Bailey and Brad Hershbein, both of the University of Michigan, to conduct research specifically into whether the pill drove a narrowing in the gender pay gap across the United States. The median annual wage and salary earnings of full-time, full-year female workers, as a percentage of men's earnings, was relatively stable at around 60 percent during the 1960s and 1970s. Between 1979 and 1989, however, the figure rose rapidly to about 69 percent. In fact, the speed of wage convergence between men and women in that decade was faster, even, than during the 1990s and the 2000s.

But how much of this can be attributed to the pill? Through careful statistical analysis, the academics concluded that the effect of the birth control pill on wages amounted to roughly one-third of the total wage gains for women in their forties, born between the mid-1940s and early 1950s. In other words, 10 percent of the narrowing in the gender gap during the 1980s could be attributed to early access to the pill, and 31 percent during the 1990s. The researchers also acknowledged, however, that it was impossible to place a true and undisputed value on the pill as a conduit for female economic empowerment. Still, its availability altered norms and expectations about marriage and childbearing and likely even influenced firms' decisions to hire and promote women.

In many cases, the fear of hiring a woman who might immediately get pregnant had been sufficient reason to disqualify a female job candidate. Suspecting that a woman had access to the pill might well have allayed such fears. So, the actual economic effects of the pill might be even more significant than Miller and her colleagues established. "Even these conservative estimates," the scholars wrote at the end of their paper, "suggest that the pill's power to transform childbearing from probabilistic to planned shifted women's career decisions and compensation for decades to come."

# CHAPTER 3

*Giving the Problem a Name*

By noon I'm ready for a padded cell.
—Nebraska mother of three with a PhD in anthropology, quoted in
Betty Friedan's *The Feminine Mystique*

It was meant to be an occasion for celebration and joyful reminiscence, and for many it certainly was, but it also ended up being one of the most socially consequential college reunions in American history. In June 1957, Smith College alumni gathered to mark the fifteenth anniversary of their graduation from the elite women's liberal arts school in Northampton, Massachusetts. Among the many housewives in attendance was a mother of three who lived in Rockland County, just north of New York City, and occasionally supplemented her husband's income with cash earned as a freelance journalist for women's magazines. She had majored in psychology and graduated summa cum laude in 1942. She'd then spent a year on a fellowship, she told the other alumni that day, training as a psychologist at the University of California, Berkeley, before moving back East, getting married, and having kids.

Betty Friedan was eager to hear what everyone else had spent the past decade and a half of their lives doing, but her curiosity wasn't superficial or sparked by an appetite for frivolous gossip. Her goal was to understand how educated women in America were faring: whether they were satisfied, or whether their often-suburban life—structured around unyielding social and cultural norms—felt as smothering to them as it was starting to feel to her.

Friedan was born Bettye Naomi Goldstein in the city of Peoria in central Illinois in February 1921. She was the oldest of three children and the daughter of a Russian jeweler called Harry and his Hungarian wife, Miriam, who had worked as a journalist but quit when Bettye was born. Bettye was tremendously intelligent and as ferociously principled as she was outspoken. She read books from the local library with a vengeance and displayed her intellectualism with an unabashed pride, using long, complicated words just for the sake of it—though she mispronounced many of them because she'd never heard anyone say them out loud.

Bettye wrote for her school newspaper. When she was thirteen, she won an essay competition. Under the assigned title of "Why I am Proud to Be an American," she ruminated on her heritage: how her grandparents escaped persecution by fleeing Eastern Europe and living first in St. Louis before settling in Peoria; how her grandfather got into medical school; and the opportunities that paved the way for her father to launch his own business.

Even though books took Bettye around the globe, Peoria's city limits for the most part marked the frontier of her world. On vacations, the Goldsteins ventured as far as Wisconsin. But Bettye didn't mind. She knew nothing else. Geeky, and one of the only Jewish students at Peoria High School, she didn't have many friends, but she was acquainted with several girls, and only one had a mother who worked outside the home. That woman—a widow—ran a travel agency, and Bettye adored her warmth and nurturing personality. She was spirited, witty, exciting; she was everything that Miriam Goldstein—Bettye's own stern and moody mother—was not.

In 1938, after graduating high school, armed with a handful of books and an appetite for adventure, Bettye got on the Rock Island Railroad, changed trains in Chicago, and boarded a sleeper car to Northampton and a new life at Smith. In her first year, she won an academic scholarship. The creative vibrancy of the town electrified her. The diversity of the student body, compared to the homogeneity of Peoria, chipped away at an often-paralyzing self-consciousness that had stemmed from always having been so obviously different from everyone else. She read Virginia Woolf, Thomas Mann, James Joyce, and Gustave Flaubert, and by her third year Bettye was editor-in-chief of the college newspaper, tilting its editorial stance to the left, occasionally inciting controversy. She advocated for the unionization of maids on campus and started a literary magazine. She began reading the *New York Times* and dropped the *e* from the end of her name. Her mother had loved that final silent letter, so this was a gesture, perhaps, that symbolically severed the umbilical cord. After graduating, and before leaving to start that psychology fellowship at Berkeley, Betty signed up to become a member of the Communist Party.

In California, Betty became more political, drifting even further to the left, fueled by a blossoming confidence and audacity rarely displayed by women of the time. She studied under the renowned psychologist Erik Erikson—best known for coining the term "identity crisis"—and, after her first year-long fellowship, was offered a second, this one even more prestigious than the first. It would have paved the way to a doctorate, but Betty had started dating a physicist who was intimidated by her success. Many years later, in her memoir, she would imply that he pressured her to turn down that second fellowship. Soon after, Betty broke off her relationship with him and moved into a small house that her Smith friends were renting in New York's Greenwich Village, a bohemian haunt loved by creative types.

She started working for the Federated Press, a news service that produced articles for labor newspapers across the country. She interviewed Eleanor Roosevelt and navigated a steep learning curve, training herself to craft succinct copy to deadline. In 1946, she joined the *UE News*, the publication of the United Electrical, Radio & Machine Workers of America, and regularly authored pamphlets calling for gender equality and improved workers' rights.

It was a year after the end of World War II. During the 1930s and early 1940s, Frances Perkins, who had served as U.S. Secretary of Labor under President Roosevelt and had been the first woman ever to hold a Cabinet post, had spearheaded the implementation of some extremely important labor laws. She crafted a safety net for a society still bitterly bruised by the Great Depression, and she secured an extensive array of benefits for workers; however, women were still, unquestionably, lesser citizens.

Few employers had done anything to dismantle entrenched gender norms, even in the face of the rapid influx of women into the labor market over the preceding five years. In some states, a married woman could not get a job without the permission of her husband, and access to credit was a matter of gender too. Rules that allowed employers to fire or discriminate against a single woman when she married—called marriage bars—were still commonplace, particularly in jobs like teaching and clerical work. Many women concealed their marital status in a bid to stay employed, at least until they could no longer hide a pregnancy, but marriage bars were not officially outlawed in the private sector until decades later.

One article published in 1946 in the British conservative magazine *The Spectator* reasoned that marriage bars made sense for several reasons: Married women are supported by their husbands, so they don't need jobs; bans also ensure that single women who actually need to work in order to earn a living have more opportunities to do so; and finally, unmarried women are simply more reliable and are more willing to follow jobs to other locations than married women. In other words, they're less likely to get pregnant.

\*\*\*

The first man Betty dated after the war was a South African banker. It didn't work out, and he was followed in short order by a dentist and, eventually, by Carl Friedan. Carl, a childhood friend of one of Betty's colleagues, had been a theater director in the Special Services Unit, the entertainment branch of the military, during the war. On their first date, he gifted Betty an apple, and it made her laugh. It was a blind date at Barney Greengrass, a deli on Manhattan's Upper West Side, where they ordered sturgeon sandwiches. Not long after, the two moved in together.

Betty and Carl married on June 12, 1947, and a year later she gave birth to Daniel. Four years after that, Jonathan was born, but about five months into her second pregnancy, Betty was fired from the union newspaper where she'd been working. It wasn't until 1978, with the Pregnancy Discrimination Act, an amendment to the Civil Rights Act of 1964, that discrimination on the basis of pregnancy was outlawed.

Betty found out later that her editor hadn't wanted her to take a second maternity leave, so he had ruthlessly decided to fill her position with a man. This placed the financial burden on Carl, still working in theater, to support his growing family, and he grudgingly admitted that he would have to turn his back on the volatile arts industry in favor of something more lucrative. Through a friend, Carl secured work in advertising and quickly proved he had a knack for it. He worked on Fifth Avenue and even had a secretary, but despite the couple's newfound economic stability, rifts were starting to form in the Friedan marriage, opening more dramatically when Betty discovered that her husband was having an affair.

Pregnant, furious, and embarrassed at having lost her job to a man, Betty became a housewife by default and despised it. She was irritable and short-tempered. Ever since she was a young girl she'd suffered from asthma, and for the most part she had learned to keep it under control, but when she stopped working, her attacks became more severe and more frequent. She started seeing a therapist, who, much to her annoyance, only pointed out what was plainly obvious to her. "Why are you pretending to be just a housewife?" he asked her. "Didn't you graduate summa cum laude in psychology? Aren't you a writer?" She had, and she was, but there was nothing she felt she was able to structurally change about her life to make it more fulfilling.

One evening in 1956, after three martinis, Betty had sex with Carl, forgetting that she'd already removed her diaphragm. Nine months later, their third child and first daughter, Emily, was born. The family had outgrown the apartment in Queens, where they'd been living for the last few years, and moved to a converted barn in a hamlet—then known as

Sneden's Landing and now as Palisades—in Rockland County on the Hudson River, about a forty-minute drive from the city.

Carl worked constantly. Occasionally, Betty wrote articles as a free-lancer for women's magazines, and deep down inside, her political convictions remained fiery, but something—a sense of self, an element of identity—was fading. She wanted desperately to be a happy housewife, the kind her own mercurial mother seemed incapable of being, but in her memoir, she later recalled the grimness of those first few months in the suburbs and how at least twice—once while on a hike with a church group, and once in a supermarket parking lot—she had a sudden, terrifying panic attack.

She was also getting tired of the pieces she was submitting to women's publications—articles about all the joys and none of the annoyances of cooking and parenting. They felt inane and inconsequential. She wanted to write meaty features rooted in research and policy and international affairs, about the development of the hydrogen bomb or nuclear testing in the Pacific, but editors consistently responded with the same line: American women simply can't identify with those topics. They're not interested. Want to write about surging commodity prices because of geopolitical tensions? Then file a story on the creative ways in which housewives might deal with the rising cost of coffee, Betty Friedan was told. Anything else would, quite simply, be wasted on women.

\*\*\*

In 1947, Marynia Farnham and Ferdinand Lundberg, two Freudian psychoanalysts, published a book called *Modern Woman: The Lost Sex*, which posited that something had gone awfully awry in society. Women had become overeducated, the pair argued, and this affliction was preventing them from being able to perform their roles as obedient housewives and good mothers. Reading the book made Friedan's blood boil. She valued her education immensely. How dare someone suggest otherwise? Granted, she felt like she wasn't leveraging her degree to maximize her career and economic potential. And, no, she hadn't done the momentous things her professors and advisors—first at Smith and then at Berkeley—had urged and even expected her to do, but that didn't mean she should never have gone to college. Education was not the root of anyone's problem, she seethed.

It was 1957 by then, and ahead of her fifteenth-anniversary reunion at Smith, Friedan had been asked to conduct a survey of her former classmates. Riled up by *Modern Woman*, she decided that she would use a questionnaire as the basis for an article to refute the thesis put forward in the book. She agonized over the questions, seeking input from some of her college girlfriends, and eventually settled on a set of thirty-eight, covering a spectrum of subjects from politics and fashion to parenthood and books. They were designed to elicit information on everything from a respondent's attitude toward sex and the satisfaction she derived from her marriage, to whether the women considered themselves to be good cooks and even whether they used paper napkins. Several of the questions related to money. Some were open-ended but others entirely binary: *Are you a Republican? Are you a Democrat? Do you believe in God? Do you hate getting old?*

To her surprise, Friedan received about two hundred completed surveys and realized that, rather than producing answers, the responses left her with more questions than she'd started with. As she pored over the papers, two distinct trends emerged. The women who expressed the most appreciation for their education and those who were explicitly using it in some way were least likely to comply with the stereotype of the ideal woman at the time, a woman who, first and foremost, was a wife and mother. But these women also tended to be more satisfied, to have more joie de vivre, and, over all, to be more appreciative of their husbands and children. On the other hand, the women who resembled or even matched the stereotype of the deferential, compliant housewife—a model mother and acquiescent spouse—were more likely to be depressed and frustrated: a shadow, in some ways, of the spritely, sharp-witted graduates she'd tossed her cap with a decade and a half earlier.

The night of the reunion, some of the women from the class of 1942 planned to stay over in Hubbard House, a dormitory on campus, but when the celebrations wound down, they arrived to find the doors locked. The women congregated outside in the dark and were joined by some of the resident seniors who also couldn't get in. Gradually, the alumni—now in their mid- to late thirties—struck up a conversation, bonding with the soon-to-be graduates, over the absurdity of the situation. Friedan, nostalgic for her years of editing the student newspaper and rallying behind a political cause, took the opportunity to ask some of the younger women what they were arguing about these days, what got them angry. And the responses floored her. They weren't angry. "I'm going to get married straight after graduation," one young woman told her. Others already knew they wanted to have three children—or perhaps four—and most envisioned a quiet life in the suburbs, a life not unlike the one that Friedan had somehow come to find herself leading.

Eventually, the janitor arrived and unlocked the door, allowing everyone to retire to bed, but Friedan couldn't sleep. Something was wrong. The responses to the survey were still noisily bustling around her brain, but at the same time she couldn't silence the voices of the younger women echoing in her head. How could these imminent Smith graduates—individuals who were about to embark on their adult lives armed with a degree from an elite educational institution—be so devoid of professional ambition? she wondered. Had the definition of an ideal American woman really come to this? Was her existence—the life of what Betty Friedan considered to be a mundane suburban housewife— actually enviable? Did these girls really know what they were pining for?

Back home in Rockland Country, Friedan channeled her bewilderment into an article she titled "Are Women Wasting Their Time in College?" In it, she provocatively suggested that it might not be higher education that was frustrating American women in their roles as mothers and housewives, but the prevailing definition of the role of women and the prescribed ideals they were told to aspire to that were driving them to despair.

An editor at *McCall's*, the monthly magazine that had bought and published much of Friedan's work up until that point, was shocked and rejected the piece on the spot. *Ladies' Home Journal* suggested a dramatic rewrite that flipped the article's argument on its head, and another editor at *Redbook* told Friedan's agent that she must be "going off her rocker." The rejections added fuel to her determination to air what she was starting to think of as the American housewife's awkward secret, and to corroborate her case, she collected more data. She did interviews and surveyed women who'd studied at Radcliffe and other colleges to rule out the possibility of Smith graduates being anomalies, and what she found only cemented her initial conclusions.

One April morning in 1959, Betty Friedan was observing a conversation among five suburban mothers, one of whom had four children. The woman in question was Jim's wife and Janey's mom. She was the server of meals and putter-on of snowsuits, she explained to her friends, but if you were to strip away her spouse and kids, she'd have no idea who she really was. "It's almost like"—the woman stumbled forth in a disjointed, tortuous stream of consciousness—"the world is going on without me."

At that very moment, inspired by the woman's words, which were rich with feeble frustration, Friedan knew that she was on to something—and that this was the problem with no name. Magazines had been so quick and firm to reject her pitch simply because, by highlighting this nameless problem, she was threatening the very foundations upon which these publications were established. She was trying to get them to publish something that would instantly explode the myth of the fulfilled domestic female, a myth these magazines feasted on. Later that day, while taking her own children to the doctor, Friedan stopped at a pay phone and called her agent. Stop pitching the piece, she instructed her. This project had to be bigger. We're onto something, she said: This has to become a book.

\*\*\*

George Brockway became president of the Manhattan-based publisher W. W. Norton & Company in 1958. The following year Brockway's wife, who'd been a brilliant student at Bryn Mawr College in Pennsylvania, gave birth to their thirteenth child. Also that year, Betty Friedan and her agent approached him with a proposal for a book that would soon come to be called *The Feminine Mystique*.

When Friedan initially ran her idea by him, Brockway simply listened in silent fascination. Friedan hadn't expected it, but Brockway agreed instantly with the premise and conceded that she really had touched on something important. As she spoke, all he could think of was his own wife and her daily existence, designed entirely around getting the children up and dressed, cooking them meals and feeding them, cleaning the house, changing the bedsheets, making peanut butter sandwiches, shuttling them to school or nursery and then back again, cooking some more, feeding some more, cleaning some more, smiling at her husband, lying in bed at night exhausted but restless, and then doing everything all over again the next day and the day after that. Perhaps a little shell-shocked, Brockway offered Betty Friedan a three-thousand-dollar advance. She planned to deliver a manuscript in a year.

It ended up taking her five. Friedan proved to be a meticulous researcher. Now in total defiance of what a good mother and wife should spend her days doing, she travelled to New Jersey, Boston, and Chicago—trips that were carefully engineered around childcare and domestic duties. She managed to get a desk in the public library in New York City and caught a bus there three days a week to write and research. She hired a babysitter to help her with her three children. She drew on her knowledge of psychology and interviewed experts in economics, sociology, and history to piece together a picture of the gradual and tragic evolution of American women through recent history: from the spirited and career-focused feminist ideal of the 1920s New Woman to the affluent-but-shackled stay-at-home-wife-and-mother of the postwar era, plagued by unfulfilled potential and a deep yearning for something that she couldn't put a name to.

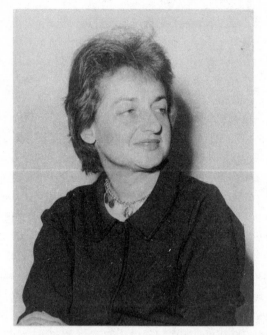

Betty Friedan, the journalist and activist who cofounded the National
Organization for Women, pictured here in 1960.

This latter woman, Betty Friedan found, was eloquent, educated, and often quite pretty, though not intimidatingly so. She had exquisite manners and a sweet disposition but was also entirely consumed with household chores and myopically focused on being the best wife and the best mother possible. Her days were geared toward keeping her husband and children healthy, happy, and fulfilled. Much like Brockway's wife, she washed and cleaned and sewed and cooked and gardened, and she picked up her children and dropped them off where they needed to be and exactly on time. Mostly, she smiled through inconvenience and stress, through the strangling feeling of anxiety that occasionally crept across her chest and into her throat, admitting graciously that her wonderful spouse was always right. And when he told her yet again that he'd be late back from work, she tucked the children into bed and didn't mind a jot keeping his dinner warm, all the while trying to push away the thought that he might well be having an affair.

The message in the mass media, in *Redbook* and *Ladies' Home Journal* and *Woman's Home Companion*, was that this woman was living the dream—that by conquering a man's heart she had fulfilled the primary goal any woman in this country, the greatest country in the world, should aspire to. What those magazines didn't convey was that the American housewife felt lonely, melancholy, and one-dimensional, but also like she didn't have the right to feel that way. Occasionally, in the dead of night, she wondered what it would be like to have a sordid affair herself, or to run away, or to throw herself in front of a hurtling freight train. When it became intolerable, she popped a pill or two, took a sharp breath in, knocked back some of the liquor she kept secretly stashed in her undergarment drawer, and just got on with it. Miltown, a tranquilizer pill dubbed "mother's little helper," had hit the market in 1955 and swiftly became the first blockbuster psychotropic drug in American history. It was a dependable companion, a confidante who couldn't tell.

One of Friedan's former classmates had written on the Smith reunion questionnaire that the problem was "always being the children's mommy, or the minister's wife, and never being myself." A housewife from Nebraska with a PhD in anthropology and three children told Friedan during a later interview that a film made of a typical morning in her house would look like an old Marx Brothers comedy. "I wash the [breakfast] dishes, rush the older children off to school, dash out in[to] the yard to cultivate the chrysanthemums, run back in[side] to make a phone call about a committee meeting, help the youngest child build a blockhouse, spend fifteen minutes skimming the newspapers so I can be well-informed, then scamper down to the washing machines, where my thrice-weekly laundry includes enough clothes to keep a primitive village going for an entire year," the woman said according to Friedan's account. "By noon I'm ready for a padded cell [. . .] yet I look upon myself as one of the more relaxed housewives in the neighborhood."

In the prologue to the final manuscript, Betty Friedan commented that the "problem that has no name burst like a boil through the image of the happy American housewife." Sharply, she asserted that we can "no longer ignore that voice within women that says: 'I want something more than my husband and my children in my home.'"

\*\*\*

Through a stroke of misfortune, *The Feminine Mystique* appeared on bookstore shelves in February 1963 during a newspaper printers' strike, meaning that it wasn't reviewed in the *New York Times* or in many of the other major papers. But as soon as a critical mass of readers got their hands on a copy, word swept across the country—hushed but excited—that this was a seminal, brave, even revolutionary and deliciously dangerous piece of writing.

Betty Friedan embarked on a book tour and started appearing on talk shows, which supercharged sales. Hundreds of middle-class and affluent women wrote to her in the weeks and months after they hungrily tore through it—between bathing the baby and cooking dinner and setting their hair—and admitted that they, too, suffered from the problem with no name. Some said that they considered themselves to be nothing more than an "appliance" or that they felt "brain dead" despite being highly educated. One woman admitted in a letter that she felt so depressed, it was almost drowning her.

But others took a different view. For each letter of thanks, respect, or adoration, Friedan received at least one complaining that she was putting stupid, perilously risky ideas in the pretty little heads of daughters and wives. One letter accused *The Feminine Mystique* of posing a greater threat to America than the Russians, because it questioned women's "sacred role as housewife." Whatever side of the debate people came down on, though, there was no doubt that the book had struck a timely chord and opened the valve on a topic that no one before Friedan had had the nerve, the awareness, or the gumption to breach in such a fervid manner.

More than just a social commentary or even a manifesto, *The Feminine Mystique* was a cri de coeur, a thrilling sign that there might be an alternative to female submissiveness, to women being what Simone de

Beauvoir in 1949 had dubbed "The Second Sex." It also planted a flag for the feminist movement. Betty Friedan, little known until then, was hailed as a chief architect of what later would be called second-wave feminism.

Decades earlier, in 1920, women had won the right to vote—the most basic democratic right. During the Second World War, many of them had worked jobs previously only held by men. With the birth control pill now slowly becoming available to a chosen few, they'd been offered the prospect, at least, of being able to take control of their bodies. Now, they wanted to be treated as full-fledged humans. They wanted to break out of this mystique in which, during the postwar years of national victory and pride, they had become seemingly irreversibly ensnared.

***

In 1960, four decades after being granted the right to vote, women accounted for about a third of the paid labor market but were still all but absent from managerial and executive roles, and the average female wage was still only about 60 percent of the average male wage. During the 1960 presidential campaign, Senator John F. Kennedy and his team had vocally expressed their support for gender equality and the Civil Rights Movement. One of Kennedy's closest allies was consumer champion Esther Peterson, a Utah-born daughter of Danish immigrant Mormons, who was a fierce advocate of making equal pay for equal work the law. It was women—particularly women in unions—who played a decisive role in helping Kennedy clinch one of the most closely fought election battles in U.S. history, but when the new administration settled in, only a tiny minority of women were given leadership roles.

Women held fewer than 3 percent of appointed positions in the Kennedy administration, and for the first time since Herbert Hoover's presidency, not a single woman was included in the Cabinet. Esther Peterson's appointment, to head the Women's Bureau of the U.S. Department of Labor, was an important exception. It was upon Peterson's recommendation that Kennedy established the President's Commission on the Status of Women late in 1961. Chaired by Eleanor Roosevelt, its mission—in Kennedy's own words—was to "indicate what remains to be done to demolish prejudices and outmoded customs which act as barriers to the full partnership of women in our democracy."

The Commission's first meeting took place in February 1962, and a legislative initiative on equal pay dominated the agenda. Almost a century earlier, in 1870, Congress had passed an amendment to an appropriations bill that required that female clerks working for the government get the same amount of pay as their male counterparts. In 1938, the Fair Labor Standards Act—the FLSA—had been signed into law, designed to eliminate "labor conditions detrimental to the maintenance of the minimum standards of living necessary for health, efficiency, and general well-being of workers." It was the last piece of New Deal legislation passed, and it established a minimum wage, overtime pay, recordkeeping, and child labor standards in both the private and public sector. But when World War II broke out, leading to women flooding the paid labor market, it became apparent that the FLSA was fundamentally inadequate in that it did nothing to ensure that women—now in large numbers doing men's jobs—were being compensated at the same level as their male counterparts.

The National War Labor Board in 1942 encouraged industry leaders to make "adjustments which [would] equalize wage or salary rates paid to females with the rates paid to males for comparable quality and quantity of work on the same or similar operation," but it was just that: encouragement, ineffectual urging that was easy to dismiss. In 1945, a comprehensive Women's Pay Act was introduced to Congress but failed to pass, and when women in the 1950s started working outside the home in growing numbers, pay discrimination based on gender remained pervasive and overt. Gender-specific help-wanted ads were still a norm. In fact, it wasn't until 1973 that the Supreme Court upheld a 1968 ruling by the Equal Employment Opportunity Commission (EEOC) making such ads illegal.

At its inaugural meeting in 1962, the President's Commission on the Status of Women endorsed a fresh effort to pass some kind of equal pay act, and Roosevelt proudly told the press that different wages for comparable work were "contrary to the concept of equality and justice in which we believe." But everyone also knew that it would be an uphill battle. For one thing, many in the business community—including the U.S. Chamber of Commerce—opposed the legislation and argued that women were simply more expensive to employ. In a statement submitted to the Senate hearing on the equal-pay legislation, the National Retail Merchant Association (NRMA) said that legislation "which is fair and equitable to both employers and employees" would "necessarily be confusing, complex, and virtually unenforceable." Citing an industrial study on absenteeism, the association also argued that the rate of time lost due to absenteeism is "much higher for women than for men workers."

Cognizant of how much work would be needed to make equal-pay legislation a reality, Peterson, Roosevelt, and other members of the President's Commission set out on a fact-finding mission. Meticulously, they amassed data on pay and collected information and anecdotes on attitudes and norms across the country. In March 1962 they hosted a series of hearings at which members of a plethora of interest groups testified and shared their insights and experiences: labor leaders, academics, businesspeople, and media professionals. But although evidence was mounting that the structures of the American economy entirely failed to adequately support women's opportunities to fully participate in society, progress toward achieving real change was slow. One sticking point was the wording in the Commission's draft legislation around equal pay for "comparable work." Opponents of the legislation argued that proving comparability would be challenging if not impossible, while advocates, on the other hand, said that using the word "equal" would allow employers to pay unequal wages even if two roles differed only in the slightest.

Eventually, the phrase "equal pay for equal work" was settled on, and the legislation specified that employers had to enforce gender-based pay equity for "jobs requiring equal skill, effort, and responsibility, which are performed under similar working conditions." Congress passed the legislation as an amendment to the FLSA. By some accounts it did so only as a concession to male unionists, who were nervous that their wages might be undercut by employers who were increasingly hiring female workers. But whatever the impetus, on June 10, 1963, Kennedy signed the bill into law. The Equal Pay Act, he noted in his remarks that day, "represents many years of effort . . . to call attention to the unconscionable practice of paying female employees less wages than male employees for the same job. This measure adds to our laws another structure basic to democracy." He acknowledged that "much remains to be done to achieve full equality of economic opportunity" but determined that "this legislation is a significant first step forward."

Much did indeed remain to be done. By Kennedy's own admission, for example, childcare facilities were grossly under-resourced and lacking. About 25 million women at the time were employed outside the home, and that number was rising rapidly. One out of five working mothers had a child under the age of three, and two out of every five had a child of school age. The total facilities of all the licensed day-care centers in the country at the time had the capacity to accommodate about 185,000 children, meaning that about 500,000 children under the age of twelve had to look after themselves, or be watched by another family member, friend, or acquaintance, for at least a portion of the day while their mothers worked. "This, it seems to me," Kennedy said, "is a recipe for disaster."

\*\*\*

Of all the years in the twentieth century, 1963 was unquestionably one of the most pivotal in U.S. history. The year dawned with George Wallace becoming governor of Alabama and declaring, from the steps of the state capitol, "segregation now, segregation tomorrow, segregation forever." By August, Martin Luther King Jr. was announcing, to the March on Washington during his "I Have a Dream" speech, that "1963 is not an end, but a beginning."

The momentum building up in the Civil Rights Movement propelled the Women's Movement. In January, a striking freelance journalist from Toledo, Ohio, named Gloria Steinem, who'd graduated from
Smith in 1956, turned up at an audition to become a Playboy Bunny. It
was a stunt in the name of journalism, and in an undercover assign-
ment for *Show* magazine she shone a light on a world of toxic masculinity, sexual harassment, pitiful pay, and racism, lorded over by a savvy
Chicago businessman named Hugh Hefner. A year earlier, dazzling
movie star Marilyn Monroe, whose nude image had been used, without her consent, on the cover of the first-ever issue of *Playboy*, had died
of a barbiturate overdose, and in February 1963, writer Sylvia Plath—
Smith class of 1955—killed herself in London. Barely a month earlier,
Plath had published *The Bell Jar*, a semi-autobiographical novel about
a woman who moves to New York City for a prestigious internship at a
women's magazine but—in the face of societal pressures to conform to
a stereotype—loses her grip on sanity.

Friedan's *The Feminine Mystique* hit stores eight days after Plath's
death, and it left many women shocked, angry, sad, or just entirely
discombobulated. After reading it, some grappled with their own existence and identity, with their place in this man's world. Self-proclaimed
feminists were fired up by the fact that it was suddenly patently clear
what the wider effect of women being yoked to men—economically
and otherwise—really looked like. The approval of the birth control pill
had instilled in some of them a sense of optimism, but in much of the
cultural mainstream, not even a semblance of effort was being made to
address what was truly going on: the problem that was still nameless
but now being avidly discussed—albeit quietly—at school gates, around
kitchen counters, and in the checkout lines of grocery stores across the
country and beyond.

While Margaret Sanger and Katharine McCormick had been
hustling to make their "magic pill" accessible to the masses, another
revolution—technological in nature—had materialized. Between 1949
and 1959, the number of households in the United States with at least
one television soared from about a million to 50 million, while the

number of commercial TV stations soared. TV became a new fulcrum of many Americans' pastimes, and, as such, it dictated norms and social expectations. On TV, women played predictable parts. Shows like *Leave It to Beaver* and *Bewitched* set the tone. Even though, in the real world, women were now working outside the home far more than they had ever done in history, on the small screen they were almost entirely confined to their houses, a paradox that was emboldening a growing group of women—and a few men—to demand change.

On November 22, 1963, Kennedy, the first president who had acted decisively to address gender discrimination on a national scale, was assassinated while riding in a motorcade through Dealey Plaza in Dallas. Esther Peterson and Eleanor Roosevelt had been the driving forces behind the President's Commission on the Status of Women, and arguably the Equal Pay Act never would have passed without them, but it was Kennedy's allyship and political clout that had gotten everything onto the table to begin with.

It was around that time that Betty Friedan had a dream, the memory of which would stick with her for decades to come. In it, she was standing behind the curtain on an empty stage peeking out at a huge audience of women who were all waiting expectantly for the show to start and for something to happen. But it never did. They were being offered no hope for progress toward achieving the rights they wanted: equal pay, equal opportunities, and equal respect.

Friedan had been reading about the Civil Rights Movement, about "when those ministers, priests and rabbis went down to Alabama, when they marched with the Blacks, when that Sheriff 'Bull' Connor with his bullwhip hosed down those protestors," she later wrote. She was fascinated by the way that a movement, a mass of diverse individuals with a common goal, had succeeded in exerting pressure on President Lyndon B. Johnson, enough to push the Civil Rights Act of 1964 through Congress, prohibiting discrimination on the basis of race, color, religion, sex, or national origin. And though she never identified as a political activist—only ever as an angry journalist—Friedan knew that much more had to, and could, be done to meet the expectations of the sprawling number of women, not just the audience in her dream, who were waiting for action. Through Title VII of the Civil Rights Act, women and workers of color could now sue employers for discriminating against them in terms of pay and when making hiring decisions, but Friedan was worried about enforcement—a fear that was compounded sometime later when she happened upon an article in the *New York Times*.

Under the headline PROTEST PROPOSED ON WOMEN'S JOBS, the report cited an African American law school professor named Pauli Murray warning that unless demonstrators were prepared to march on Washington for women's rights in the same way they had done for African American rights in August 1963, the sex discrimination provisions in Title VII would never get enforced. Yes, the Act committed to the creation of the EEOC—a government body explicitly tasked with enforcing Title VII—but women, Murray warned, were still at risk of squandering this historic chance. Friedan, who often thought of herself as having an inner Geiger counter, now felt it clicking insistently. She looked up Murray, and the two arranged to meet.

\*\*\*

In a 2005 book about notable American women, scholar Susan Ware argues that when historians reflect on twentieth-century American history, "all roads lead to Pauli Murray." Murray defied convention in almost everything she did to advance the causes of civil rights, feminism, and sexual freedom immeasurably. But she never earned celebrity and has, to a great extent, been written out of history, which may well be testament to how threatened people in positions of power felt by her ability to spotlight the inequities that existed under their watch.

Anna Pauline Murray was born in Baltimore on November 20, 1910, the fourth of six children. Her mother, Agnes Fitzgerald, died of a cerebral hemorrhage in 1914, and her father, William Murray, a graduate of Howard University and a teacher who eventually became a principal in the Baltimore public school system, suffered from depression throughout much of Anna Pauline's early life. It was an affliction exacerbated by the long-term effects of typhoid fever, and William was eventually confined to Crownsville State Hospital, where he was taunted by a racist white guard and, in 1923, beaten to death with a baseball bat.

After her mother's death and amid her father's declining health, Anna Pauline moved to Durham, North Carolina, to live with her aunt and maternal grandparents, Cornelia and Robert Fitzgerald. Cornelia had been born into bondage (her mother, Harriet, had been enslaved, and her father had been the son of Harriet's enslaver), but Robert had grown up in Pennsylvania, where he'd gone to antislavery meetings, crossing paths with people like Harriet Tubman and Frederick Douglass. Anna Pauline had unbounded admiration for her grandfather.

In 1926, at age fifteen, Anna Pauline graduated high school with a certificate of distinction, an accomplishment that would have guaranteed her a spot at the North Carolina College for Negroes (now North Carolina Central University), but she was determined to move away from the South and from the punishing segregation laws she had hated ever since she could remember. Even as a child, she had chosen to walk rather than set foot in segregated streetcars or buses. The degradation sickened her, and to preserve her sanity, she knew she had to head north.

Rejected from Columbia University because it didn't admit women at the time, and unable to afford the fees at affiliated Barnard across the street, she eventually enrolled at Hunter College, earning a degree in English. It was around that time that Anna Pauline assumed the more gender-neutral "Pauli"—a nod, perhaps, to her unwillingness to subscribe to a single gender identity. Even as a child, Barnard historian Rosalind Rosenberg notes in her 2017 biography, Murray preferred wearing boys' over girls' clothes and favored doing chores that were generally expected to be done by boys. As young as fifteen, she started referring to herself as Paul, and a brief marriage to a man when she was twenty was annulled. "Why is it when men try to make love to me, something in me fights?" she wrote in her diary shortly after the marriage ended. Historian Brittney Cooper observes in her 2017 book *Beyond Respectability: The Intellectual Thought of Race Women*

A photograph that Pauli Murray sent to Eleanor Roosevelt in 1955.

that Murray "always resisted a strict feminine gender performance, but she did come to identify as a woman. In this way, her strategies of negotiation and survival constitute a form of disidentification with the dominant gender norms she encountered during the 1930s and 1940s." After college Murray repeatedly sought gender-affirming treatments, including hormone therapy, which she was denied.

In 1933, with a degree in hand but broke on account of the dismal job market that followed the 1929 Wall Street crash, Murray started working at the Works Progress Administration, an agency established under the New Deal that employed millions of job seekers to work on public projects. She also started writing prolifically. Her articles and poems appeared in a slew of outlets, including the political magazine *Common Sense* and *The Crisis*, a publication of the National Association for the Advancement of Colored People (NAACP).

Scarred by the experiences of her youth, Murray used her platform to lend a voice to the Civil Rights Movement. In 1938, drifting in and out of insecure work and concerned about the health of some of her aging relatives back home, she campaigned to gain admission to a PhD program at the all-white University of North Carolina. Although the NAACP didn't support her when she appealed to them, her efforts caught the attention of the national media, and she later wrote a letter to President Roosevelt, informing him of her situation after he'd praised the university as a "great liberal institution." He didn't respond, but Eleanor Roosevelt saw a copy of the letter, and the First Lady invited Murray to meet with her in New York to discuss the matter. The university administration didn't change its stance, but Eleanor Roosevelt and Pauli Murray started corresponding regularly, forging a friendship that would last until Roosevelt's death.

Murray was particularly passionate about ending segregation on public transportation and was arrested in March 1940 for refusing to sit at the back of the bus in Richmond, Virginia—almost fifteen years before Rosa Parks was arrested and fined for refusing to give up her bus seat to a white man in Montgomery, Alabama. After hearing Murray speak at a Workers Defense League rally, Thurgood Marshall—a young Black lawyer who in 1967 would become the first African American U.S. Supreme Court justice—wrote a letter of recommendation to Howard University School of Law, his alma mater, and in 1941, Murray was awarded a scholarship.

At Howard, a historically Black university, the color of Murray's skin was no longer remarkable, but the perils of being identified as a woman did become painfully apparent. She graduated top of her class in 1944 with a Bachelor of Laws degree, which she'd pursued because she was determined to forge a career in civil rights law, but she was angry. Not enough attention was being paid, she contended, to the experience of being a Black woman in America. She coined the term "Jane Crow" to describe that intersection, alluding to the Jim Crow laws across the South that enforced racial segregation and relegated Black Americans to the status of second-class citizens—the very laws that had encouraged her to go to New York in the first place.

Top graduates of Howard frequently received a Julius Rosenwald Fellowship to do graduate work at Harvard, but Harvard Law, like Columbia, didn't accept women. "Gentlemen," Murray wrote in a letter responding to the rejection she received, "I would gladly change my sex to meet your requirements, but since the way to such change has not been revealed to me, I have no recourse but to appeal to you to change your minds on this subject. Are you to tell me that one is as difficult as the other?"

Resigned to the intransigency of the system, Murray earned an LLM, or Master of Laws degree, from the University of California, Berkeley, School of Law and briefly served as California's first African American deputy attorney general before moving back to New York, where she was commissioned by the Methodist Church—a staunch opposer of segregation—to author a short pamphlet on the ways in which segregation laws were impacting its mission.

Whenever Murray was given an opportunity to expatiate on the causes she cared deeply about, she did so with unchecked enthusiasm. And so, by the time she finished writing the pamphlet, it had exploded far beyond the parameters of the Methodist Church's initial brief. In 1950, she published a tome spanning well over seven hundred pages entitled *States' Laws on Race and Color*, which the American Civil Liberties Union (ACLU) distributed to law offices around the country, as well as to schools, universities, and human rights organizations. Thurgood Marshall dubbed it the bible of the Civil Rights Movement for the way in which it demonstrated the social implications and unconstitutional nature of segregation law. Later it was widely cited as the basis for many of the arguments brought in the 1954 *Brown v. Board of Education* Supreme Court case, in which the justices ruled racial segregation of students in public schools unconstitutional.

In 1956, Murray was offered a job at the prestigious law firm Paul, Weiss, Rifkind, Wharton & Garrison, which she joined as the first Black woman to be employed as an associate by a major New York law practice. She made a particular impression on one summer clerk. In decades to come, that clerk, named Ruth Bader Ginsburg, would not only credit Murray's work for advancing the causes of African Americans and women, but she would also refer to Murray as her personal legal hero.

In a 2017 interview, Justice Ginsburg, who served on the Supreme Court from 1993 until her death in 2020, said that Murray's work directly inspired an amicus brief she wrote for the historic 1971 Supreme Court case *Reed v. Reed*—the first time in U.S. history that the highest court recognized women as the victims of sex discrimination. "We knew when we wrote that brief," she said when asked about Murray, "that we were standing on her shoulders."

That case concerned the death of nineteen-year-old Richard Reed from Idaho, who was understood to have shot himself in his father's house with one of his father's hunting rifles. Sally Reed, Richard Reed's mother, who was separated from Cecil Reed, his father, filed to be the executor of her son's estate. But Idaho law at the time stipulated that "males must be preferred to females" when more than one person was equally qualified to administer an estate. Cecil's application was granted without even allowing Sally a hearing to prove why she might be better qualified.

Sally was determined to appeal, but a raft of lawyers refused to take her on, deeming her case hopeless. The estate in question comprised about $495 and a few personal belongings. Eventually, an attorney named Allen Derr agreed to represent her. He cautioned that she would probably lose but did concede that there was a slim chance that the case might present a viable constitutional issue. The case ended up reaching the Supreme Court, where it presented the nine justices with an entirely unfamiliar prospect: that of declaring a law that discriminates on the basis of sex to be unconstitutional.

The American Civil Liberties Union joined Derr's side, and Ginsburg, who in 1971 cofounded the ACLU's Women's Rights Project, was the principal author of the brief. Drawing on Murray's work, Ginsburg argued that Sally Reed had been denied "equal protection of the laws" that she should have been afforded under the Fourteenth Amendment. On November 22, 1971, the Supreme Court agreed, holding that the decisions made in favor of men by the Idaho code were an example of the "very kind of arbitrary legislative choice forbidden by the Equal Protection Clause of the Fourteenth Amendment."

This was only one example of the power that Murray's work quietly wielded, but her career and her success mirrored the stop-start progress of both the women's movement and the Civil Rights Movement. In 1961, John Kennedy appointed Murray to the Presidential Commission on the Status of Women, and in 1963 she joined the March on Washington, but she was disheartened by the lack of intersection between the two movements. In one letter to the prominent trade unionist and civil rights leader A. Philip Randolph, who was instrumental in organizing the March on Washington for Jobs and Freedom, Murray said that she had been "increasingly perturbed over the blatant disparity between the major role which Negro women have played and are playing in the crucial grass-roots levels of our struggle and the minor role of leadership they have been assigned in the national policy-making decisions."

When on July 2, 1964, President Lyndon Johnson signed the Civil Rights Act into law, Murray published an article in the *George Washington Law Review* under the headline JANE CROW AND THE LAW: SEX DISCRIMINATION AND TITLE VII, explaining how certain legal statutes, designed to guarantee the civil rights of African Americans, still clearly limited the scope of liberties afforded to women. And so, in October 1965, deeply frustrated by the lack of progress and in a speech about Title VII deemed worthy of a prominently placed write-up in the *New York Times*, Murray urged women across the country to organize another March on Washington, not dissimilar to the one that had occurred two years earlier. Betty Friedan's phone call followed, and the two struck up a relationship that led to an evening meeting in June 1966 during a conference on women's rights that was taking place in Washington, D.C.

Both Friedan and Murray were attending the conference, but the speakers and panels did little to assuage their concern that the advancement toward greater rights for all women was stalling. Disheartened, the pair joined a dozen or so other women in Friedan's hotel room for a late-evening summit to discuss what could possibly be done. The next day, during a luncheon marking the final day of the conference, the women gathered around two tables and, in hushed tones, continued their conversations from the night before, while conference dignitaries made their closing remarks. A sense of urgency was now palpable, and at one point, Friedan pulled out a napkin upon which she started scribbling notes, including the letters N-O-W. Catherine Conroy, a union leader from Wisconsin, slid a five-dollar bill out of her purse and placed it on the table in front of her. "Put your money down and sign your name," she ordered the others. By the end of the afternoon, twenty-eight women had done just that, and the National Organization for Women (NOW) was born.

A few months later, at the end of October, NOW adopted its Statement of Purpose, a document jointly authored by Friedan and Murray but frequently attributed to Friedan alone. NOW's mission, the document stipulated, was "to take action to bring women into full participation in the mainstream of American society now, exercising all privileges and responsibilities thereof in truly equal partnership with men." It stated that "the time has come to move beyond the abstract argument, discussion and symposia over the status and special nature of women which has raged in America in recent years," and also that "the time has come to confront, with concrete action, the conditions that now prevent women from enjoying the equality of opportunity and freedom of choice which is their right, as individual Americans, and as human beings." Childbearing and child-rearing, it noted, "which continues to be a most important part of most women's lives," was still "used to justify barring women from equal professional and economic participation and advance."

The statement outlined that although just shy of half of all American women between the ages of eighteen and sixty-five by that point worked outside the home, two-thirds were in routine clerical, sales, or factory jobs or were household workers, cleaning women, or hospital attendants—occupations that, like today, tended to command only the lowest level of pay. With alarm, the statement noted that working women were actually becoming increasingly concentrated at the lower level of the pay spectrum.

***

Pauli Murray kept diaries throughout most of her life. In later years, these proved invaluable to historians trying to disentangle her complex feelings about identity, gender, and race, which, as she admitted in her posthumously published memoir, *Song in a Weary Throat*, limited her intellectual brilliance and ability to fight for the causes she cared about. In one diary entry, she wrote that she hated "to be fragmented into Negro at one time, woman at another, or worker at another." Decades before Kimberlé Crenshaw, a professor at Columbia Law School and cofounder of the African American Policy Forum, coined the term "intersectionality," that's exactly what Murray was referring to. But to Murray's dismay, the movements she dedicated her life to didn't speak to each other in a meaningful way. The Civil Rights Movement, for all the awesome progress it had achieved, sidelined women. The women's movement was, for the most part, a movement for affluent white women.

Today, Pauli Murray is not a household name. She's celebrated in some circles and in parts of her North Carolina hometown of Durham, where the Pauli Murray Center invites tourists and historians to learn about her life and legacy, but she enjoys nowhere near the degree of celebrity afforded to Betty Friedan or Eleanor Roosevelt for their efforts to fight gender inequality. Rosa Parks has claimed an unchallenged spot in history curricula around the world; Murray might feature as a footnote. As Kathryn Schulz wrote for *The New Yorker* in April 2017, Murray's lifelong fate was to be both ahead of her time and behind the scenes. Her boldness, her gender fluidity, and her readiness to defy every stereotype and norm that she encountered throughout her life made her so unquantifiable and impossible to categorize that many scholars and academics, rather than attempting to do so, wrote around her. Some scratched her from their books entirely.

But even though her legacy hasn't been visible, it has endured. The *Reed v. Reed* decision was a watershed moment in the centuries-long quest for female economic empowerment and equality. It opened the door for countless other women—and men—to successfully challenge discriminatory laws under the Equal Protection Clause of the Fourteenth Amendment. But it also signaled a profound shift in attitude. It indicated that the Supreme Court was slowly catching up with where the rest of society was heading. With women entering the workforce at such a rapid clip, *Reed v. Reed* underscored the extent to which statutes like Idaho's were little more than a quaint artifact from a bygone era.

Betty Friedan's *The Feminine Mystique* struck America like a comet. But if she really was, as countless history books and mainstream media articles claim, the mother of second-wave feminism, then Pauli Murray was the patron saint of equality more generally. And indeed, in 1973, after Murray's life partner of almost a quarter of a century, Irene Barlow, died of a brain tumor, Murray sought solace in the Christian faith and enrolled in a seminary. In 1977, the Episcopal Church ordained her as their first Black woman priest—the last of many firsts in Murray's remarkable life.

Murray died of pancreatic cancer on July 1, 1985, in Pittsburgh, Pennsylvania, at the age of seventy-four, and in 2012 she was named an Episcopal saint. In its entry, the church described her as an advocate of "the universal cause of freedom."

Murray's life also provides an important and underutilized lens through which we should acknowledge the shortcomings of the second wave of feminism that Betty Friedan championed so boldly and so bravely. Friedan's was a feminism that spoke to an upper crust of society—white women who were relatively affluent and mostly educated—and while these limitations don't in any way render what she did socially and historically unimportant, it is critical to appreciate that the women she considered in her book represented but a fraction of women across America then, as they still do today. In a 1963 letter to Friedan, the historian Gerda Lerner praised *The Feminine Mystique* but also wrote that "working women, especially Negro women, labor not only under the disadvantages imposed by the feminine mystique, but under the more pressing disadvantages of economic discrimination." Betty Friedan planted an extremely visible seed from which a movement was able to grow that challenged the status quo and demonstrated that no cultural norm was incontrovertible. But while her book addressed discrimination that was happening to a small slice of the population, Murray confronted systemic oppression on a much higher level and often from an invisible place. Friedan's weapon was the mass media. Murray's was the law.

In April 1960, at age seventy-five, Eleanor Roosevelt got sick. After a protracted illness and much suffering, she died in November 1962. She was seventy-eight. The final weeks of the former First Lady's life were miserable. She was in pain and wanted to die, but she mustered up the strength to write, including one final letter to her dear friend Pauli Murray. "For many years you have been one of my most important models—one who combines graciousness with moral principle, straightforwardness with kindliness, political shrewdness with idealism, courage with generosity, and most of all an ongoingness which never falters, no matter what the difficulties may be."

Years later, in 1970, Murray wrote that "if anyone should ask a Negro woman in America what has been her greatest achievement, her honest answer would be, 'I survived!'" But throughout her life, Pauli Murray did far more than survive, and what she achieved—the barriers she broke down and the fights she fought—allowed others, who might have merely survived as minorities and outsiders, to prosper and excel.

The pay gap between Black women and white men particularly, but also between Black and white women, remains huge. In 2021 in the United States, Black women only earned about 63 percent of what white, non-Hispanic men made. Even today, scant data is available on the pay gap faced by those who live—as Murray did—at the intersections of race, sexual orientation, and gender identity. Data that does exist is often patchy and based on nonrepresentative sample sizes. But in 2011, the National Gay and Lesbian Task Force and the National Center for Transgender Equality published a 228-page report for which the authors questioned 6,450 transgender and gender-nonconforming individuals from all U.S. states. They concluded that transgender and gender-nonconforming people face injustices at every single twist and turn in life: "in childhood homes, in school systems that promise to shelter and educate, in harsh and exclusionary workplaces, at the grocery store, the hotel front desk, in doctors' offices and emergency rooms, before judges and at the hands of landlords, police officers, health care workers, and other service providers." Respondents indicated that they experienced unemployment at twice the rate of the general population, and rates for people of color were up to four times the national unemployment rate. One in nine of those surveyed reported experiencing harassment, mistreatment, or discrimination at work.

Murray's story is unlikely to help many of the respondents to that survey feel different about the world around them. But she deserves recognition for the role she played in laying the legal foundations for eradicating at least one of the forces that has historically perpetuated pay and employment gaps: blatant discrimination. In her critique of America, Murray zoomed out to show the whole picture, while keeping *The Feminine Mystique,* as a part of it, in sharp and necessary focus. Friedan's privilege helped her shout loudly and be heard widely. But the effects of Murray's efforts to legally enshrine equality in law will long endure.

# CHAPTER 4

*Progress in Failure*

We, the women of America, tell you that America is not a democracy.

—Alice Paul

For all the credit owed to Pauli Murray, Betty Friedan, Katharine Dexter McCormick, and all of their contemporaries who dedicated their lives to advancing gender equality, it's important to remember that each trod a path that—to a greater or lesser extent—was paved by a person who came before her. They were all pioneers. But they all built on foundations, however feeble or basic, created by someone else. Searching for the original feminist—the person who actually started the fight for female economic empowerment in a meaningful way—would be like disassembling a Russian doll with a seemingly limitless number of figurines inside.

Perhaps one of the most powerful symbols of the fight for gender equality in twentieth-century America was the thwarted Equal Rights Amendment. The author of its first iteration, women's rights activist Alice Paul, thus categorically deserves a place in that long line of frequently unassuming and often silenced but astonishingly influential individuals. Born in January 1885 in Burlington County, New Jersey, Paul was the first child of William and Tacie Paul, Quakers who raised their four children according to their faith's staunch belief in gender equality. From an early age, Paul's parents impressed upon their children that, regardless of gender, each had a duty to contribute to the betterment of society as a whole. In a 1974 interview, not long before her death, Paul said that equality of the sexes was a founding principle of the Quakers, so she never believed otherwise: "The principle was always there."

The Quaker belief in gender equality was unusual for that time, and that helps to explain why so many of the individuals who were active in the fight for women's suffrage were Quakers. Throughout her life, Paul expressed admiration for Susan B. Anthony, an early suffragist who cofounded the National Woman Suffrage Association (NWSA) and who was arrested for voting as early as 1872, and Lucretia Mott, an abolitionist who had become committed to reforming the position of women in society when she was excluded from the World Anti-Slavery Convention in London in 1840. Mott had also collaborated with Elizabeth Cady Stanton to organize the Seneca Falls Convention—the first women's rights convention—in 1848. Both Anthony and Mott were also Quakers.

Paul went to a Quaker school in Moorestown, New Jersey, and then enrolled at the coeducational Swarthmore College, a school cofounded by her maternal grandfather. Her mother had for a while attended Swarthmore herself but dropped out when she married William Paul. Alice Paul excelled academically and was inspired by many of her teachers, including a mathematics professor named Susan Cunningham, who would later become one of the first women to be admitted to the precursor organization to the American Mathematical Society. After graduating, Paul moved to New York, where she developed an interest in the emerging field of social work, learning about the detrimental effects of economic and gender disparities on communities. Eventually, this would inspire her to move to England, where a small group of militant suffragists was attracting media attention for resorting to violence to raise public awareness of their demands for equal rights.

She struck up a friendship with Christabel Pankhurst, the daughter of Emmeline Pankhurst, one of England's most radical suffragists, and joined their movement. The women were regularly arrested for smashing windows and other acts of civil disobedience, which on several occasions landed them in prison. When that happened, they staged hunger strikes and were force-fed, but Paul firmly believed that the approach was working. "The militant policy is bringing success," she wrote of the Pankhurst strategy when she eventually returned to the United States

Alice Paul, pictured in 1915.

in 1910. "The agitation has brought England out of her lethargy, and women of England are now talking of the time when they will vote, instead of the time when their children would vote, as was the custom a year or two back," she added.

When Paul returned to America, she started studying at the University of Pennsylvania and joined the National American Woman Suffrage Association (NAWSA), created in 1890 as a merger of two rival factions, the National Woman Suffrage Association (NWSA), led by Elizabeth Cady Stanton and Susan B. Anthony, and the American Woman Suffrage Association (AWSA), led by Lucy Stone, Henry Blackwell, and Julia Ward Howe. Soon Paul was appointed head of the group's Congressional Committee, effectively handing her responsibility for leading a federal suffrage movement. In 1912, she moved to Washington, D.C., where she collaborated with other NAWSA members, including Lucy Burns and Crystal Eastman, to organize and stage a massive women's march for nationwide suffrage on March 3, 1913, the eve of president-elect Woodrow Wilson's inauguration day. Crowds of outraged onlookers, mostly men, attacked the parading women, bringing the event to a violent end, but the march drew extensive media coverage, alerting the public to the women's demands and introducing the issue of voting rights into mainstream conversation and consciousness.

Paul had been working closely with NAWSA president Carrie Chapman Catt in the lead-up to the march, but as time went on, the differences in their political strategies and approaches became evident. Catt and others in NAWSA's leadership wanted to focus their efforts on state campaigns. Paul believed that pushing for constitutional change was more effective. NAWSA, as an organization, endorsed President Wilson, but Paul considered him and his fellow Democrats in power to be responsible for female disenfranchisement. Their disagreement proved irreconcilable, and in 1914, Paul and a group of women who championed her strategy split from NAWSA and two years later established the National Woman's Party (NWP).

Inspired by Pankhurst's grit and willingness to throw physical and metaphorical rocks, the NWP in 1917 organized the first-ever public picketing in front of the White House. So-called Silent Sentinels bearing protest banners stood outside the gates of the White House to shame President Wilson for his inaction and apathy on the cause of women's rights. MR. PRESIDENT, HOW LONG MUST WOMEN WAIT FOR LIBERTY? one banner read. Others sharply parroted Wilson's own words directly back at him. WE SHALL FIGHT FOR THE THINGS WHICH WE HAVE ALWAYS CARRIED NEAREST OUR HEARTS—FOR DEMOCRACY, FOR THE RIGHT OF THOSE WHO SUBMIT TO AUTHORITY TO HAVE A VOICE IN THEIR OWN GOVERNMENTS, one woman had written on a sign, a passage lifted straight from a recent presidential speech.

Six days a week and with no concern for inclement weather, the women congregated in nonviolent protest. Quietly they stood in defiance of passersby who initially offered little more than half-hearted heckles and insults. Wilson himself at first treated Paul and her fellow protestors with condescension or simply ignored them, but as the

An anti-women's-suffrage cartoon from the 1920s intended to show that, for a
woman, love and marriage were incompatible with having a career and being
professionally ambitious.

months drew on and the women persisted, tensions rose. When America entered World War I, a shift occurred.

While the suffragists had up until that point been regarded by many as disrespectful nuisances at worst—pesky gadflies—they suddenly drew wrath from members of the public who considered their actions to be entirely unacceptable and insultingly disloyal to the country. Angry mobs attacked them, and some of the women were arrested, purportedly for the crime of obstructing traffic. As had happened in England, Paul was imprisoned and, upon starting a hunger strike, force-fed. Well over a hundred women were arrested and kept in dire conditions: in freezing, unsanitary, and rat-infested cells. Paul ended up being moved to a sanatorium, where prison officials hoped she would be declared insane; however, around that same time, information about the conditions under which the female prisoners were being held began to leak to the press. Appalled that anyone would be forced to live in such squalor, members of the public started to sympathize with the suffragists, demanding their release and exerting pressure on politicians to intervene.

When Paul was eventually released, she encountered a groundswell of support that was entirely new to her and that heaped pressure on President Wilson to reverse his position on the prospect of women voting. Finally, at the end of 1917, he did. In the subsequent months, Wilson met with members of Congress to drum up support for a suffrage amendment, presenting it as a "war measure"—the war, he claimed, couldn't be fought effectively without female participation. In 1919, members of the House of Representatives and the Senate voted to pass the Nineteenth Amendment, which was sent to the states for ratification. Three-quarters of states were needed for the amendment to pass, and in the summer of 1920, with thirty-five states having voted to ratify the amendment and thirty-six needed, the deciding vote landed on Tennessee.

Supporters from opposing sides set up camp at The Hermitage Hotel in Nashville and lobbied intensely in what became known as the War of the Roses. Suffragists and their supporters wore yellow roses in their lapels, while anti-suffragists sported red ones. Eventually, Harry T. Burn—who, two years earlier, at the age of just twenty-two, had become the youngest member ever to be elected to the Tennessee General Assembly—cast the deciding vote to ratify the Nineteenth Amendment to the U.S. Constitution. Burn came from a conservative district. Twice he had voted to table the amendment, and on the day of the deciding vote, a red rose was affixed to his lapel. At the last minute, however, Burn changed his allegiance, seemingly swayed by a letter he'd received from his mother, which he was carrying in his pocket at the time. "Hurrah and vote for suffrage and don't keep them in doubt," his mother, a college-educated widow who reportedly read three newspapers a day, had written to her son. "Don't forget to be a good boy and help Mrs. Catt." As Burn declared his historic "aye," he ripped off the red rose, and the battle for women's suffrage was over.

Many suffragists turned away from activism and public life after the enactment of the Nineteenth Amendment, considering their work to be done. But Alice Paul was adamant that gender equality was far from guaranteed, even by the noteworthy progress made in August 1920. Having gained a sense of what changing the law entailed, Paul was hungry to learn more. In the years that followed, she earned three law degrees at the American University in Washington, D.C., arming herself with the skills, experience, and reputation to craft legislation. In 1923, as celebrations marking the seventy-fifth anniversary of the Seneca Falls Convention got underway, Paul announced that she had authored what she called the Lucretia Mott Amendment, in homage to the abolitionist she so admired. The amendment called for absolute gender equality and stated that "men and women shall have equal rights throughout the United States and every place subject to its jurisdiction."

Every year from then until 1942, Paul and her supporters submitted the Lucretia Mott Amendment to Congress. It never passed. By 1943, with her patience running thin, Paul had reworded the original draft of the amendment to better reflect the language of the Fifteenth and Nineteenth Amendments, which she hoped would make it more palatable to lawmakers. The new version stated that "equality of rights under the law shall not be denied or abridged by the United States or by any state on account of sex." It became known as the Alice Paul Amendment, and Paul continued to submit it to Congress annually. Finally, on March 22, 1972, the proposed Twenty-Seventh Amendment to the Constitution, now known as the Equal Rights Amendment, or ERA, passed the U.S. Senate and then the House of Representatives and was sent to the states for ratification. Congresswoman Martha Griffiths, the principal House proponent of the amendment, predicted that it would be "ratified almost immediately." Congress placed a seven-year deadline on ratification. The countdown was on.

\*\*\*

As the author of the document that formed the basis of the ERA, Paul blazed a trail for the women's movement with her assiduous understanding of the power of the legislature to effect real change, but a new cast of characters took up the baton as Paul grew older and lost the strength to sustain the fight. Some advocates were less obvious than others.

In an August 20, 1969, memo to President Richard Nixon, Daniel Patrick Moynihan, an assistant to the president on domestic policy—despite not referring explicitly to the ERA—observed that "the essential fact is that we have educated women for equality in America but have not really given it to them. Not at all." He asserted that "inequality is so great that the dominant group either doesn't notice it or assumes the dominated group likes it that way," and he urged Nixon to consider what it might be like to have a woman as president. "Male dominance is so deeply a part of American life that males don't even notice it." Nixon did eventually become a fierce advocate for the amendment.

Betty Ford, even beyond her relatively short term as First Lady, was a champion of the ERA. At the 1980 Republican National Convention, when a debate commenced over the removal of the ERA from the GOP platform, Ford stormed out of the convention and joined the National Organization for Women's protest. Some other Republican women publicly supported it, too, as did Justice Sandra Day O'Connor. But it was Shirley Anita St. Hill Chisholm—a former community activist and educator from Brooklyn who, in 1964, had become the second African American to enter the New York State Legislature and who, four years later, had become the first woman to seek the Democratic presidential nomination—who delivered perhaps history's most impassioned endorsement of the ERA.

In a speech in 1970, Chisholm described the ERA as "one of the most clear-cut opportunities" that Americans were likely to have to declare their "faith in the principles that shaped our Constitution." She noted that, while "prejudice on the basis of race is, at least, under systematic attack," discrimination against women purely on account of their gender "is so widespread that it seems to many persons normal, natural, and right." The congresswoman reeled off a laundry list of rights that women, by that point, were still denied: "Women are

Shirley Anita St. Hill Chisholm, a former community activist and educator from Brooklyn, in 1968 became the first woman to seek the Democratic presidential nomination.

excluded from some state colleges and universities," she said. "In some states, restrictions are placed on a married woman who engages in an independent business. Women may not be chosen for some juries. Women even receive heavier criminal penalties than men who commit the same crime," she went on.

She took aim at the labor laws in place that were ostensibly designed to protect women, laws that were sometimes referred to as examples of judicial paternalism. "The physical characteristics of men and women are not fixed but cover two wide spans that have a great deal of overlap," she reasoned. "It is obvious, I think, that a robust woman could be more fit for physical labor than a weak man. The choice of occupation would be determined by individual capabilities, and the rewards for equal work should be equal."

Ultimately, she said, what it comes down to is that "artificial distinctions between persons must be wiped out of the law. Legal discrimination between the sexes is, in almost every instance, founded on outmoded views of society and the pre-scientific beliefs about psychology and physiology. It is time to sweep away these relics of the past and set future generations free of them."

In January of that year, in a case known as *Schultz v. Wheaton Glass Co.*, the Supreme Court had determined that a job that is "substantially equal" in terms of tasks but not necessarily in terms of job description or title is protected by the Equal Pay Act of 1963. The outcome made it illegal for an employer to pay a woman lower wages than a man for completing a similar task. However, even though the ruling was a watershed moment in the fight for gender equal employment rights, the law in countless other respects remained deficient. It wasn't until 1988, and the Women's Business Ownership Act, for example, that all women were able to get a business loan without a male cosigner. A witness in a federal legislation hearing before that act was passed explained that she had been forced to ask her seventeen-year-old son to cosign for a loan because she didn't have a living husband, father, or brother who was able to do so.

One of Chisholm's most notable qualities as a politician was her consistent effort to find common ground with even her staunchest opponents. In that spirit, she also used that 1970 speech to underscore that the ERA would be economically advantageous for men. Survivorship benefits, she noted, would be available to husbands of female workers just as they already were to the wives of male workers. As it happened, it wasn't until 1975 that the Supreme Court unanimously decided that the gender-based distinction of the Social Security Act of 1935—which permitted widows but not widowers to collect special benefits while caring for minor children—violated the right to equal protection guaranteed by the Fifth Amendment.

The case that led to that decision concerned a twenty-nine-year-old computer consultant named Stephen Wiesenfeld. His wife, Paula, who had earned a higher income than he did as a math teacher, died from an embolism while giving birth to their son, Jason. To care for Jason as a single parent, Wiesenfeld cut back his hours but was not eligible for Social Security survivors' benefits that would have been available to Paula if he had been the spouse who died. Wiesenfeld's legal team was headed by Ruth Bader Ginsburg, at the time a practicing attorney and a professor at Columbia Law School. Ginsburg argued that Paula herself was being discriminated against in this situation, because her contributions to Social Security were not being treated on an equal basis to those of a salaried man.

Eight of the nine Supreme Court justices voted in favor of Wiesenfeld, with only Justice William Orville Douglas abstaining on account of being absent for health reasons. Ginsburg's role, in this case in particular, helped draw attention to the extent to which Social Security provisions had, up until that point, not only discriminated against men who were caregivers, but also women and wives who—in the face of entrenched norms and social expectations of the time—were breadwinners.

\*\*\*

By 1970, about half of all single women and 40 percent of married women in the United States were working outside the home in paid employment, creating a tide of awareness that fueled swelling discontent with the barriers still faced by this growing portion of the labor market. The year 1970 was also the fiftieth anniversary of the ratification of the Nineteenth Amendment, but rather than celebrating, many supporters of the women's movement seized on the half-century milestone to draw attention to how little had actually changed since Harry T. Burn had cast that all-important vote in 1920. In 1920, not a single woman had been in Congress, and in the space of fifty years, that number had risen to only eleven.

It had been seven years since the passage of the Equal Pay Act, but the average woman working full-time, year-round still made only fifty-nine cents for each dollar a man in an equivalent job made. And even though outright discrimination had, in many respects, been out-lawed, it was still rampant, fortified by habits, beliefs, and a culture of misogyny that underpinned many industries and organizations. In no state was marital rape a crime in 1970—Nebraska was the first to com-pletely outlaw it, in 1976—and as late as 1977, two-thirds of Americans believed that it was a man's job in a household to earn money, while women should be responsible for taking care of the home.

Betty Friedan—by then forty-nine years old and divorced—was among the feminist leaders whose frustration was bubbling over. Much of the criticism that she'd levelled at society in *The Feminine Mystique* seven years earlier had remained unaddressed, something that over a hundred feminists decided to spotlight on March 18, 1970, when they charged into the offices of the *Ladies' Home Journal* to protest the way in which the magazine's mostly male staff—managed by a male editor-in-chief—depicted women's interests and aspirations. An irony the protes-tors enjoyed underscoring was that the magazine's motto was "Never Underestimate the Power of a Woman."

The demonstrators made concrete suggestions and even presented a mock-up of a cover they said they wished to see on a future issue of the *Ladies' Home Journal*. Their demands included that the magazine hire a female editor-in-chief, provide free childcare for its staff, and put an end to the "basic orientation of the *Journal* toward the concept of Kinder, Küche, Kirche"—a reference to the Nazi propaganda slogan widely used to describe the ideal woman's purview in society: children, kitchen, and the church. Two days later, speaking at a NOW conference in Chicago, Friedan called for a Women's Strike for Equality to be hosted simultane-ously in cities across the country on the anniversary of the passage of the Nineteenth Amendment. "I decided we ought to have some sort of women's strike, one that would show that discrimination still exists in employment and education, and that consciousness is exploding in the minds of women," she later recalled.

What followed was a series of meetings in New York to which members of all kinds of women's groups were invited. The attendees, according to an account in the *New York Times* at the time, resembled a cross section of the city's female population. "There were dumpy, gray-haired grandmother types who arrived at the meetings toting shopping bags. There were braless, long-haired teenyboppers in T-shirts and jeans. There were well-groomed Pucci-ed and Gucci-ed women who looked as though they had just left the bridge table in Rye. And there were always a few Blacks—but never more than a handful."

The air in Manhattan on August 26, characteristic for that time of year, was muggy and oppressive, but that didn't deter the crowds. Thousands filled Fifth Avenue, many chanting, singing, and carrying signs. Organizers of the march had obtained a permit but paid no attention to a city order to stay in a single traffic lane. The crowd exploded. The *Times* again enthused that "every kind of woman you ever see in New York was there. Limping octogenarians, braless teenagers, Black Panther women, telephone operators, waitresses, Westchester matrons, fashion models, Puerto Rican factory workers, nurses in uniform, young mothers carrying babies on their backs." Traffic stood still for hours as the streets were claimed by women who were tired of being stuck indoors and who shared three distinct demands: free, around-the-clock childcare; equal opportunities in education and employment; and access to abortion for all. To that end, Friedan urged work stoppages to coincide with the march of "everyone who is doing a job for which a man would be paid more," as well as of any woman doing unpaid domestic labor.

The roster of speakers was lengthy and diverse. Kate Millett, a Columbia PhD and author of the bestselling book *Sexual Politics*, which provocatively analyzed the pervasive subjugation of women in art and literature, declared: "At last we have a movement." Congresswoman Bella Abzug—nicknamed "Battling Bella" for her fearlessly confrontational demeanor—addressed the crowd. Eleanor Holmes Norton, a lawyer who had recently sued *Newsweek* for gender discrimination on behalf of dozens of female employees, demanded from the podium that the U.S. Senate pass the ERA. And even Alice Paul, frail at the age of eighty-five, made an appearance.

Witnesses estimated that as many as fifty thousand people took to the streets in New York City alone, with thousands gathering in Boston, San Francisco, and Los Angeles, and hundreds more in places like Baltimore and Seattle. A newspaper in Louisiana reportedly replaced pictures of brides with pictures of grooms in the day's wedding announcements to mark the occasion, while male preachers in Massachusetts asked women to make the sermons that day. Countless housewives turned their backs on their daily chores, refusing to cook, clean, and look after the children, shedding light on the extent of their unpaid—and often under-recognized—work.

Some hecklers in New York City, mostly men (of which a few mockingly wore bras), stood along the edges of the marching crowds, throwing pennies, but opponents on the day attracted little attention, and by the time the women congregated in Bryant Park in the evening, it was clear that the event had been a success. In the weeks and months that followed, NOW became a household name. Its membership increased by 50 percent in the aftermath of the strike, and a CBS News poll found that four-fifths of all Americans had heard of women's liberation in the weeks that followed.

Later, "women's lib" would be as frequently mocked as it was celebrated and as often criticized as it was championed. It was a label that was used derisively and complimentarily, and it came to sum up not just feminists who took to the streets with megaphones and placards, but an entire social movement—an era, even. Women and supporters of gender equality had successfully forced policymakers, business executives, educators, and community leaders to acknowledge that they were serious in their demands and that they would not stop disrupting the status quo until change materialized.

Nonetheless, that day in August 1970 did not represent the revolution that some had billed it to be. The three core demands of the marching masses were not met and, in part, remain unmet today. America's feminist undercurrent was undoubtedly getting stronger, and select battles were being won, but real progress, in many respects, was elusive. Women, in the minds of many, remained the weaker sex. The movement was promising but also polarizing. For every champion of equality was someone who was aggressively warning of the risks associated with any sort of change in that direction: an erosion of traditional values.

\*\*\*

Within a year of the ERA passing the Senate and the House of Representatives by the required two-thirds majority in 1972, thirty states of the thirty-eight required had ratified it. But then momentum abruptly slowed, curbed by a powerful alliance between conservative activists and the religious right. William H. Rehnquist, who was head of the Justice Department's Office of Legal Counsel at the time and who would subsequently serve as associate justice and then chief justice of the Supreme Court, in an internal memo warned that the ERA would "virtually abolish all legal distinctions between men and women" and "hasten the dissolution of the family." Rehnquist wrote in the memo that he could not help thinking that there was, within the women's movement, "a virtually fanatical desire to obscure not only legal differentiation between men and women, but insofar as possible, physical distinctions between the sexes."

Years later, Ruth Bader Ginsburg reflected that arguments against the ERA were also frequently rooted in a belief that women did actually have it better than men. "Judges and legislators in the 1960s and at the start of the 1970s regarded differential treatment of men and women not as malign, but as operating benignly in women's favor," she said. "Women, they thought, had the best of all possible worlds. Women could work if they wished; they could stay home if they chose. They could avoid jury duty if they were so inclined, or they could serve if they elected to do so. They could escape military duty, or they could enlist." She added that she considered it her mission to educate both the public and the country's decision-makers in the legislatures and courts. "We tried to convey to them that something was wrong with their perception of the world," she said. "We sought to spark judges' and lawmakers' understanding that their own daughters and granddaughters could be disadvantaged by the way things were."

Phyllis Schlafly, a conservative, antifeminist attorney, spearheaded a movement to block the ERA, claiming that its passage would lead to the introduction of, among other things, gender-neutral bathrooms and same-sex marriages. Schlafly, who hailed from St. Louis, Missouri, had entered electoral politics in 1952 in an unconventional manner. Republicans had encouraged her husband, John Fred Schlafly Jr., a conservative lawyer from Alton, Illinois, to run for Congress, but he turned them down. Schlafly herself had studied on a scholarship for a master's degree at Radcliffe and then found employment at a conservative think tank before working on the successful congressional campaign of Republican Claude I. Bakewell. Resolutely, she offered to run for Congress in her husband's stead. She won the Republican primary and, despite losing the general election, rapidly gained prominence in conservative circles. She made countless speeches as an officer of the Daughters of the American Revolution, and she built and fostered a national network of hundreds of friends and acquaintances who shared her values and convictions. Between 1956 and 1964, Schlafly served as the president of the Illinois Federation of Republican Women.

When Congress passed the ERA, Schlafly was barely aware of it. In fact, when she learned about it, her initial inclination was to support it. But in December 1971, she read up on it and decided that it posed a serious threat to America's sacred values and safety. In October of the following year, she founded and became chairwoman of STOP ERA, a precursor organization to the conservative Eagle Forum. The first part of the organization's name was an acronym for "Stop Taking Our Privileges," summing up members' concerns that the amendment would scrap earlier laws that were implemented to protect women, guarantee alimony, and exempt them from combat. In fact, according to the U.S. Constitution, Congress at that point already had the power to draft both men and women into combat. Without the ERA, however, there was nothing that could provide a guarantee that women would be protected against sex discrimination in any professional field, including in the military.

In 1978, when the ERA had secured only thirty-five of the necessary thirty-eight approvals, Congress passed a bill by a simple majority extending the deadline to June 30, 1982, but while this prolonged proponents' hope for change, it did little more than that. By the final deadline, fifteen states had not ratified it: Alabama, Arizona, Arkansas, Florida, Georgia, Illinois, Louisiana, Mississippi, Missouri, Nevada, North Carolina, Oklahoma, South Carolina, Utah, and Virginia.

The amendment's death was described alternately as a tragedy, a great accomplishment, a disgrace, and a vindication for the right, but most agreed that Schlafly's vehement campaign against it had played a huge part in its ultimate demise. Speaking to reporters from Alton that day, Schlafly described the defeat as a "tremendous victory for women and for families."

Phyllis Schlafly, the conservative antifeminist attorney who spearheaded a movement to block the ERA.

# CHAPTER 5

## Winds of Legal Change

[Women] may be cops, judges, military officers, telephone linemen, cab drivers, pipefitters, editors, business executives—or mothers and housewives, but not quite the same subordinate creatures they were before.

—*TIME* magazine, January 1976

Members of the women's movement reflected on the 1970s as a decade of empowerment and progress followed by bitter setback, of hope and headway and then brutal defeat. The Women's Strike for Equality in 1970 had ignited a determination that this era would go down in history as a turning point. It had also demonstrated a democratization of the movement, as it attracted support from individuals of different races, backgrounds, political persuasions, and sexual orientations. Feminism was sweeping across the country and transforming itself from an ideology claimed by wealthy suburban housewives to an all-encompassing political, cultural, and social movement that might have spoken to the majority. The ERA's failure in 1982, however, suggested otherwise.

Still, there had been a series of significant legal breakthroughs, beyond the *Weinberger v. Wiesenfeld* and *Schultz v. Wheaton Glass Co.* cases already mentioned. In January 1971, in a landmark Supreme Court decision—*Phillips v. Martin Marietta Corp.*—the court held that under Title VII of the Civil Rights Act, an employer could not refuse to hire a mother with young children if that same employer was prepared to hire a father with young children. A year later, in 1972, largely thanks to the grit and determination of a Brooklyn-born preschool teacher and guitar instructor–turned campaigner named Bernice Sandler, Title IX of the Education Amendments was enacted, prohibiting sex discrimination in educational institutions that received federal funding. That extended to most schools and pertained to the funding of sports teams and facilities, but it also protected students from sexual harassment and sexual violence and made it an educational institution's legal duty to respond and remedy hostile educational environments.

In 1973, a female lieutenant serving as a physical therapist in the United States Air Force named Sharron Frontiero brought a case claiming that benefits given by the U.S. military to the family of service members could not be awarded differently because of sex. Ruth Bader Ginsburg, working for the ACLU, presented oral arguments in favor of Frontiero, whose husband, Joseph, had been denied the housing and medical benefits that female spouses of male Air Force officers at the time automatically received. According to a federal statute, a married *woman* in the armed services could receive spousal benefits only if she was contributing more than half of her husband's living expenses.

Joseph was a full-time college student, and Sharron's annual income of 8,200 dollars provided about three-quarters of their joint income, but Joseph—as a U.S. Navy veteran—was receiving a monthly veteran's payment under the G.I. bill of 205 dollars, as well as 30 dollars each month for pulling shifts as a part-time night watchman. Combined, that money tipped him over the limit, rendering him ineligible for the spousal benefits he would have received if he had been a woman and if Sharron had been a man. "Our idea," Sharron said, "was that men don't depend on women, and women don't depend on men. Men and women depend on each other."

It was Ginsburg's first time giving oral arguments in front of the Supreme Court, and it proved to be a pivotal moment in her career. Clad in her mother's gold earrings and a matching circle pin—jewelry she always wore on important occasions—the future justice used the opportunity to summarize the history of women's subjugation poignantly and elegantly. "Sex, like race, has been made the basis for unjustified, or at least unproved, assumptions concerning an individual's potential to perform or to contribute to society," she said. She drew on the work of Pauli Murray on the intersection of sex and race and the similarities between the two in terms of discrimination. She explained that sex bears no more relationship to ability than skin color and distilled a complex set of arguments down to something simple, adroitly quoting the nineteenth-century feminist and abolitionist Sarah Grimké: "I ask no favors for my sex. All I ask of our brethren is, that they take their feet off our necks."

"That's when it dawned on me how brilliant she is," Brenda Feigen, who at the time was codirecting the Women's Rights Project with Ginsburg, later recalled. "She told the story of sex discrimination—how it had been and how it had to end." In May 1973, the Supreme Court delivered a decision in *Frontiero v. Richardson*. Eight of the justices agreed that distinguishing between men and women in the military service was unsustainable. Justice William H. Rehnquist was the only dissenter.

The following year, in 1974, Congress passed the Equal Credit Opportunity Act (ECOA) designed to ensure that banks and lenders make credit equally available to all customers who are deemed creditworthy, but its passage might not have been as noteworthy for proponents of female economic empowerment if it hadn't been for Congresswoman Lindy Boggs from Louisiana.

Boggs—born Marie Corinne Claiborne—who today might be best known as the mother of the late journalist and broadcaster "Cokie" Roberts, began her political career in the late 1930s and early 1940s as a founding member of the Independent Women's Organization, a volunteer-based group that supported Democratic candidates considered to be allies in the struggle for women's equality. In 1941, when her husband, Thomas Hale Boggs, was elected to the House of Representatives, she became an active campaigner and volunteer. She served as president of the Democratic Wives' Forum and the Woman's National Democratic Club. Armed with Southern charm and a strategically brilliant mind, she unabashedly threw herself into the murky world of Capitol Hill, advising not only her husband, but other politicians, too, and making a name for herself beyond being a political spouse. In 1973, when a plane her husband was flying in went missing over Alaska, Boggs filled his House seat as the first woman ever to represent Louisiana.

Boggs served on the powerful Banking and Currency Committee, which in 1974 was tasked with marking up what would become the Equal Credit Opportunity Act, making it illegal for creditors to discriminate against applicants based on race, age, or status as veterans. Boggs took a pen to the document and manually added a provision banning discrimination based on sex and marital status. As a newly widowed woman, she was learning firsthand what it was like to seek credit and manage your own finances without a husband. She reportedly didn't tell any of her colleagues before making photocopies of the annotated document and handing it out to the other committee members. "Knowing the members composing this committee as well as I do, I'm sure it was just an oversight that we didn't have 'sex' or 'marital status' included," Boggs told her colleagues, according to her memoir. "I've taken care of that, and I trust it meets with the committee's approval," she reportedly said. It passed unanimously.

Also during the 1970s, advocates Elizabeth Rindskopf and Dorothy Toth Beasley became the first two women to argue against each other in front of the Supreme Court. Significantly, in 1972, Congress also passed the Equal Employment Opportunity Act, which amended Title VII, giving the EEOC the right to conduct its own enforcement litigation and to sue private employers. In 1976, the U.S. Military Academy at West Point, the U.S. Naval Academy at Annapolis, and the U.S. Air Force Academy at Colorado Springs admitted their first women students under a law passed a year earlier directing them to do so. And then there was the Pregnancy Discrimination Act of 1978—yet another amendment to Title VII—making it illegal for a woman to be fired for becoming pregnant.

No court case during the decade, however, was arguably more significant for women's social and, by extension, economic empowerment than *Roe v. Wade.* In June 1969, a young high school dropout named Norma McCorvey from Simmesport, Louisiana, found out that she was pregnant with her third child. McCorvey was twenty-one years old and did not feel capable of raising a child. Two daughters that she'd given birth to had already been placed for adoption. She was living in Texas, where a pregnancy could only legally be terminated if the mother's life was in danger, so, in desperation, she sought an illegal abortion but failed to find a way to have one. Eventually, McCorvey was introduced to two attorneys, Linda Coffee and Sarah Weddington, who were trying to find a plaintiff in a case they were preparing to contest the Texas law that made it illegal to have an abortion.

Hoping that it would ease the burden of her own personal situation, McCorvey signed the suit that challenged the law on the grounds that it violated the Ninth Amendment to the U.S. Constitution, which guarantees the right to free choice and privacy. To avoid public scrutiny, she used the alias "Jane Roe." The case moved at a sluggish pace, though, from Dallas District Court and eventually to the Supreme Court. The "Roe Baby," as the infant later became known, had long since been born and placed for adoption by the time the case was decided. In January 1973, the Supreme Court ruled seven votes to two that making abortion illegal violates the U.S. Constitution. The court explained that it recognized the right to liberty in the Constitution, which protects personal privacy, including the right to decide whether to continue a pregnancy or not.

As she had been with the ERA, Shirley Chisholm was a vocal supporter of *Roe v. Wade*. One of her most courageous acts, in fact, was expressing public support for legalized abortion. It put her at odds with both the traditional civil rights leaders and supporters of the more militant Black freedom struggle, who charged that abortion and birth control were tools of white America to commit genocide on African Americans. It was a decision that might well have curtailed Chisholm's political life, but for her, the sacrifice was worth it. In her 1970 memoir, *Unbought and Unbossed*, Chisholm wrote that she particularly took issue with this idea of genocide. "To label family planning and legal abortion programs 'genocide' is male rhetoric, for male ears," she wrote, noting that in 1969, 49 percent of the deaths of pregnant Black women and 65 percent of deaths of pregnant Puerto Rican women were due to "criminal, amateur abortions."

Much like determining the financial effect of contraception, measuring the economic impact of *Roe v. Wade* on women's lives in both the short and long run is far from a straightforward task. Nonetheless, researchers have tried. While *Roe* legalized abortion federally, five states—Alaska, California, Hawaii, New York, and Washington—as well as the District of Columbia had repealed their abortion bans several years before. This allowed researchers to use a methodology known as "difference-in-difference estimation" to study the impact that the change in law had. They compared what happened in those five states when abortion bans were lifted to changes in outcomes across the rest of the country. They also compared changes in outcomes in the rest of the country in 1973, when *Roe* passed, to changes in outcomes in the five states where abortion already was legal. This approach, academics writing for the Brookings Institution argue, allows the states where abortion access is not changing to serve as a sort of control group that accounts for other forces that were impacting fertility and women's lives in 1973, when *Roe* was being decided.

In 1999, that's exactly what a team of economists did, leading them to conclude that the legalization of abortion in the states that changed their laws before *Roe* led to a decline of between 4 and 11 percent in births in those states relative to the rest of the country. The economists found that these effects were particularly large for teenagers and women of color. In fact, these demographics experienced birth rate reductions that were nearly three times greater than the overall population's as a result of abortion being legalized. Subsequent studies corroborated this. One, from 2017, found that legalizing abortion cut the number of girls who became teen mothers by 34 percent and the number who got married while still teenagers by one-fifth. Again, the effect was strongest among young Black women. Digging even further and using the same methodology, many teams of academics have, in recent decades, presented evidence that legalizing abortion does not only increase a woman's access to education, but also bolsters female workforce participation and earnings. Other studies have found that children born to women with abortion access experienced lower rates of poverty and received less public assistance during childhood—predominantly because they were less likely to live in a single-parent household—and were more likely to graduate from college.

*\*\*\**

The defeat of the ERA haunted the women's movement in the years and decades that followed. Its failure to be ratified by the necessary states was on one level a symbolic loss, but on another a distinctly practical one. The first and—at the time of this book's writing—only right that the U.S. Constitution specifically affirms equally for women and men is the right to vote. Legal experts have also noted that passage of the ERA would provide a clear judicial standard for deciding cases of sex discrimination by providing consistency across all states. It would save women—and sometimes men—from having to engage in long, arduous, and costly legal battles just to prove that their rights are equal to those of the opposite sex. In a 2020 letter to the *New York Times*, Toni Van Pelt, then the president of NOW, also noted that because the Constitution does not in its current form mention women, "women can go unseen by our judicial system." She wrote that "laws like the Equal Pay Act are not protected by the Constitution and can be repealed or rescinded at any time based on political whims."

In March 2017, Nevada ratified the ERA, making it the first state to do so since the expiration of the 1982 deadline. Illinois followed in 2018, and, in 2020, Virginia passed a ratification resolution, technically bringing the number of state ratifications to the necessary thirty-eight. But what was celebrated by women's groups as a major milestone and victory—almost a century after the ERA was first conceived by Alice Paul—did not provide any level of constitutional guarantee of legal rights regardless of sex. The same month that Virginia ratified it, the Justice Department released an opinion in which it concluded that the state's efforts had come too late. It stated that the entire legislative approval process would have to be restarted in order for a proposed amendment to be legally binding. A further factor complicating the issue was that between 1982 and the moment of Virginia's ratification, five states had rescinded their initial approval of the ERA: Idaho, Kentucky, Nebraska, Tennessee, and South Dakota.

Despite the ERA not being ratified, however, it would be entirely wrong to call it a failure or to deem the efforts by the cast of thousands to get it enshrined in the law unsuccessful. Public opinion regarding the need for change shifted substantially during the years that the ERA was on the table. Surveys taken by Louis Harris and by the Roper Organization between 1970 and 1985 provide evidence of the growing support for strengthening the status of women in American society during those years. According to the Library of Congress, pollsters in 1970 asked members of the public: "Do you favor most of the efforts to strengthen and change women's status in society today?" Of all those questioned, 40 percent of women and 44 percent of men responded in the affirmative, but by 1985 the proportions agreeing to the question had risen to 73 percent of women and 69 percent of men respectively.

Between the ninety-second Congress, starting in 1971, and the ninety-fifth, which ended in 1978, a total of ten statutes were enacted that prohibited discrimination on the basis of sex in education, employment, credit, and housing. And the ERA set the tone for decades to come. Legal historians and scholars also argue that debate over the ERA was a driving force behind the Supreme Court adopting a more rigorous standard of review in sex discrimination cases.

Culturally, the ERA's ability to ignite such impassioned campaigning and debate demonstrated that women's issues were actually human rights issues—and that human rights issues were mainstream political issues that couldn't be suppressed or ignored. Richard Nixon's support of the ERA made the idea of it more tolerable for those fearful that passing the amendment would contribute to the erosion of family values and tradition: that it would make America un-American. The ERA provided the impetus and scaffolding for conversations to be had about gender and equality that otherwise might not have occurred for decades.

In 1975, *TIME* awarded its "Man of the Year" honor to "American women." The cover article, entitled GREAT CHANGES, NEW CHANCES,

TOUGH CHOICES, noted that women "have arrived like a new immigrant wave in male America," and that "they may be cops, judges, military officers, telephone linemen, cab drivers, pipefitters, editors, business executives—or mothers and housewives, but not quite the same subordinate creatures they were before."

In the two decades following 1970, the number of women winning an elective office surged. Between 1973 and 1993, the proportion of women mayors in U.S. cities with populations greater than 30,000 increased from less than 2 percent to 18 percent. The percentage of women in state legislatures almost quadrupled, and the percentage of women in the U.S. House of Representatives more than doubled.

The increase in female political representation is particularly relevant to a broader understanding of female economic empowerment, because it has historically tended to be women—and women from both ends of the political spectrum, at that—who have championed legislation that directly affects the lives of women, children, families, and minorities, in areas including but not limited to health, education, and welfare. A 2020 study by The Global Institute for Women's Leadership at King's College London found that women in politics are more likely than men to consider representing women to be part of their purview, and they also tend to legislate more than men on women's priority issues. The academics also found that women in politics are better able to propose and pass women-friendly legislation when there is a greater proportion of women in the legislature and when there is a women's caucus, or women's parliamentary body. In conclusion, and in the words of the academics, more women leaders seem to make for more equal and caring societies.

***

For all the setbacks in the 1970s, it was definitively an era of planting seeds and building foundations. Chisholm's presidential candidacy—characterized by speeches that cast a light on the uncomfortable truth about sexism and racism in America—provided a wake-up call and sent a signal that politics did not have to be the way it had always been; that politicians could look and sound different than they had historically. The echoes of her advocacy have proved far more important and consequential than her political defeat.

Almost five decades after Chisholm's run for the presidency, Kamala Harris, in her bid for the Democratic presidential nomination, ran under the slogan "For the People," which her campaign explicitly acknowledged was a nod to Chisholm. Harris, a former San Francisco district attorney, was elected in 2011 as the first Black woman to serve as California's attorney general. In 2016, she became the second Black woman to be elected a United States senator, and in 2020, she became both the country's first female and first Black vice president. Of Chisholm, she said, "I stand, as so many of us do, on her shoulders."

Ruth Bader Ginsburg's legislative efforts in the 1970s, which in no small part built on the earlier work of Pauli Murray, set invaluable precedents for legal battles that followed and tested the Constitution in a meaningful way.

Culturally, the 1970s elevated the issue of gender equality and female economic empowerment enormously. The August 1970 Women's Strike for Equality sent shock waves not only through America, but around the world. Different national women's movements fed off and inspired one another. In October 1975, an estimated 25,000 women in Iceland joined a strike demanding gender equality. The country's economy ground to a halt, underscoring the critical and underappreciated nature of women's contributions to the economy. The following year, the country enacted a sweeping gender equality law, and five years later Vigdís Finnbogadóttir became the world's first democratically elected female president. The United Nations General Assembly declared 1975 International Women's Year and organized the first World Conference on Women, held in Mexico City. It subsequently declared the years 1976 until 1985 the United Nations Decade for Women.

Back in the United States, by 1980, the gender pay gap had narrowed from ten years earlier but only by a tiny fraction. Women were earning 60.2 cents on every man's dollar compared to 59.4 cents a decade before. The trajectory was pointing in the right direction, but progress was agonizingly slow—at that pace it would take until the twenty-fifth century for parity.

Alice Paul died in 1977 at the age of ninety-two. In one of the last interviews she ever gave, she stated that the adoption of the Nineteenth Amendment in 1920 had been the high point of her life. Chisholm turned her back on politics in 1982. After seven terms in the House, she told interviewers that she'd become disappointed by "moderate and liberal" lawmakers who were "running for cover from the new right."

Chisholm was principled to a fault, and it was her decision not to allow political belief and affiliations to compromise human decency that distinguished her as a vanguard. Her determination, as a Black woman, to run for president at a time when America was not ready to be led by either a Black president or a female one demonstrated an ability to tolerate personal defeat in the name of common progress. As she departed Washington for a life of teaching, playing the piano, and spending time with her second husband, who'd been injured in a car accident shortly after their marriage, she asserted that she was "at peace" with herself. "It's been a remarkable challenge," she declared. "I am not looking back."

# CHAPTER 6

## 1,365 Men and Me

When I'm right, no one remembers. When I'm wrong, no one forgets.

—Muriel Siebert's memo pad, 1968

Between the late 1970s and the late 1980s, a woman's role in America's society and in the economy changed perhaps more dramatically than in any other decade of the twentieth century. By the 1970s, thanks to growing female labor force participation, the country had started to become somewhat comfortable with the idea of a woman working outside the home. But it wasn't until the early 1980s that the concept of a woman having a career started to become widely accepted.

In 1981, a magazine article in *Mademoiselle* asked whether men would still love women as much now that "we dare to love ourselves and our work as much as we love them." The answer—mercifully—was yes.

Around the same time, research conducted by the President's Advisory Committee for Women, a commission established by Jimmy Carter in 1978, concluded that most Americans felt, or at least proclaimed to feel, comfortable with the idea of their doctor, lawyer, political representative, or boss being a woman. By that time, it had been almost a hundred years since Susanna Salter had in 1887 been elected the first female mayor of any U.S. city—Argonia, Kansas—and more than half a century had passed since Bertha Knight Landes had in 1926 in Seattle been elected as the first female mayor of a major city in the United States. Although women made up just 2 percent of senators and about 4 percent of all voting members of the House of Representatives, the trajectory by 1980 was clear: When it came to positions of power, women were here to stay.

In 1982, *Cagney & Lacey*, the first television drama with two female leads, debuted to much critical acclaim. The NYPD detective duo, a single woman and a working mother, developed a sizable and loyal public following by redefining, as scholar and author Julie D'Acci put it, the "notions of what women could or could not be—not only on television but in society at large."

Even a female U.S. president was starting to become less of an outlandish prospect than it had been, no doubt on account of heads of state like Indira Gandhi in India, Golda Meir in Israel, Isabel Perón in Argentina, and Margaret Thatcher in the United Kingdom. In 1987, Gallup asked Americans whether, if the party whose candidate they most often supported were to nominate a woman for president, they would vote for her. Eighty-two percent said that they would, up from just sixty-six percent in 1971.

Women were starting to account for a growing proportion of the higher education population, too. Emboldened by the women's movement, the wide availability of birth control, and a realization that the prospect of building a career—rather than just holding down a series of jobs—was well within their reach, women surged into colleges. Throughout the 1960s and 1970s, helped also by the 1972 passage of Title IX, female college enrollment and graduation rates soared relative to those of their male counterparts. In the seven years between 1975 and 1982, for example, the number of women attending law schools more than doubled, according to the American Bar Association.

It was no longer widely assumed that all women harbored the dream that those college students had recounted to Betty Freidan at her 1957 Smith college reunion. It wasn't a given that they would want to get married, have kids, and then become housewives. Women no longer defaulted to aspiring to follow in their mothers' footsteps. The birth control pill was becoming more easily available, as were other methods of contraception, meaning that it had never been simpler for a woman to plan when—and if—she wanted to have children, and to tailor whatever choice she made around professional ambitions and other personal projects.

A particularly notable development of the late 1970s and early 1980s was that even one of the greatest vestiges of the patriarchy, the financial services sector, was starting to show signs of transformation, albeit tentative ones. Women were still decades away from securing a permanent spot in the boardrooms and on the trading floors of Wall Street, but in select corners of the world of money—in securities trading and retail investing—a smattering of women were starting to stake out a path.

In December 1967, Muriel Siebert had become the first woman to buy a seat and become a member of the New York Stock Exchange (NYSE), allowing her to trade. Her achievement was hailed a glass-ceiling-smashing moment, but it would be nearly ten more years before she was joined by a second female on the iconic trading floor. For almost an entire decade, she wrote in her memoir, it was just "1,365 men and me."

***

Muriel was born on September 12, 1928, as the second daughter of Margaret and Irwin Siebert, a Jewish couple living in Cleveland, Ohio. The Siebert family rarely traveled; vacations were too expensive. So, in 1953, when Muriel, known as Mickie, made a trip to New York City with two girlfriends, her imagination in terms of the possibilities that lay before her ran wild.

On a touristy excursion to the New York Stock Exchange in the heart of the world's busiest financial district, she peered down from the visitors' gallery. The NYSE was the ultimate symbol of American capitalism and, by extension, power. By 1960, at least a billion shares would trade hands there every year, cementing it as an unshakable bastion of commerce and a nerve center of the global economy. The sprawling floor—two-thirds the size of a football field—was covered with slips of paper and buzzing with a hive of activity: men in dark suits—footmen to the captains of industry—shouting and gesticulating frantically, as if the future of the world depended on them clinching that next trade.

The five-story-high ceiling, embellished with gold leaf, the lavish Georgian marble, and the energy that throbbed through the entire building enchanted her. "Now *this* is exciting," she told her friends. "Maybe I'll come back here and look for a job." At the time, every tourist who paid a visit to the exchange was given a piece of ticker tape printed with their name as a souvenir. WELCOME TO THE NYSE, Siebert's read. In the years that followed, the irony of that statement—the implication that she, a woman, should feel welcome in this place of overt toxic masculinity—would never fail to amuse her.

Ever since 1624, when the Dutch founded New Amsterdam on the southern tip of Manhattan and constructed a stockade, from which Wall Street got its name, men had been in charge here. The intoxicating mix of adrenaline and risk-taking that working on the stock exchange necessarily entailed fueled a specific type of individualism and hypermasculinity, later glamorized in movies like *Wall Street* and *American Psycho*. It was a peculiar world, an industry entirely unlike any other, and it intrigued Siebert. It even had its own language—its own cultures and mores. It was primitive in many ways—you ate what you hunted—and she realized early on that being able to navigate it could lead to immense personal fortune and power. The potential upside was exhilarating.

A year after that first visit, just before Thanksgiving 1954, Siebert returned to New York with five hundred dollars, a used Studebaker, and few other material belongings but a steadfast dream. She had intended to graduate from college first and had in the early 1950s enrolled in Flora Stone Mather College, a women's school that was later absorbed into Cleveland's Case Western Reserve University. In fact, she'd been the only woman to take classes on the topics of finance and banking at the affiliated men's school, but she had dropped out when her father died. In the vastness of New York City, she now sought a new beginning away from familial tragedy.

Without a college degree, though, Siebert's job prospects looked bleak. Her applications to the United Nations and Merrill Lynch were summarily rejected. Eventually, after lying and saying she had a degree, she was hired as a trainee in the research department of Bache & Company, a securities firm that provided stockbroking and investment banking services, on a weekly paycheck of sixty-five dollars.

Incredulous that she'd secured something that would pay her rent, Siebert embraced her new role as a junior analyst—the grunt work and all—and her perseverance earned her incremental pay raises and, over time, more responsibility. If a seasoned researcher's interest in an industry began to fade—if he was starting to get bored with a particular stock—he might dump that company on her. That way Siebert was handed responsibility for researching airlines and some media companies, and she did so assiduously, combing through investor updates, accounts, balance sheet and audit reports. There were one or two other female analysts in the company, but they covered what Siebert thought of as female industries: retail and cosmetics. "I was certainly the only woman reading *Civil Aeronautics Board Reports* and *Missile and Space Daily* in the beauty parlor," she remembered.

The young woman from Cleveland established her place at Bache, impressing managers with piercing and often fearless questions to corporate executives rooted in a solid, if largely self-taught, understanding of accounting. But despite being encouraged by the slowly rising trajectory of her pay, Siebert knew she was getting, in many cases, significantly less than her male colleagues. Grudgingly, she started casting her eye around for other opportunities. A contact introduced her to bankers at Kuhn, Loeb & Co. and at Smith Barney, but she was told that neither institution had ever hired a woman as anything other than a secretary. And now they were meant to take a chance on a woman analyst? What a ludicrous idea.

Insulted and disheartened, Siebert eventually left Bache without another job lined up. More desperate now, she fired off applications en masse, but all were rejected or went unanswered completely, until she decided to start tweaking them ever so slightly. Rather than sending out the résumé of Muriel Siebert, she applied under the name of M. F. Siebert, initials that belied her gender. And it worked. In 1958 she started as a research analyst at brokerage firm Shields & Company, on a salary of 9,500 dollars a year—almost double the median income of a U.S. family at the time.

Siebert's initial enthusiasm was short-lived, however. A year into the job and having already generated a huge amount of revenue from commissions, her income was flatlining, and she became aware of two men who had recently been hired straight out of business school as analysts at 8,800 dollars a year. Their salaries were less than hers, but in her opinion the gap did not reflect the chasm between her experience level and theirs. And quite aside from that, a male analyst of Siebert's experience level was making 20,000 dollars a year, more than double what she was earning, which her managing partner justified by saying that he, unlike she, had a family to support. *That's take-a-vacation money or buy-a-new-car money or start-investing-your-own-money money,* Siebert thought. It was the anger and frustration that stemmed from that realization that gave her the gumption to, once again, move on. A stint at investment bank Bear Stearns followed, before Siebert joined Finkle & Co, a brokerage set up by an erstwhile senior partner and bond trader at Bear Stearns, and it was there that she got her first taste of trading.

To Siebert it seemed that traders and analysts were different species entirely, but she wasn't intimidated by the vulgar vernacular and brash tone of the trading fraternity—surprised, perhaps, but not intimidated. Still working as a stock analyst but now shoulder-to-shoulder with traders, she learned to navigate the profanities that were hurled around the room nonchalantly. She became accustomed to brushing off misogynistic remarks and being dismissed as "the girl." Instead, she focused on the commissions she was reaping. By 1965, Siebert was earning more than a quarter of a million dollars a year, or well over two million in today's dollars. By any measure at the time, she was now rich and successful, and that dream that she had so keenly harbored when she first moved to New York was no longer an aspiration. But still, she felt confined and not infrequently a little lonely.

\*\*\*

In 1839, French feminist and novelist Amantine Lucile Aurore Dupin, better known by her pen name George Sand, wrote a play called *Gabriel*. It was never performed, but the script survived. One passage in it translates as "I was a woman; for suddenly my wings went numb, ether closed in around my head like an impenetrable crystal vault, and I fell." The play's heroine, an Icarus-like character, holds a dream of using her wings to soar above the role that society affords her. Unceremoniously, she fails.

More than a century later, the impenetrable crystal vault that curtails a woman's potential became the invisible "glass ceiling": in 1978 management consultant Marilyn Loden used the term at a conference during a panel discussion about women's professional aspirations.

"As I listened, I noted how the [female] panelists focused on the deficiencies in women's socialization, the self-deprecating ways in which women behaved, and the poor self-image that many women allegedly carried," Loden said in an interview in 2017. "It was a struggle to sit quietly and listen to the criticisms," she continued. "True, women did seem unable to climb the career ladder beyond the lowest rung of middle management, but I argued that the 'invisible glass ceiling'—the barriers to advancement that were cultural, not personal—was doing the bulk of the damage to women's career aspirations and opportunities."

Loden's experiences mirrored exactly what Siebert seemed to be enduring. One time, Loden recalled, she, an experienced human resource professional within the telecommunications industry, was told that despite her better performance record, a promotion she was aiming for would be awarded to a male peer. "The reason given was that he was a 'family man,'" she said. "He was the main breadwinner and so needed the money more."

In the mid-1960s, Siebert didn't have a phrase for it, but the glass ceiling stubbornly hovered right above her head, and she was aware of it all the time. One day, while chatting after lunch with a male client whom she both liked and trusted, she was bemoaning the inequity of the job market across the financial services sector. "What large firm can I go to and get credit for the business I'm doing?" she asked dispiritedly.

Traders on the floor of the New York Stock Exchange in the 1930s.

"Don't be ridiculous," he retorted. "Buy a seat on the Stock Exchange and work for yourself."

Now Siebert thought that he was the one being ridiculous. Women simply didn't work on the stock exchange. It wasn't their terrain. Victoria Claflin Woodhull and her sister, Tennessee, had in the 1800s operated a Wall Street brokerage firm that briefly earned them the moniker "Queens of Finance," but the backlash the pair endured had been brutal. Some men's journals graphically mocked the sisters, publishing sexualized images of them and associating the idea of free-spirited independent women with the concepts of sexual immorality and prostitution.

If anything, men's angry reactions to Woodhull's foray into stockbroking seemed to more deeply entrench unfair gender norms across the industry, norms that only calcified in the decades that followed, coming to permeate every bank, investment firm, trading house, and, most visibly perhaps, trading floors.

Of course, Siebert appreciated her lunch companion's vote of confidence, but she also thought that his proposal was crazy. Nonetheless, the idea lingered. That evening, she sourced a copy of the constitution of the Stock Exchange, took it home, and pored over every line, hunting for evidence that she, a woman, would not be able to buy a seat. Nothing caught her attention: She met the requirements stipulated by the NYSE's standard regulations, and she'd passed the necessary exams. Technically, nothing was preventing her from applying. She'd simply have to make a compelling business case for herself and pay the purchase price of the seat. On the other hand, she couldn't help but think, *Why rock the boat?* She was earning handsomely: Her salary afforded her luxury vacations, she could dine out in New York's fanciest restaurants, and she lived in an affluent neighborhood. Did she really need more?

It took Siebert six months to muster up the courage to apply for permission to buy a seat, courage that was not helped when she learned that the London Stock Exchange around that time rebuked a "prospective petticoat invasion," banning women from buying seats on that trading floor. Women weren't admitted to the London Stock Exchange until 1973. In 1967, when Siebert eventually paid a visit to John J. Mulcahy Jr., the secretary of the New York exchange who controlled the sale of seats, she did so armed with an impassioned speech that she'd tried to memorize about the honor and glory that membership would bring. But when she opened her mouth, nerves pervaded, and all she found herself capable of uttering was a single question: "Can I buy a seat, or is this just a country club?" Mulcahy, a little stunned, pondered the entirely unique situation he found himself in and then contemplated out loud. No, he would not be able to turn her down on the basis of her sex, he admitted. She'd have an excuse to sue every member of the exchange's board of governors. And with that, Siebert knew she'd just cleared the first hurdle.

On December 7, 1967, Siebert signed a conditional sales contract with the NYSE and wrote a check for 89,000 dollars, or 20 percent of the purchase price of a seat. The cash, which Siebert drew from her savings, was meant to foot the bill of the exchange's investigation into a candidate's eligibility for full membership.

Conscious of having told a lie about graduating from college when she first applied for a job in the city, Siebert took precautions. Now, she only claimed to have attended college, not graduated. She said that she had "studied" rather than "obtained a bachelor of arts." An interview before the admissions committee followed, featuring a series of mostly innocuous questions that Siebert answered calmly, but other challenges remained. One of the final steps toward full membership required that she convince two existing members to sponsor her application. Almost all the individuals she approached declined to help, some conjuring up creative excuses. One said he was out of town and unavailable; another proclaimed not to know her well enough; a third didn't even try to hide his fears of being stigmatized for backing a woman. "Holy shit, Mickie," he blurted out when she asked him, "I won't have a friend left."

Two acquaintances eventually agreed to put in the requisite good word for her, but the final barrier was a significant one. The NYSE informed Siebert that in order for her application to be considered complete, she would need a letter from a bank, on official corporate stationery, stating that, in the event that the exchange were to grant her membership, the bank would stand ready to lend her 300,000 dollars of the total 445,000-dollar purchase price of the seat.

The NYSE became a publicly traded company in 2006, but before then it was a private entity, of which financial professionals could become members by buying a seat. Owners of seats were able to trade in person on the floor of the stock exchange, either on behalf of themselves or as agents of others, in which case they'd be known as floor brokers. Owning a seat and being a member was considered extremely prestigious. It gave financiers the opportunity to haggle and negotiate on objectively one of the most important financial exchanges in the world. Seats were, therefore, extremely sought after, and prices of them were dynamic, determined by supply and demand. In the mid-1800s, in the decades after twenty-four businessmen signed the Buttonwood Agreement laying down the ground rules for trading stocks and establishing the original stock exchange, the cost of a seat had hovered around 4,000 dollars. By the early 2000s prices had surged in tandem with ballooning demand, and inflation, to above 3 million dollars. The last seat ever to sell on the NYSE before it went public did so for $3.575 million in January 2006, about two months before the IPO.

It wasn't the cost that incensed Siebert, though, but the double standard she was encountering. As far as she knew, such a demand had never been made of a male applicant, but to her great relief, Chase agreed to back her and finance her acquisition through a loan secured against some stocks that she owned. Poignantly, the pronoun on the form used to codify the agreement between Siebert and Chase had to be crossed through and corrected by hand.

Three weeks after signing the conditional sales contract, Siebert received a letter from the assistant secretary of the New York Stock Exchange informing her that she'd been admitted to trade—a letter that changed her life and sent newspaper headline writers across the country into an excited frenzy. NOW THE GIRLS WANT TO PLAY TOO, Long Island's *Newsday* declared. SKIRT INVADES EXCHANGE, another crowed. But Siebert's favorite appeared in the *Minneapolis Tribune*: GOD BLESS AMERICA—FIRST WOMAN JOINS NY STOCK EXCHANGE.

\*\*\*

One of the things that amused Siebert most about the ensuing weeks and months was how many people had, seemingly overnight, developed a keen interest in her bathroom habits. For more than a century and a half, there had been no reason for a ladies' room to exist on the exchange floor of the building. It was only for a short stint during the Second World War that women had ever set foot on those hallowed wooden floorboards.

In 1945, investment bank Merrill Lynch had assigned a young woman named Helen Hanzelin to the floor as a telephone clerk, and thirty-six women were subsequently employed as quotation clerks and carrier pages, taking on the jobs of men who had been drafted into military service. They were the Rosie the Riveters of Wall Street, and just as had been the case at Mae Krier's Boeing factory in Seattle, they were promptly replaced by returning male veterans when the war ended. Later, women were briefly employed as clerks and pages during the Korean War. But when they left, the need for a women's bathroom faded, too, and as Siebert settled into her new role as a trader, media outlets delighted in pointing out that she would have to travel several stories any time she needed to go.*

There was also no ladies' bathroom on the seventh floor, where the dining club was located. Siebert took it in her stride, but a few years into her trading career, a group of women business owners attended a meeting at the exchange that was followed by lunch at the club. Several of the women were European—members of the Ferragamo and Moët & Chandon families—and they expressed outrage at the lack of ladies' facilities, proclaiming that this would never be the case in their civilized countries, France or Italy. Siebert took the opportunity to broach the subject with the chairman of the exchange and provocatively offered to haul in a portable toilet to rectify the matter. He wasn't amused, but it still took many years before management agreed to convert some of the old wooden telephone cubicles into ladies' rooms, and as recently as 2012, the NYSE made headlines for sending women on the exchange floor on a veritable trek every time they needed to use the bathroom.

In 1968, Siebert started operating as an independent seat holder on the New York Stock Exchange. She hired a secretary, who was male, and two years later was joined by two partners and granted permission to form a member corporation: Muriel Siebert & Co., Inc. She was becoming more visible, and with that prominence came attention, both good and bad. Some men patronized her, but others were intrigued by the exoticism of a female trader. A handful went as far as to ask for her hand in marriage.

Women flocked to her for other reasons. "Every young woman fresh from college who wanted a job on Wall Street walked through my doors," she recalled. And at the same time she was deluged with mail and calls from women with no interest in a career in finance but who had money worries that they hoped Siebert would be able to help them with. Some

---

* Siebert did eventually discover that there had been a small ladies' room on the same floor all along that had been built for the women working there during the Korean War.

were widows, begging for cash or advice on how to meet medical costs or mortgage expenses. None of them, she noticed, seemed to have even a basic foundation in financial education beyond a home economics class. Struck by this realization, Siebert commissioned a survey at 137 women's colleges and was shocked by the outcome. Fully 85 percent of respondents had never taken a class or course in managing money. One college administrator told her that personal finance was simply not "a proper subject for ladies." One of the things that appalled Siebert most was that subjects like laboratory sciences were still prerequisites for graduation at most institutions, but the basic concepts of managing money almost never featured. "The institutions of higher learning in this country seemed to have agreed that it was more important to know how to dissect a frog than how to manage personal finances," she asserted.

Another realization that horrified Siebert was that a general perception existed across much of the financial services industry that those few women who succeeded had done so by sleeping around. Once while out having dinner at a steakhouse in midtown Manhattan, she overheard two men she'd never met talking about "Mickie Siebert." One explained to the other that "Mickie . . . sleeps with all the customers." Siebert walked over to the pair and introduced herself. It might have embarrassed them but did nothing to erode attitudes that persisted widely and for decades.

Siebert's hair was a popular topic of conversation—its color and its style—as well as the way she dressed, but she swatted offhand comments away like flies and got on with her job. In her first year after striking out on her own, she made close to a million dollars in sales commissions and was able to afford to move her small but growing team into a new office with impressive views of Manhattan. But she prided herself on sitting with her back to the windows. She didn't have time, she explained, to look out the skyline and dream.

\*\*\*

The women of 1970s Wall Street—the ones who weren't secretaries but who traded, negotiated, and closed deals just as any male banker would—knew each other by name. Outspoken Mickie Siebert was perhaps the most prominent, but Neale Godfrey was far from obscure.

Growing up, Godfrey had entertained the idea of becoming a diplomat. Born in West Caldwell, New Jersey, in 1951, she'd graduated from the American University in Washington, D.C., majoring in international relations, and then spent time in the Middle East and South America. After marrying an aspiring lawyer when she was in her early twenties, though, she acknowledged that she would need a job to earn a living. The couple had moved back to New Jersey to accommodate his studies, and, at the age of twenty-one, Godfrey was approached by a recruiter for Chase Manhattan who was seeking a Spanish speaker to support the bank's clients in Latin America. She couldn't write shorthand and had no foundation in math or anything numerical, but the recruiter insisted she should apply for the job.

"Years later, I figured out that I was actually part of an experiment," Godfrey recalls today. "Someone at the bank had proposed the idea of hiring women into men's jobs," she explains. "I was meant to serve as evidence that women just weren't suited to these types of jobs. But as it turned out, I proved the opposite."

On the day before her final interview, Godfrey caught the subway downtown on a fact-finding mission. "I wanted to see what women who worked on Wall Street wore, but obviously all I saw was gray suits, black suits, and navy suits," she recalls. She opted for a simple A-line dress and carried an empty briefcase, unsure of what all the men she'd observed carried around in theirs.

Godfrey became one of the first women to work for Chase Manhattan as anything other than a secretary. She initially joined on an annual salary of 11,000 dollars but was soon told by the head of personnel that she should actually be paid only 6,500 dollars, "because she was taking the job of a man." But while that ignited in her a rage that's still palpable when she talks about it four decades later, there was something else that shook her to the core.

"When I was offered the position in 1972, my boss leaned across his desk, looked me in the eye, and issued a stern warning. I was not, under any circumstances, to get pregnant, he barked," Godfrey remembers. When, about a year later, she confessed that she was actually expecting a baby, his reaction terrified her. "I didn't mind him screaming at me, though," she recalls. "What deeply, deeply upset me was that he offered to pay for an abortion—for me to get rid of it. To this day, I have no words to describe how that made me feel."

But Godfrey persisted. Over the following decade, she worked her way up the ranks at Chase, chalking up achievements that included structuring and executing chemical company DuPont's multi-billion-dollar acquisition of oil giant Conoco, the most expensive corporate takeover battle in history at the time. She worked closely with barons of the industry, like David Rockefeller, with whom she struck up a friendship. Rockefeller, who served as chief executive of Chase from 1969 until 1980 and as chairman for one more year after that, developed a fond affection for Godfrey. On one occasion, she recalls, she was invited to a client meeting at a member's club in Connecticut, which Rockefeller was also attending. They traveled there together. "We were told upon arrival that I, as a woman, couldn't go in through the front door and would have to enter the club through the kitchen," she explains. "I was annoyed but didn't want to make a scene, so I started heading toward the kitchen, but David didn't skip a beat," she remembers. "'If Neale goes through the kitchen, so do I,' he said. And off we went."

It was this sort of allyship and championing—amid the all-too-frequent pernicious toxicity and misogyny—that kept Godfrey at the bank for more than thirteen years. But when the opportunity arose to do something entrepreneurial, to lead, and particularly to do so in the name of democratizing the world of money, she couldn't resist. In 1985, she was asked to head up the First Women's Bank—founded in 1975 as the first full-service commercial bank in the country that was operated and majority owned by women—as chief executive and president. The idea for the bank, headquartered at 111 East Fifty-Seventh Street in Manhattan, had been conceived in 1973, before the passage of the Equal Credit Opportunity Act a year later banned creditors from discriminating against applicants on the basis of sex, marital status, and a number of other characteristics. Its first president had been Madeline H. McWhinney, who in 1960 had become the first female officer of the Federal Reserve and who later was the first woman to run for election to the board of trustees of the Federal Reserve Retirement System.

By the time the First Women's Bank opened—and in recognition of the recent legislative changes—management maintained that the bank's core mission was to help women become financially literate and independent but also billed it as "totally nondiscriminatory" and maintained that it wouldn't compromise its fiduciary duties solely in order to lend money to women who needed it. "It doesn't do the woman a favor or our shareholders a favor to give a loan to a woman who cannot repay it," McWhinney told the *New York Times* in 1975.

The bank was celebrated enthusiastically in feminist circles, and the day it opened its doors, hundreds swarmed to its chic offices—likened by the press to the interiors of an Upper East Side art gallery—either with the explicit goal of opening an account or just out of curiosity: Were women really capable of owning and running a fully functioning bank?

"Everyone in the Women's Movement had an account there—Gloria Steinem, Betty Friedan, Bella Abzug, even Madonna—you name them, they were there," Godfrey says. "To be part of creating this symbol of a changing world of big money was just so exciting."

\*\*\*

In the meantime, Mickie Siebert's reputation had continued to surge as her sales commissions did, and in 1977 she received an unexpected call from Robert Morgado, secretary and top aide to Hugh Carey, the Democratic governor of New York. He was looking for a new superintendent of banking, and she'd caught his attention. He was calling to tell her that Carey was trying to hire more women. The job was hers if she wanted it.

In many ways, the timing could not have been worse. Siebert's mother was in poor health after having suffered a stroke, and Siebert was now paying the cost of her care in a private nursing home on

Manhattan's Upper East Side. The job would command a salary of just under 48,000 dollars a year, which was about a tenth of what Siebert was taking home thanks to her dealings on the stock market. It would also require her to put Muriel Siebert & Co., Inc., in a blind trust. Nonetheless, she couldn't resist the new challenge and opportunity to once again step into a position never before held by a woman.

The jurisdiction of the superintendent was immense: about five hundred banks with no less than four hundred billion dollars in combined assets under management, as well as another one hundred billion dollars in trust accounts. After a series of interviews and a two-hour confirmation hearing before the finance committee of the state senate, Siebert—Bible and bottles of champagne in hand—headed to the banking department offices located in the World Trade Center on July 7, 1977, and was sworn in. Four days later, her mother died.

For all her confidence and experience, Siebert readily admitted that it was somewhat daunting being hailed "the most powerful woman in New York" by a newspaper as highly regarded as the *Financial Times* of London. She was intimidated by the scope of her new job, and even more so when she started to better understand the state of some of the institutions that she was responsible for overseeing. The Municipal Credit Union for employees of the City of New York was of particular concern. In August 1977, just a month after she officially took up her new post, two MCU employees were arrested and charged for taking kickbacks on loan applications. Not long after, headlines appeared about loan delinquencies and corruption of board members. By November, things were looking so bad for MCU that Siebert decided the New York State Banking Department would have to take control of MCU, something that no banking superintendent had done since the Depression.

Siebert's tenure as superintendent was tumultuous. She attracted attention and criticism for personally engineering mergers and acquisitions in a manner that her predecessor had never attempted. But by the end of a five-year term, she proudly reminded anyone who would listen that no New York bank had gone under during her time in the job despite a slew of nationwide bank failures.

On May 25, 1982, Muriel Siebert resigned as New York State's superintendent of banks and promptly announced her next goal. At a news conference at the Helmsley Palace Hotel in midtown Manhattan, she launched her campaign for the Republican nomination for the U.S. Senate. In addition to her experience in state service, she cited the twenty-two years she had spent on Wall Street.

Standing on a milk crate in stockinged feet so that she could see over the top of the lectern, she declared that America was like a family living beyond its means. The Vietnam War, which had ended in 1975, had never really been paid for. When bonds covering the cost of it came due, they would demand double or even triple the interest rate at which they had been issued. It was a terrible situation, Siebert warned, and she would use her platform to make the hard choices necessary to "cure the nation's economic ills."

But even in that moment, Siebert's gender was the most relevant thing to some members of the assembled audience. "Aren't you going to be a bitch like other women?" one man barked from the audience. Another noted that "it's about time we had a broad on the ticket." She didn't object to the offensive term, just bit her tongue and moved on. After all, she needed his support.

Other elements of campaigning concerned her more: the issues on which she and some influential Republicans clashed most. She needed their backing, but sometimes compromise wasn't an option. Siebert supported the Equal Rights Amendment, for example, and she was passionately pro-choice, which alienated vast swaths of the party. In the end, assemblywoman Florence M. Sullivan clinched the primary and was subsequently defeated by a thirty-point margin by Democratic candidate Daniel Patrick Moynihan. Siebert had to resign herself to the idea that her future might not be in public office, but moneymaking was one thing she was confident she could still do.

Her time away from Muriel Siebert & Co., Inc., was one of the most volatile for markets in recent history. A slew of new, complex financial products had launched in the intervening years, creating a landscape that was aggressively competitive. Siebert and her eponymous business were trailing notably behind, but she was delighted to be back in a familiar place doing what she knew best. By 1987, the firm was thriving again, capital-rich and preparing to expand, but the market had other ideas. On August 25 of that year, the Dow Jones Industrial Average, a price-weighted index of thirty of the biggest companies listed on stock exchanges nationwide, hit an all-time high. Two months later, in October, it suffered its largest single-day drop in history, bigger even than the decline before the Great Depression. The plunge, on what would become known as Black Monday, followed several weeks of slipping markets. The trajectory triggered floods of computer-driven futures orders that overwhelmed trading systems and dramatically depressed prices. As a result of complicated algorithms, selling accelerated, sending indices in financial hubs all around the world into free fall. Billions of dollars were wiped off the value of markets in a matter of hours, and days of intense fluctuations followed. Siebert, whiplashed by the drama, found comfort only in peering out her second-floor office window at the street below, at the people doing what they had always done: buying a hotdog or smoking a cigarette. It reminded her that the world was still turning and that all was not lost.

By the end of 1987, remarkably, Muriel Siebert & Co., Inc., had still managed to chalk up a small profit despite having been forced to write off millions of dollars. And the experience taught Siebert a lesson that would help her shape the firm's success in the decades that followed. In 1996, through a savvy deal with a publicly listed furniture company that was being liquidated, Siebert Financial Corporation started trading on the NASDAQ stock exchange.

In 2007, she celebrated the fortieth anniversary of buying her seat on the New York Stock Exchange by ringing the closing bell. At her side was her loyal companion: a long-haired Chihuahua named Monster Girl, with whom she claimed an important affinity: Neither of them was scared of the big dogs.

In August 2013, Siebert died in Manhattan from cancer. In her later years she'd often been called upon by broadcasters as a market pundit. Her sound bites were punchy, underscoring her fearlessness and a sense that she had nothing to lose, that she'd achieved everything she'd set out to. In testament to her legacy, the NYSE in 2016 announced that it was renaming one of its trading halls Siebert Hall. It marked the first time in history that a room at the exchange had ever been named after an individual.

Neale Godfrey left the First Women's Bank in 1989. The bank had struggled financially, and a newly appointed board made the decision that it should change its name to target a broader customer base. Female depositors and borrowers, the board reasoned, no longer faced discrimination from other banks, so the First Women's Bank became the First New York Bank for Business, and Godfrey sought out her next challenge.

Beyond giving different genders equal opportunities in the world of money, Godfrey also shared Siebert's belief that financial literacy should be taught broadly and across all generations, starting with the very young. That passion inspired her to form the Children's Financial Network, a company with the express mission of educating children and their parents about money in an accessible and unintimidating way. She started writing books and appearing on television talk shows and radio programs. Today, she bills herself as the "financial voice of grandparents and Baby Boomers" and mentors many female graduate school students, particularly those staking out career paths in the finance industry. She's encouraged by the progress the sector has made since the 1970s—since the days of overt discrimination, of harassment that was a given, and of women being made to walk through kitchens to be able to attend meetings with their male equivalents. But the remnants of what she endured remain, she says. "Every generation has a responsibility to call out and do what they can to fix the mistakes of the last," she says. "There's so much more work to do."

In 2021, Women in Banking and Finance, a nonprofit, and the London School of Economics surveyed women working in the industry and found that a significant proportion felt that they were expected to be exceptional in order to achieve the same level of success as "mediocre" men. When prompted to explain, the respondents said that their ability to progress was limited by factors including men belonging to a social group in which other men served as gatekeepers; men always being around, while a woman was more likely to take parental leave; and—almost unbelievably—a lingering reluctance among team leaders to "manage out" men, because they were still more frequently viewed as breadwinners.

\*\*\*

Muriel Siebert's and Neale Godfrey's hard-fought journeys to the uppermost echelons of finance coincided with more legislative changes that buttressed female economic empowerment at home and in the workplace.

In 1978, the United States passed the Pregnancy Discrimination Act, making it illegal for a woman to be dismissed from her job for becoming pregnant, as Godfrey might have been. In 1980, sexual harassment was first defined by the Equal Employment Opportunity Commission, and in 1981, the Supreme Court ruled in favor of Joan Feenstra in a case that would have repercussions in decades to come. In 1974, Feenstra of Louisiana filed a criminal complaint against her then-husband, Harold Feenstra, accusing him of molesting their daughter, who was a minor at the time. While in jail awaiting trial, Harold, who denied the charges, hired an attorney, Karl Kirchberg, to represent him, signing a three-thousand-dollar promissory note in prepayment for legal services. As security on that note, Harold took out a mortgage on the home he jointly owned with Joan—without telling her. Under Louisiana "Head and Master" laws at the time, her consent was not required.

The couple eventually separated. Harold moved out of the state, and Joan dropped the charges, but it wasn't until 1976 that she found out about the mortgage. One day, Kirchberg showed up at her house threatening to foreclose on her home unless she paid him the amount outstanding on the promissory note Harold had signed. Joan refused to pay, at which Kirchberg obtained an order of executory process directing the local sheriff to seize and sell the Feenstra home.

Joan Feenstra and Karl Kirchberg ended up in court, where, in addition to fighting foreclosure, she challenged the constitutionality of the statutory scheme that empowered her husband to execute a mortgage on their jointly owned home without her even knowing about it. The district court upheld the state of Louisiana's law, and, on appeal, the Fifth Circuit overturned that decision, declaring the law unconstitutional, but it limited the application of their decision to future rulings. Feenstra then appealed to the U.S. Supreme Court, which decided in March 1981 that the Louisiana law that the district court had acted upon lacked an "exceedingly persuasive justification" for its sex-based classification. As a result, the justices unanimously deemed the decision to have been a violation of the Equal Protection Clause of the Fourteenth Amendment.

More than thirty years after that decision, in 2015, Supreme Court Justice Ginsburg referred to the case of *Kirchberg v. Feenstra* to illustrate during oral arguments in a same-sex marriage case how "traditional" concepts of marriage have changed and evolved over time, requiring the law to shift too. In *Obergefell v. Hodges*, a landmark civil rights case, the Supreme Court ruled that the fundamental right to get married is guaranteed to same-sex couples by the Constitution.

During the 1970s and 1980s, women like Siebert and Godfrey were defying conventions in an obvious and extreme way as they climbed the rungs of seniority in their respective fields. Women like Joan Feenstra and Justice Ginsburg were examining and highlighting ways in which the law was inadequate. But elsewhere women who would never make the headlines were starting to consider and realize their earnings potential and right to take not only their education and career, but also their finances, into their own hands.

In 1983, in the small Illinois city of Beardstown, a bank teller named Betty Sinnock and fifteen other women, with an average age of seventy, developed a fledgling interest in the stock market and what investing in it might be able to offer them.

Officially, they called themselves the Beardstown Business and Professional Women's Investment Club, but soon they became known locally simply as the Beardstown Ladies. Aside from surging equity prices, they were motivated to start dabbling in the world of stocks on account of the men in their lives constantly telling them they shouldn't bother their pretty little heads about money and such, that it was a man's world.

Things moved quickly. Initially each member of the club put down a hundred dollars, followed by twenty-five a month later. And then the fun really started. To begin with, they bought stocks in companies they all knew, household names. A Walmart opened in Beardstown, and the ladies noticed that its parking lot tended to be fuller than that of a nearby Kmart, for example, so they snapped up some of its stock. When one of the women had a Medtronic pacemaker put in, she bought some Medtronic shares from her hospital bed after surgery. Many of them had never read a copy of the *Wall Street Journal*, but they relied on intuition and experience to make their picks.

And that back-to-basics approach seemed to work. For six consecutive years they were recognized as one of the National Association of Investors' "All-Star Investment Clubs." CBS, charmed by the folksy, quirky nature of the club, put the women on the *This Morning* show in 1991 and again the following year. By 1993 they were making a video, which led to calls for more TV appearances and finally a book that appeared in 1994, *The Beardstown Ladies' Common-Sense Investment Guide*, a collection of stock-picking tips interspersed with recipes for hearty meals curated by each of the ladies: Helen's Springtime Pie, Elsie's Prizewinning Angel Food Cake, and Buffy's Busy Woman's Dream, the last a casserole made by mixing a can of vegetables with a can of cream-of-chicken soup and a pound of ground turkey, topping it with Tater Tots, and baking it for an hour.

Within four years, the guide had sold more than 800,000 copies. It was translated into several languages, and other books followed as the Beardstown Ladies went global. Speaking engagements in Brazil, Germany, and the United Kingdom followed. For a brief spell, they were TV stars in Japan; they let a crew from the country film their monthly meetings. "I always used to see limos go by and say, 'I wonder who's in there,'" Betty Sinnock, the erstwhile bank teller, told the *Wall Street Journal* in 2006, reflecting on that time. "Well, now it was me in there."

The celebrity status the ladies assumed conveyed a powerful message to women across America: namely, that investing was for everyone. It could be as much a hobby for the grandmother who delights in crafting the perfect apple pie and perfecting her cross-stitch as it could be for the Ivy League–educated insurance broker who lives in a five-bedroom suburban house and provides for a stay-at-home wife and three children. Money was exciting and enticing for the masses, and anyone could make a fortune on the stock market; it was a great economic and social enabler. By the mid-1990s, helped by the resurging bull market after the 1987 crash, stock picking became one of the nation's favorite pastimes, and women were very much in the game.

What provided the metaphorical icing on the cake when it came to the story of the Beardstown Ladies was that they were not only likable and entertaining but also, seemingly, exceptionally skilled at their activity of choice. The cover of their first book proudly proclaimed that the group had averaged 23.4 percent returns each year from 1984 to 1993, significantly more than the S&P had returned over the same period. But something quite literally didn't add up.

In 1998, a *Chicago* magazine reporter wondered whether the returns that looked too good to be true actually were, and he conducted a thorough audit, which confirmed his suspicion. It showed actual returns of 9.1 percent per year during the period. The S&P 500 had returned about 14.6 percent annually.

It was a bitter end to a marvelous tale, which culminated in the ladies' publisher, Hyperion, part of Disney, being sued and pulling their book from print, but the buzz they had caused endured in an altogether positive way. They had proven prominently that women—and any woman of any age, at that—could at least try her hand at trading. Like Muriel Siebert and Neale Godfrey, they had demonstrated that doing something that few—if any—women historically did could be exciting and rewarding, even if it did involve taking on all manner of personal and professional risks. The narrative was changing. An undercurrent was swelling. Prudently but emphatically, women were claiming finance as an interest of their own.

# CHAPTER 7

## Old Dreams, New Realities

I don't think a woman should have to choose between having a baby and having an income.

—Lillian Garland

During the 1980s, the U.S. gender wage gap narrowed more than during any other decade of the twentieth century. Women's earnings were being bolstered by shifting parameters in the job market and beyond. Radically changing norms and expectations were helping to elevate women in business, as were the shrinking gender gaps in education. The law was finally working more as a tailwind than a headwind, and some women were making it to the highest echelons of business, proving that they were just as capable and ambitious as any man. On the one hand, there was a sense that women were reaping the early rewards of monumental social, judicial, and cultural change. On the other hand, women were starting to realize that the goal of economic empowerment was far more complicated than they might have originally thought.

In 1996, two researchers—Lesley Lazin Novack and David R. Novack, of Mary Baldwin College and Washington and Lee University respectively—published a paper presenting evidence that while women by the 1980s had theoretically made great strides toward matching men professionally and economically, they were, more than ever before, being presented with "conflicting images which nurture new career-related expectations while simultaneously stressing traditional expressions of femininity, especially marriage and motherhood."

The academics concluded that for many women who attended college, life after college was exceedingly frustrating. Some, they wrote, were finding themselves on a veritable collision course with potential romantic partners—partners who pretended to, or even thought that they did, believe in gender equality in marriage but, when challenged, proved "unwilling or psychologically unable to yield or even to share the power that traditionally has resided within the male domain."

In other words, women had finally been granted the rights that men had enjoyed for centuries but were now being condemned—or at least silently stigmatized—for taking advantage of them. "Cultural 'genetic' blueprints are strong and not easily changed," Novack and Novack wrote. "They are deeply ingrained within each of us, often presenting situations rife with cognitive dissonance." Some years earlier, in 1988, sociologist Rosanna Hertz had viscerally summed up the same predicament. Women, she wrote, were being "caught in the middle between an old dream and a new reality."

In 1982, Helen Gurley Brown published a book with a title that would become a culturally iconic phrase, a book that, by many accounts, only served to exacerbate the situation for women trying to navigate the competing forces of expectations, ambition, needs, wants, and mundane reality. In *Having It All: Love, Success, Sex, Money, Even If You're Starting with Nothing*, the longtime editor of *Cosmopolitan* professed that, yes, of course women could thrive professionally, look fantastic, have a deeply fulfilling marriage and sex life, and be an exemplary mother at the same time. They just had to have the right attitude; they just had to be ambitious and determined enough.

Gurley Brown's advice was specific and actionable, accompanied by a drumbeat reminder that if she—someone who had grown up poor in Arkansas—could do it, then anyone could. "Mouseburgers," she called women like herself, women who are "not prepossessing, not pretty, don't have a particularly high I.Q., a decent education, good family background or other noticeable assets." By following some simple steps, she argued, these women could "mouseburger" their way to the top. Should you sleep with your boss? There's no reason not to, she concluded. And what should you eat? Ideally, not much. "You may have to have a tiny touch of anorexia nervosa to maintain an ideal weight," she wrote. "Not a heavy case, just a little one!"

Helen Gurley Brown, who edited *Cosmopolitan* from 1965 until 1997.

The narrative was nearly as toxic as it was confusing, and it planted the seed for a notion that would be popularized decades later by Sheryl Sandberg: Women have the power to remedy gender inequality; they just need to "lean in."

In 1984, the *New York Times Magazine* reported that from 1960 to 1983 the percentage of female lawyers had risen from about 2 to 15 percent, and the percentage of jobs in banking and financial management held by women had risen from 9 to 39 percent. Women were shifting into traditionally male-dominated blue-collar work too. The same article observed that, from 1970 to 1984, the number of female butchers in packinghouses had increased by more than a third, and that by 1984 nearly 80 percent of new bartending jobs were going to women. On the other hand, however, as academics Gloria Sorensen and Lois M. Verbrugge observed in a 1987 paper, employed women were still spending many more hours on family and household tasks than were their husbands. Citing other research, the pair also found that the amount of time that husbands spent on family did not vary significantly based on the employment status of their wives. And they found that the role of "wife" frequently included the expectation that she contribute to her husband's career through direct and indirect support of his work role, regardless of whether she herself was employed in a paid occupation outside the home or not.

But Sorensen and Verbrugge also concluded—perhaps even quietly echoing Gurley Brown's sentiments—that "the task of juggling home and job responsibilities is not always stressful." Indeed, they observed that "many women appear to be very resourceful in coping with these potentially conflicting demands" and the "multiple roles of mother, wife, and worker actually may benefit health by providing alternative sources of personal identity and satisfaction."

Reams of research conducted in the decades since then have concluded that it is, of course, not that simple. The impact of the personal-professional balancing act on any woman's mental and physical health is perhaps best represented on a vast spectrum. The point a woman occupies on that spectrum at any given moment is determined by factors—which themselves are constantly changing—too numerous and too varied to summarize.

Most recently and starkly, this was demonstrated in 2020, when the COVID-19 pandemic started to ricochet around the world, shutting schools and childcare facilities. The parameters of the labor market—of the working world—transformed in many cases literally overnight. Women in many countries emerged as the default caregivers, while men—frequently the higher earner in a household—focused on retaining their family's income. "Is the coronavirus crisis taking women back to the 1950s?" journalists Emma Jacobs and Laura Noonan asked in an article for the *Financial Times*. One woman the pair interviewed described the nature of her pandemic existence, balancing an executive job in finance with being a parent to two school-age children, by saying that her only goal in that moment was simple: "just survival."

Early on, estimates put the number of women who dropped out of the workforce at about four times the number of men. A few months into the pandemic, economist Ernie Tedeschi put the number of mothers who had quit the U.S. workforce between February and September 2020 at 900,000, and the number of fathers at 300,000. But Claudia Goldin of Harvard, in a paper published in March 2021, noted that actually—and despite widespread reports of what countless media outlets around the world portrayed as a female exodus from the labor market—most women managed to keep their jobs during the COVID-19 pandemic, which turned out to be a double-edged sword. "Far more mothers, and other women who are caregivers, have been stressed, frustrated, and anxious because they did *not* leave their jobs than have been forced to exit the workforce or cut back their hours," she wrote.

Even well before the pandemic, though, in 2018, academics from the University of Montreal published a study tracking more than 2,000 workers over the course of four years. They concluded that women, and particularly mothers, were more vulnerable to burnout than men. Women, they found, were less likely to be promoted than men, making them more likely to be in positions with less authority, which more frequently leads to increased stress levels and frustration. The researchers also found that women were more likely to head single-parent families, experience child-related strains, invest time in domestic tasks, and have lower self-esteem—all things that can exacerbate burnout.

***

Back in the 1980s—and around the time the term "burnout," coined by psychologist Herbert J. Freudenberger in 1974, was becoming common parlance—many women were, perhaps against all odds, muddling through.

In 1983, the *New York Times* ran an article about Patricia Cremer's daily routine. Cremer, a reservations agent for Delta Air Lines and mother of one, lived in Jonesboro, Georgia, with her husband, Richard, who was a mechanic for the same airline. On weekdays, Patricia, whose shift finished at 2:30 P.M., and Richard, who started work at 2:50 P.M., would drive their respective cars to a point midway between the airport and their home. On the side of the road, he would hand her the baby, give her a flighty kiss, and be on his way. It was a changing of the guard, ships passing in the night, and it lasted for two years before her schedule changed slightly, allowing the couple twenty minutes in their house together after Patricia got home and before Richard had to be on his way. The article cited research from the Bureau of Labor Statistics that found that, at the time, at least 1.1 million American working couples with children had only one spouse employed during what would be considered regular working hours. In 330,000 of these families, the data found that parents worked different shifts with no overlapping hours at all.

Another couple introduced in the article was Elizabeth and Ramon Ortiz, living in New York City and saving for a house in the suburbs. Elizabeth was a registered nurse and Ramon a junior police officer. "When I get home, he's sleeping, and when he gets up, I'm sleeping," Elizabeth is quoted as saying. "We talk a lot by phone." And finally, in San Jose, California, Randall and Eileen Phares were interviewed. Both worked as deputy sheriffs. She worked nights at a women's jail, while he worked during the day at a men's jail. They had three children. When asked why she did all the housework despite working just as much as her husband in paid employment, she is quoted as having said that Randall is "not domestic."

\*\*\*

So why did women do it? Why did they attempt the balancing act of full-time paid work outside the home while simultaneously taking on the bulk—if not all—of the unpaid work inside the home? For one thing, the meaning of paid work was becoming weightier. For many women, having a job had evolved from being a family's second source of income to being an integral part of who she was as a person. In the 1960s, academics had started surveying college freshmen about their future and what they anticipated personal satisfaction might look like. The students were asked about the relative roles of family, finances, and community and about their philosophy of life, their attitude toward helping others, and their vision for, and definition of, career success. Early in the 1970s, more and more female respondents started to indicate that they anticipated that "coworker recognition" and "career success" would play a big part in how personally satisfied they would feel in life. Gradually, women's answers started to resemble men's more, and by the early 1980s, according to Harvard's Claudia Goldin, women's and men's responses were practically identical.

The median woman graduating from college between the 1950s and the early 1970s was married by the age of twenty-two, or within a year of graduating, but by the 1980s she was, on average, twenty-five at the time of marriage, meaning that she was more likely to have worked for several years before starting a family, if she chose to do so. In 1970, the average or mean—age of first-time motherhood for all mothers, both college graduates and not, was 21.4 years. By 1990, it had risen to 24.2.

A lot of research, including Goldin's, also shows that by the 1980s, and despite the problematic narrative that glamorized the prospect of "having it all," women were staking more on their careers, even if that meant neglecting other parts of their lives—not, actually, having it *all*.

To many women, a job became a potential puzzle piece in a long-term career, a stepping-stone to the next professional opportunity. They also started to view their workplace as an important part of the social world they inhabited. Goldin explains that, because of this, women were becoming "stickier" in terms of their labor force attachment. For a woman, leaving the workplace increasingly began to involve a loss of, or at least a change in, identity—just as being unemployed or retired had, up until then, involved a loss of prestige or sense of social belonging for many men.

Probably as both a cause and effect of this strengthening connection between occupation and identity, a shift occurred in the types of jobs that women were pursuing. Women were migrating from jobs that had been considered traditional for them—teacher, nurse, librarian, and social worker—to a more varied array: lawyer, physician, manager, and professor, according to U.S. Census data. And their choices when it came to college majors were changing, too: Increasingly, they were picking those that were more sought after and better compensated in the labor market and regarded as less valuable in a domestic setting, and, to a far greater extent than before, they were opting for post-graduate education too.

Another reason women were finding themselves stretched across the worlds of work and home in a manner that was often unsustainable had to do with the gendered roles that men typically assumed—and in many cases still assume—both in the labor market and at home.

In his 2022 book, *Of Boys and Men: Why the Modern Male Is Struggling, Why It Matters, and What to Do About It*, scholar Richard V. Reeves argues that while women have made great strides into the paid labor market in recent decades—a shift that was particularly pronounced during the 1970s and 1980s—men have not experienced anything even akin to that sort of change. As women became more likely to work outside the home, men didn't—or at least not to the same degree—become more likely to pick up domestic chores, like childcare. This was not necessarily solely their fault but also due to social norms: New fathers were not expected to take paternity leave, and young men were not expected to pursue careers in fields that might be perceived as unmanly, like nursing or early childcare. Reeves writes of a "male malaise" and a phenomenon that the sociologist David Morgan terms "ontological insecurity": a loss of a sense of being in the world, a sort of existential identity crisis.

In the 1980s, women working outside the home all day long, earning money, advocating for themselves, and making decisions independently of men was becoming more normal. Men not working outside the home but, instead, ferrying the children to and from daycare and school, cooking dinner, and singing the kids to sleep with a lullaby at night, was not. One side of the equation was changing. The other was stagnant.

At the same time, men started to understand that to succeed professionally, they now weren't competing only with other men, but with women, too. This ran counter to familiar, patriarchal norms and thus created a degree of cognitive dissonance that was hard for them to navigate. Even today, such norms—no matter how informed by biases—exist and shape our beliefs, behaviors, and attitudes. However enlightened we think we are, and whatever gender we identify as, our biases inform what we consider to be right and wrong, even if our rational selves tell us otherwise. These also inform how much we trust someone, how much we like someone, and how much we choose to invest in a relationship.

In 2016, a study by Swedish academics published in the *American Economic Journal* shed some light on the correlation between female labor market participation and marriages that end. The writers found that a woman who earns less than her partner or does not work at all at the time of their marriage is significantly more likely to be divorced if her career suddenly takes off. "The main thing we saw from doing this research is the continued prevalence of gender nuance," Johanna Rickne, one of the authors of the study, explained. "Women still marry up, and men marry down—in terms of education, but also image and income," she added.

If "having it all" broadly means figuring out how to balance work, children, and marriage, then it's often the case that two out of three may be attainable, but all three are not. Around the time that women were starting to figure out the work bit, and perhaps even the children part, often the marriage or relationship component was revealing itself to be both a problem within its own right and a trigger for other complexities.

In 1969, Ronald Reagan, then governor of California, signed the country's first no-fault divorce bill, removing the need for married couples to prove spousal wrongdoing in order to be granted the right to divorce. A number of states followed California's example, and across the country divorce rates reflected these legal changes. Between 1960 and 1980, the divorce rate doubled from 9.2 divorces per 1,000 married women to 22.6. It wasn't acknowledged or even widely understood at the time, but, at least in part, marriages were crumbling because the preponderance of professionally ambitious women, with a desire for financial independence and a career from which they could derive personal satisfaction, was threatening age-old norms and entrenched mores. The uptick in women's employment led to many women feeling emboldened to leave marriages that were unsatisfying or abusive.

The climbing divorce rate in the late 1970s and 1980s also elicited a change in public perception. In 1970, the producers of *The Mary Tyler Moore Show* had been forced to alter the show's original plot. Instead of the protagonist being recently divorced, her story was changed so that she was simply jilted by her boyfriend. Network executives were scared that audiences wouldn't sympathize with, or even accept, a divorcée. A heartbroken reject was much more palatable. Ten years later, however, TV studios and Hollywood were churning out content that prominently featured divorce—and not in an apologetic or parenthetical way. The romantic comedy *An Unmarried Woman* of 1978 told the story of a wealthy Manhattanite, Erica Benton, whose husband leaves her for another woman. When he later changes his mind and begs for her back, Erica rebuffs him unceremoniously. (The film was nominated for Best Picture and Best Original Screenplay at the Academy Awards, and Jill Clayburgh, who played Erica, was nominated for Best Actress.)

But divorce in the real world rarely resembled divorce on the big screen. It was often painful, messy, and traumatic. And in many cases, it became painfully clear that society—the legal system, for example— had not caught up with the concept of a divorced mother.

In February 1982, Lillian Garland took leave from her job as a receptionist at the California Federal Savings and Loan Association to give birth to her daughter, Kekere. She had been in an abusive marriage from which she had fled not long before the birth, forcing her to support herself and her child on her single, modest income. But in April of that year, when Garland reported back to work after recovering from a cesarean section, she was told that her job was no longer available and that there were no openings for her. "I just felt faint, I was cold all over," she told reporters. "Before the baby was born, my supervisor kept asking when I was leaving and when I'd be coming back, so it never occurred to me that I might lose my job because I'd had a child. I was in total shock. I don't think a woman should have to choose between having a baby and having an income."

Garland's situation spiraled. As a single mother, with no savings and no earnings, she was evicted from her apartment and forced to sleep on a friend's couch. Then Garland lost custody of her baby girl to the child's father. Totally distraught, she turned to California's Department of Fair Employment and Housing for help, who told her that, no, what her employer had done was not legal, and, yes, she should try to challenge it in court. The state's law entitled every woman to up to four months of unpaid leave without losing her job for medical disability caused by pregnancy or childbirth. But the California Federal Savings and Loan Association had other ideas. It decided to use the Garland case to challenge that law. It argued that if an employer had to grant disability leave to pregnant women, that was an act of sex discrimination because it afforded women preferential treatment over men. If disabled men did not have the right to reinstatement, neither should women who have just had babies, it posited.

To Garland's utter dismay, a federal district judge agreed with the association and declared the California law null and void, but she was not prepared to give up. Eventually, in 1987, the case wound up in the U.S. Supreme Court, where the justices ruled six to three in favor of Garland, declaring that states could indeed require businesses to guarantee job protection for pregnant women. Justice Thurgood Marshall commented that the California law did not violate the federal law or discriminate against men as Garland's former employer had claimed. Rather, it "promotes equal employment opportunity" by allowing "women, as well as men, to have families without losing their jobs."

Justice Marshall also noted that the statute "does not compel employers to treat pregnant workers better than other disabled employees; it merely establishes benefits that employers must, at a minimum, provide to pregnant workers. Employers are free to give comparable benefits to other disabled employees." "It's a wonderful victory," Betty Friedan, who had lost her first job when she became pregnant, told

*TIME* magazine. "It says that equality does not mean women have to fit the male model."

Lillian Garland ultimately won her case in court, but her experiences as a single mother were emblematic of what countless women were enduring, women whose stories would never be told. Several studies conducted during that time showed that wives with the highest income during marriage, experienced the most dramatic fall in income after separation or divorce, but that a decline in wealth occurred across every income category and frequently pushed women below the poverty line. Teresa Mauldin, of the University of Georgia, concluded in a 1990 research paper that "perhaps the most obvious way for women to improve their economic situation following marital disruption is to remarry."

Indeed, while married women generally continued to grow their income during the 1980s, divorcées' income lagged. It was the case then, as it is today, that in the overwhelming majority of marital separations that ended up in court, the mother became the primary custodial parent. A tiny minority of fathers paid adequate child support, and even today that hasn't changed much. As of 2015, over 70 percent of single mothers were believed not to be receiving any child support at all, and almost 37 percent were estimated to be living in poverty.

Generally speaking, the only demographic group making less economic progress than divorced mothers was never-married mothers. As Nicholas Wolfinger of the University of Utah writes: "In the 1980s, divorcées had median incomes more than double those of never-married mothers. Thirty years later, the disparity hasn't changed much. All women have higher incomes, as measured in inflation-adjusted dollars, but only married mothers have seen really big gains."

While staying single and not having children might have been one way of avoiding the earnings-inhibiting push-and-pull of being a working mother in the 1980s, that route had drawbacks of its own.

In her 2005 book *Marriage, A History*, historian Stephanie Coontz explains the etymology of the word "spinster," originally a term of respect used to describe women who achieved financial independence by earning money spinning wool. In 2000, UCLA sociologist Zsuzsa Berend published a paper analyzing diary entries of forty single women in the nineteenth century and concluded that they "remained unmarried not because of individual shortcomings but because they didn't find the one 'who could be all things to the heart.'" Being a spinster, at that time, was frequently a choice, and in many parts of the country, unmarried women were celebrated as "champions of uncompromising morality," Berend writes. "There was a respectability to spinsterhood," historian Pat Palmieri elaborates in a 2012 interview with *Boston* magazine. "It was fashionable, these women were going on to higher ed and becoming professionals, they could have their own income."

But by the twentieth century, as paragons of the ideal housewife were celebrated, all of that had changed. While the Civil Rights Act of 1964, and particularly the passage of Title VII, prohibited discrimination on the basis of race, color, religion, sex, or national origin, marital status was not—and is not—considered an "immutable" characteristic, and was therefore never widely included in civil rights laws.

In a 1987 article for the *Chicago Tribune*, one woman documented her experience of her own wedding, describing it as a "sign of maturity and progress, as inevitable to us as losing baby teeth or matriculating in school. It's a rite of passage, like losing your virginity," she wrote. And one particularly good thing about it? "You only have to do it once to have that aura of wisdom and responsibility about you."

Even today, as a women's right to autonomy is generally—in Western society, at least—considered a given, "choosing to remain single continues to be, as it has in the past, interpreted as a problem for women," writes Shelley Budgeon, of the University of Birmingham in the United Kingdom. "Because successfully performing femininity according to dominant cultural norms means having a sexual connection to a man, single women confront the knowledge that their identities are 'tainted' by their unpartnered status," she adds. In the introduction to a 2005 academic paper entitled "Caught in the Cultural Lag: The Stigma of Singlehood," Anne Byrne and Deborah Carr, of the National University of Ireland and Rutgers University respectively, state that "popular

'reality' television shows, situation comedies, and films owe a posthu-
mous screenwriter's credit to Jane Austen, as their final scenes often
fade to a dreamily enamored couple at (or on their way to) the altar."
Byrne and Carr go on to explain the concept of "singlism," which they
define as a pernicious attitude of prejudice and discrimination targeted
at the unmarried, and particularly unmarried women.

In 2020, according to government data, women who were full-time
wage and salary workers had median weekly earnings that were 82 percent of those of male full-time wage and salary workers. For full-time
single workers who had never married, however, women earned 94 percent of men's earnings. But, as ever, the statistics tell only part of the
story. Yes, single women who don't have children may take home—on
average—bigger paychecks, but that doesn't necessarily translate into
being wealthier. Across America, dozens of laws today provide explicit
legal or financial benefits to married couples. And in 2018, more than a
third of Americans aged twenty-five to fifty—equating to about 39 million people—had never been married, up from just 9 percent in 1970.

Marital privileges pervade almost every part of daily life, from
when we obtain an insurance policy to when we rent a home. In 2013,
Lisa Arnold and Christina Campbell, cofounders of an organization
called Onely.org, dedicated to deconstructing stereotypes around sin-
gles, crunched the numbers for an article published in the *Atlantic*.
They conjured up four fictional characters living in Virginia: two single women and two married women of equivalent means. The single
women earned 40,000 and 80,000 dollars annually, exactly as much
as their married counterparts—salaries that, at the time, represented
relatively middle- and high-income levels in the state, where 2011 per
capita income was 44,700 dollars. Through careful analysis that took
into account everything from taxes to Social Security privileges, from
IRA policies to health spending, the authors concluded that, over a lifetime, the lower-earning fictional woman would pay what is, in effect,
a penalty of 484,368 dollars for being single, while the higher-earning
unmarried female would pay 1,022,096. And those figures were based
on conservative estimates.

\*\*\*

It is, of course, comforting to think of the great strides we've made since the 1980s toward the ultimate goal of gender equality. But it only takes a little digging—a closer look at the numbers, some gentle questioning, or, of course, a pandemic shock—to understand the full, raging extent of the structural inequalities that persist. Women who work outside the house full-time, or even part-time, and manage to raise and provide the necessary care for young children frequently have to make certain sacrifices. Women who don't marry and don't have children have to tolerate the societal and economic consequences of living that way, just as women who divorce must. If having it all means being able to thrive professionally as well as personally, as a parent and as a spouse, unconditionally and all the time, then no one will ever have it all, regardless of their gender. The structures of our world just won't allow it. Telling a woman that it is possible just as long as she tries hard enough, is as misguided as it is damaging.

The purportedly innocent comments that substantiate, even legitimize, gender stereotypes can still be heard in classrooms, offices, homes, restaurants, and bars, nearly every day and everywhere. *She's a woman, but she's extremely smart. She's out of town, so her husband's babysitting. She's a real girlboss.* Embedded assumptions that women aren't as intellectual or technically minded as men, or that a father is an on-occasion "babysitter" rather than a default caregiver, continue to dim expectations and hopes for change. The infantilizing rhetoric of the "girlboss" or even "mompreneur" casts a woman pursuing a professional ambition or prioritizing her career into the role of the anomaly, of somebody who is stepping out of line.

In 2013, more than three decades after Helen Gurley Brown's *Having It All* hit the shelves, Facebook chief operating officer Sheryl Sandberg's *Lean In* was published. "The manifesto felt like a cross between a playbook and a bible," journalist Katherine Goldstein reflected in a 2018 essay. Millions of adoring readers at the time agreed, creating a cultural buzz around the book and its message of fierce, unapologetic, and proudly female self-empowerment. So-called Lean In Circles sprang up across the country, and the term itself swiftly became part of a global vernacular, often without attention paid to some of the important nuances in Sandberg's original words. The movement extolled the virtues of hustling like mad for success, of aggressively promoting oneself whatever the cost, with the end goal of, indeed, having it all.

It didn't take long until the glowing reputation of the Lean In brand began to tarnish. Criticism, first tentative and cautious, was initially leveled at Sandberg for not adequately acknowledging the privileges she had that enabled her to do the leaning in that got her to the highest echelons of one of the most powerful corporations in the world. That critique was compounded by a major investigation published in 2018 by the *New York Times*, surveying Facebook's missteps. It included an account of attempts by Sandberg to divert attention from the fact that Facebook had been used by Russians to try to influence the 2016 U.S. presidential election.

But it was a speech by Michelle Obama a few weeks later that dealt perhaps the most bruising and perhaps necessary blow to the Lean In movement. Addressing Brooklyn's sold-out Barclays Center stadium on a tour promoting her own memoir, the former First Lady said that she tells women that the "you can have it all" narrative is nothing short of a lie. "It's not always enough to lean in," she said. "Because that shit doesn't work all the time." The message instead, she explained, is that the onus should never be on the woman alone to fix things, to fix herself. Instead, it needs to be acknowledged that something bigger is broken: society at large.

Goldstein was deeply relieved. "I nodded my head vigorously," she told the *Washington Post* after the Obama event. Other women in the audience, working mothers particularly, said that it was refreshing to finally hear an extremely prominent feminist icon acknowledge a truth that was so widely known for decades but never spoken of. What was particularly poignant for some was that Obama was speaking about the concept of leaning in and the damaging myth of having it all from the perspective of a Black woman. Minda Harts, founder of The Memo, an organization that supports women of color in the workplace, told the *Post* that, like Goldstein, she had initially celebrated *Lean In*, avidly buying copies for colleagues to spread its message. But as time passed, she realized that Sandberg's writing stopped short of addressing the dimension of race. Without doing that, she said, you can't adequately talk about gender discrimination in the workplace. "When you have someone like Michelle Obama shining a light on this, people listen."

While the Obama speech was a critical moment in feminist history—a pointing of the finger at the spirit of the 1980s—it didn't manage to decidedly change the landscape. That spirit still haunts America. "Girlbosses" are still revered. Women who multitask to the point of debilitating exhaustion are still considered prestigious, admirable, and successful—whatever "success" actually means.

In early 2022, a forty-year-old woman from New York who had spent a decade on Wall Street before launching her own company addressed a cohort of female MBA students at an Ivy League business school. "If you really want to succeed professionally, you have to be prepared to go through absolute hell," she told the crowd in their twenties and early thirties. "Don't think about having kids until you're really well established and respected, and be prepared to be sleep-deprived and bullied for years," she warned. "Of course, you can have it all, but only if you're willing to drive yourself to the brink and if you're ready to give 110 percent in everything you do and at any cost," she said. "Lean in as much as you can," she concluded. "Otherwise—honestly—I just wouldn't recommend it."

# CHAPTER 8

## A Bimbo or a Bitch

An employer who objects to aggressiveness in women but whose positions require this trait places women in an intolerable and impermissible Catch-22: out of a job if they behave aggressively and out of a job if they don't.

—Supreme Court Justice William J. Brennan Jr., 1989

By the late 1980s, hopes for a more gender-equal world were swelling. The daughters of second-wave feminists were coming of age. Emboldened by their mothers' tales of resistance and rebellion, they were determined to claim their place in society, culture, politics, and the economy. Encouraging marks of progress seemed to be everywhere.

By 1993, marital rape had finally been outlawed in all fifty states, and a year later, Congress passed the Violence Against Women Act, the first comprehensive package of legislation designed to prevent violent criminal acts against women. On June 15, 1993, President Bill Clinton announced that he was nominating Ruth Bader Ginsburg to the Supreme Court, ending the drought in Democratic appointments to the highest court that had endured since president Lyndon B. Johnson's nomination of Thurgood Marshall more than a quarter century earlier.

As a young lawyer, Ginsburg had been rejected by practically every law firm in New York on account of her gender, but in the 1970s she garnered public attention and respect for litigating in a series of high-profile equal rights cases, including, perhaps most prominently, Stephen Wiesenfeld's 1975 case on widowers' Social Security benefits.

Ginsburg, a soft-spoken, sixty-year-old Brooklynite, was not unanimously loved by proponents of gender equality. Although she fervently championed abortion rights, she had also been a critic of the 1973 *Roe v.*

*Wade* Supreme Court decision making abortion a Constitutional right, saying that it went too far, too fast. Instead, she favored a more incremental approach to legalizing abortion.

The friendships she fostered with conservative colleagues with whom she had previously served on the federal appeals court also left some feminists wondering whether she was a good idea for America. But her nomination was, nonetheless, celebrated as a watershed moment for women. Ginsburg had been one of only nine women in a Harvard Law School class of over five hundred, and she had been the first woman to serve on both the *Harvard Law Review* and the *Columbia Law Review*. She had also been the cofounder of and chief litigator for the Women's Rights Project of the ACLU. Twelve years after Sandra Day O'Connor became the first female to serve on the country's highest court, Ginsburg was only the second.

There was a flurry of other "first women" during the decade. Also in 1993, Janet Reno became the first woman to serve as U.S. attorney general, Canadian Kim Campbell became the first female head of a North American government, and Janet Yellen—another Brooklyn-born Jewish woman—was nominated by President Clinton to the Federal Reserve Board, making her one of the country's most powerful monetary policymakers.

That same year, Judith Rodin became the first female president of an Ivy League school at the University of Pennsylvania, and in 1995, NASA astronaut Eileen Collins became the first woman to pilot a space shuttle mission.

Later—in 1997—Madeleine Albright, the daughter of Czech refugees who had fled both Nazi invaders and Communist rulers, was named the first female U.S. secretary of state, and in 1999, "Carly" Fiorina became the first woman CEO of a Fortune 100 company when she took the top spot at Hewlett-Packard. By some measures the 1990s were, in fact, boom years for women in prominent leadership positions. In 1992 alone, more women entered political office in the United States than in any year in history, with the number of women in the Senate tripling from two to six.

Across music, TV, and cinema, the picture was similar. Although complete gender parity—regardless of the metric—was still a pipe dream, women were making visible strides, and female protagonists were more common than ever before. Loud, proud, and often a little provocative, artists like Madonna, Whitney Houston, and Missy Elliott shamelessly tested the parameters of what was socially acceptable and sometimes kept going once they had determined what was not. Alanis Morissette voiced the angst of a generation coming of age and grappling with love, passion, self-discovery, and the pressures of the real world beyond the walls of the teenage bedroom.

Across the Atlantic, the Spice Girls shot to fame and promptly dominated American stereos, igniting a "girl power" movement that rewarded them with icon status. Simultaneously, sex positivity movements bubbled into the mainstream. Norms were smashed and women's bodily autonomy was celebrated. In 1996, playwright Eve Ensler debuted *The Vagina Monologues*, a theater production tackling head-on the culture of silence around sexual violence against women, which critics hailed as one of the most important pieces of political theater in modern history.

Elsewhere, the gender gaps in education had basically disappeared, and the average woman's wage had risen from about 59 percent of the average man's in 1970 to a shade above 71 percent in 1990—hardly enough but a more than 10-percentage-point gain. But when it comes to the story of American women in the twentieth century, the 1990s are perhaps the most complex chapter—a chapter that's far darker than the touched-up, airbrushed cover images of *TIME* and *Vogue* might suggest. It's riddled with paradoxes and inconsistencies. If the early and mid-1980s were an era of women being lodged between old dreams and new realities, the period that followed saw women ensnared in a web of deception, a maze of normalized—even glorified—misogyny, and dazzled by a promise of equality that turned out to be illusory.

\*\*\*

On a sunny Friday in early February 1993, Bill Clinton sat at a desk in the White House's Rose Garden and signed the Family and Medical Leave Act (FMLA) into law. This day had been a long time coming. Twice Congress had passed the legislation, and twice President George H. W. Bush had vetoed it. This third time, all hurdles had finally been cleared.

It was an immensely important act. It was the first piece of federal legislation designed explicitly to help workers manage their evolving twin responsibilities in the workplace and in the home. Its signing, and the timing of the legislation's enactment, were symbolically important too. Historically, U.S. presidents have used the first bill they sign into law as a way of signaling their priorities and emphasizing what issues they care about most, a means of indicating what sort of leader the public can expect them to be. Just over two weeks into his presidency, Clinton wanted to convey that he was profoundly concerned about the well-being of the American citizen, workers' rights, and gender equality.

The FMLA allowed employees to take up to twelve weeks of unpaid, job-protected leave in order to recover from a medical condition, to provide care for a sick family member, or to look after a newborn child. By prioritizing the bill, Clinton was demonstrating that he was attuned to changing family dynamics and demographics and that he understood the critical importance of creating better infrastructure to support new societal norms. More than half of all mothers in America were now either the family breadwinner or split that responsibility with a partner. The expectation that motherhood necessarily marked the end of a woman's career was extinct, and Clinton knew the country's policies had to be changed to reflect that.

Prior to the FMLA, if an employee was injured in a car accident, or had to take a parent to a chemotherapy appointment, or even if they had to stay at home to look after a tiny baby or adopted newborn, nothing protected them from getting fired. Indeed, cases like Lillian Garland's 1982 firing from the California Federal Savings and Loan Association demonstrated just how ruthless some employers were prepared to be.

But while the FMLA created a semblance of a security net, particularly for new mothers, it was deeply imperfect. The most obvious problem was that the leave granted to workers under the new legislation was unpaid. It was unsurprising, therefore, that almost half of workers who qualified for it did not take it on account of financial concerns. More fundamentally, about 40 percent of workers did not qualify for it in the first place. FMLA eligibility was restricted to workers who had been employed in their current roles for more than a year, who had worked at least 1,250 hours in the prior twelve months, and who had worked for a company that employed at least fifty individuals within a seventy-five-mile radius. In the end, the FMLA was an act that was passed with promise and hope, and although it was an unequivocal move in the right direction, it gravely under-delivered.

Some research indicates that the act might even have contributed to the stalling of the gender wage convergence during the 1990s—the rate at which women's incomes were closing in on men's. The FMLA was, and still is, a gender-neutral policy, but women are more likely to take advantage of it than are men, and research shows that the duration of FMLA leaves are, on average, fourteen business days longer for women than for men.

"The increased use of the FMLA by women opens the door for statistical discrimination in which a firm may differentially capitalize the expected cost of the family leave policy into current or future wages," academics Peter Blair of Harvard and Benjamin Posmanick of St. Bonaventure University wrote in a 2021 working paper. In other words, companies might moderate wage increases for women, inspired by an expectation that women will more frequently than men make use of the FMLA.

Also in 2021, economist Mallika Thomas conducted a study showing that women hired after the enactment of the FMLA were three percentage points more likely to remain employed but eight percentage points less likely to be promoted than those who were hired before the FMLA. "If women, on average, work fewer hours during child-rearing years than men, and firms cannot perfectly distinguish between workers who will work fewer hours in the future and those who will not, the firm will be less likely to invest in and train women during the early years of their careers," she explains. In other words, employers might be quick to assume that because a worker is female, she'll probably be taking time off to have a baby. Thomas reasons that, because of this, mandated maternity benefits can actually exacerbate the gender difference in promotions by changing the distribution of types of women who select into the labor force. "Therefore, the expected return on investment in any individual woman may be lower, even among those women who would have otherwise worked as many hours as men," she adds.

In 2018, academics Heather Antecol, Kelly Bedard, and Jenna Stearns published a paper examining assistant professors hired by top-fifty economics departments between 1985 and 2004. They looked at institutions that had so-called gender-neutral tenure-clock-stopping policies, which allow assistant professors to stop their tenure clock for an extended period of time, typically one year, after childbirth or adoption. In theory, the assistant professors are not expected to do any research during this time. "Compared to short family leave policies, this type of policy may better account for the extended period of reduced productivity associated with having a child, and therefore may be especially beneficial in settings in which early promotion has a large impact on later success," the academics wrote.

But through their research, Antecol, Bedard, and Stearns found that such clock-stopping policies may not actually level the playing field in terms of tenure outcomes—and, therefore, earnings—between men and women at all, if the average productivity during the period of the stopped clock differs between genders. "If men are able to use the additional time more productively or more strategically, it is possible that these policies could actually increase the gender gaps in the profession." And, indeed, that's what their research found.

From the data the researchers collected, they concluded that the probability that a man would get tenure in his first job rises by 17 percentage points after such a clock-stopping policy is adopted, while the female probability falls by 19 percentage points. The most important mechanism driving these effects is an increase in the number of journal publications by men after stopping the clock, so to speak, for a year. Women generally don't experience an increase in publications. "Our estimates," they wrote, "show that these policies help men, hurt women, and substantially increase the gender gap in tenure rates."

***

As for the women who were climbing to the top of corporations, government departments, and institutions of higher education, they shouldered an unthinkably heavy burden of expectation. Failures, or even missteps, were frequently held up as evidence that a woman was simply too weak, too flawed, too stupid, or just not tough enough, to do the job. One glaring example: Kim Campbell, who served a brief term as Canadian prime minister from June to November 1993, was characterized as unstable and unreliable as a global leader because she was twice divorced and childless. Even a female leader who perfectly matched her male counterpart in terms of competence and skill was often judged much more harshly than a man.

In 1992, academics Alice Eagly, Mona Makhijani, and Bruce Klonsky published an article in the academic journal *Psychological Bulletin* analyzing the relationship between gender and professional evaluations of corporate leaders. Although their research showed only a small overall general tendency for employees to evaluate female leaders less favorably than male leaders, this tendency was more pronounced under certain circumstances. Specifically, the authors wrote, women in leadership positions were devalued relative to their male peers when leadership was carried out in what they described as "stereotypically masculine styles." In other words, in an organization where an autocratic or directive leadership style was promoted, female leaders tended to be judged more harshly than men. The authors also found that women leaders were particularly critically assessed when they occupied roles overwhelmingly held by men, and when the individuals evaluating them were mostly male.

The conclusions Eagly, Makhijani, and Klonsky drew are perhaps most prominently illustrated by the case of Ann Hopkins. Born in Galveston, Texas, in December 1943, Hopkins graduated from Hollins College in Virginia, then obtained a master's degree in mathematics from Indiana University. In the late 1960s, she was hired to work for IBM, where she developed mathematical models to simulate the motion of scientific and weather satellites under the influence of magnetic, gravitational, and radiation forces. After several years at IBM, Hopkins was promoted from a role that was predominantly technical to one that involved project management. She eventually left IBM and worked for a series of smaller companies in the aerospace industry before accepting a job at Touche Ross & Co, one of the Big Eight national accounting firms at the time, as a management consultant.

Hopkins was the oldest of three women on the consulting staff in her office when she started. She was assigned to projects for the mayor's office in Chicago, the Federal Reserve, the Corporation for Public Broadcasting, and National Public Radio. But she most enjoyed her work for the United Mine Workers of America (UMWA). "I loved the work at Touche—the projects, the clients, the Touche teams I worked with, the travel, the way that Touche did business, the culture—all of it," she recalled years later.

She worked in one of Touche's offices in downtown Washington. The team was small and tight-knit, and she struck up a particular connection with a man named Tom Gallagher, a housing and real estate consultant who played the banjo and the guitar. Hopkins fell for his riotous sense of humor, his supreme intelligence, and his charm. After dinner dates on sixteen consecutive nights, the two decided to marry.

At Touche, their marriage represented a nepotism-policy violation, meaning that neither could be promoted to partner as long as they both worked there. After the wedding, Hopkins had given birth to their first daughter and not long after that became pregnant with a son. She decided to look for another job before her pregnancy started to show, and in December 1977 she joined a computer consulting company. Gallagher became a partner at Touche.

After years of working in a culture where she felt valued, Hopkins struggled with the transition. She found her new employer to be hierarchical and paternalistic. Decisions about almost all major matters, be they technical, administrative, or related to management, were made by a group of men she came to think of as the "founding fathers" of the company. She missed Touche but couldn't go back, so in August 1978 she joined the consulting practice of Price Waterhouse, another Big Eight accounting firm.

Hopkins thrived. She was instrumental in the firm winning a huge contract from the U.S. Department of State, the biggest Price Waterhouse had ever clinched. Partners—the most senior managers at the firm—praised her effusively, and in August 1982, in a crowning endorsement of her achievements, Hopkins was proposed by two of the partners with whom she had worked as candidate for the partner class of 1983. She was the only woman among 88 candidates, and just 6 of the firm's 667 partners at the time were women. A mere tenth of the partners were consultants, like Hopkins. Forty-seven individuals eventually made the cut. Hopkins was not one of them.

After the decision was announced, she remembers being "miserable, depressed, furious, disconsolate, and inconsolable in cycles." Joseph Connor, a senior partner who would later serve as chairman of Price Waterhouse, invited Hopkins to New York to explain the decision and provide details. Sitting in his office, she listened intently as he read out some of the transcribed comments other partners had made when asked whether to admit her to the partnership. A handful remained imprinted in her memory in the decades that followed. "[She] needs a course in charm school," was one of them. Another noted that she'd "matured from a tough-talking, somewhat masculine, hard-nosed manager to an authoritative, formidable, but much more appealing lady partner candidate." One described her as "macho," and another as "overly aggressive, unduly harsh, difficult to work with, and impatient with staff." Someone said she "overcompensated for being a woman," and, finally, one person said that she was simply "universally disliked." Dismayed, Hopkins asked Connor what he recommended she should do. Keep up the good work, and avoid being disliked was his sage advice.

When she got back to Washington and still felt that she was owed a real answer, she asked some of her other bosses the same question. One told her to walk more femininely, talk more femininely, dress more femininely, wear makeup and jewelry, and have her hair styled. When the next partner promotion cycle came and went and nothing changed, Hopkins asked her husband to try to help her understand the logic behind what she could only see as an entirely irrational business decision. His suggestion was simple and ruthless. "Sue the bastards," he said. And so she did.

In August 1983, Hopkins filed a sex discrimination claim with the EEOC alleging that Price Waterhouse had violated Title VII of the Civil Rights Act of 1964. She resigned from her job early in 1984 and worked as a consultant for the State Department and later as a budget officer at the World Bank. That same year, the U.S. Supreme Court was considering *Hishon v. King & Spalding*.

Elizabeth Anderson Hishon, originally from Cortland, New York, had filed what would become a landmark discrimination suit against the law firm King & Spalding for having rejected her as a partner. Hishon had joined the Atlanta-based firm in 1972 after graduating from Columbia Law School and was, at the time, only the second woman ever to have been hired by the firm as an associate. She had filed her suit in December 1979 claiming that she'd been passed over for partnership because of her gender. Five and a half years later, in May 1984, the U.S. Supreme Court agreed when it ruled unanimously, in reference to Hishon's case, that law firms were not allowed to discriminate on the basis of sex, race, religion, or national origin when deciding which lawyers to promote to partner.

In September 1984, *Hopkins v. Price Waterhouse* entered the legal system as a federal case before the District Court for the District of Columbia Circuit. Specifically, Hopkins and her legal team alleged that Price Waterhouse had discriminated against her by failing to make her a partner "because of gender stereotyping in the partnership evaluation process." In addition, she claimed that she had been subjected to constructive dismissal: that Price Waterhouse had, in effect, forced her to leave the firm. As a remedy, she wanted to be admitted to the partnership, to be offered back pay, and for the firm to cover her legal fees and court costs.

In September of the following year, the court held that Price Waterhouse had indeed discriminated against Hopkins but that she had not been forced to leave the firm against her will. The latter decision meant that she was not entitled to the partnership remedy she had been seeking. Price Waterhouse appealed the discrimination decision, and Hopkins appealed the constructive dismissal outcome. Two years later, the court upheld the lower court on the discrimination result, reversed it on the constructive discharge result, and remanded the matter to the lower court for trial on remedy. Price Waterhouse again appealed the discrimination issue, this time to the Supreme Court, and it was this appeal that became a historical benchmark for discrimination cases in the decades that followed.

In May 1989, the Supreme Court held Price Waterhouse liable for discriminating against Hopkins on the basis of sex under Title VII of the Civil Rights Act. What made the case particularly remarkable was the technical question it posed in relation to the evidentiary standard and burden of proof required to succeed in a case brought under Title VII. In its defense, Price Waterhouse had suggested that the issue of stereotyping that Hopkins's team had raised lacked "legal relevance" in a Title VII case. But Justice William Brennan, writing on behalf of the Supreme Court's six-to-three majority, criticized this interpretation. "We are beyond the day when an employer," he wrote, can "evaluate employees by assuming or insisting that they match the stereotype associated with their group." He added that "an employer who objects to aggressiveness in women but whose positions require this trait places women in an intolerable and impermissible Catch-22: out of a job if they behave aggressively and out of a job if they don't." In a 2007 article for the *California Law Review*, legal scholar Ilona Turner described the decision as "The Price Waterhouse Revolution." It was, she wrote, "the first time the Supreme Court gave its imprimatur to a theory of sex discrimination that includes discrimination based on an individual's perceived failure to conform to gender stereotypes."

***

Early in 1991, Hopkins, now a mother of three, rejoined Price Waterhouse as a partner with compensation and benefits set at the average of the partner group admitted in July 1983, the month she would have made partner had she been admitted after her first nomination. She received checks for court-ordered back pay and compensation for attorneys' fees that she had paid. Strictly speaking, in litigation terms, Hopkins's case was a success. But in a personal account of the entire episode that she penned in the *Hofstra Labor and Employment Law Journal* years later, she explains that it was not that cut-and-dried. After the decision, she explained, her life became a matter of public record. "Attorneys pored over my tax returns. People testified about expletives I used, people I chewed out, work I reviewed and criticized, and they did so with the most negative spin they could come up with. I'm no angel," Hopkins conceded, "but I'm not as totally lacking in interpersonal skills as the firm's attorneys made me out to be."

At some point during the course of pushing her case through the courts, Hopkins had called Elizabeth Hishon in Atlanta. Hishon, whom Hopkins came to know as Betsy, regaled her with stories of her own battle with a former employer and her eventual high-profile victory. The two women stayed in touch, struck up a friendship, and regularly met for gin and tonics when they were in the same city at the same time.

When Hopkins and Hishon spoke, they referred to their respective cases as "landmark one" and "landmark two." They frequently chuckled at the eerie coincidence that both their cases were heard on Halloween. When Hishon was diagnosed with cancer in the 1990s, Hopkins filled in for her as keynote speaker at a meeting of the South Carolina Women Lawyers Association. In 1999, Hishon passed away. Hopkins died in 2018. In an interview for her obituary, her daughter, Tela, told the *New York Times* that, yes, her mother "could be prickly," but she also "lived in accordance with her values, and one of her most firmly held beliefs was that diversity always, always, always makes something better." She added that people "either loved her fiercely" or "couldn't stand being in the same room with her."

In a 1996 memoir, Hopkins described herself as a person who was profoundly committed to her career but also determined to always be herself. She smoked and drank beer unapologetically. When she was invited to her first job interview at Touche in 1974, she wore a suit and Ferragamo pumps and rolled up to the office on a Yamaha motorbike. And she never considered herself a civil rights hero. In an interview with the *Boston Globe* in 1990, reflecting on her Supreme Court victory, she claimed that the only thing making her remarkable was that she had "happened to stand up for a particular principle at a particular time." She didn't seem to think much of the concept of feminism or the glass ceiling: "Lord knows if I put a crack in it."

History suggests it was more than a crack. Over the decades, Hopkins's case has been used on numerous occasions by employees who don't conform to a gender stereotype to protect themselves against workplace discrimination, and it has heaped pressure on partnership-based businesses—most obviously, law firms—to use more objective standards when assessing candidates for partner.

In 2004, the U.S. Court of Appeals for the Sixth Circuit considered the case of a firefighter working in Salem, Ohio. Jimmie Smith was assigned male at birth but later in life was diagnosed with gender identity disorder, or GID, which the American Psychiatric Association (APA) characterized as a disjunction between an individual's sexual organs and sexual identity. (In 2013, the APA eliminated the term and today refers to the condition as gender dysphoria.) After being diagnosed, according to court documents, Smith started "expressing a more feminine appearance on a full-time basis." Coworkers in the fire department started to ask Smith about his female appearance and his effeminate mannerisms, commenting that he didn't act or look "masculine enough."

Smith was troubled and spoke to his immediate supervisor. He told the supervisor that he was planning to have treatment that would eventually lead to his complete physical transformation from male to female. Smith explicitly asked his boss not to share that information with any other supervisors, a request that his boss ignored.

According to court documents, when the city—who was officially Smith's employer—found out about his case, representatives responded by forcing him to undergo a series of psychological evaluations, to be conducted by a physician selected by the city. According to the legal filings, the supervisors and representatives of the city "hoped that Smith would either resign or refuse to comply." If he refused to be evaluated, the defendants reasoned, they would be able to terminate Smith's employment because of insubordination. But Smith neither quit nor refused. Instead, he called a lawyer and sued the city. He claimed that, as a result of that, he was fired.

He lost in the federal trial court on the basis of the fact that, as a trans person, he was not protected under Title VII, but the Sixth Circuit ended up reversing the lower court's decision, specifically citing Ann Hopkins's Price Waterhouse case.

Discrimination "against a plaintiff who is transsexual—and therefore fails to act and/or identify with his or her gender—is no different from Ann Hopkins in Price Waterhouse, who, in sex-stereotypical terms, did not act like a woman," the appeals court ruled. It added that "sex stereotyping based on a person's gender non-conforming behavior is impermissible discrimination, irrespective of the cause of that behavior." The ruling, Ilona Turner told the *Washington Post* at the time, was "incredibly exciting." She described it as "the theory we've been thinking about for years. . . . The court recognized that discriminating against a transgender plaintiff . . . in that case someone who was perceived as a man, wearing women's makeup and women's clothing, appearing too feminine, was exactly like Price Waterhouse in reverse." It wasn't so much a matter of whether the employee was transgender, Turner commented, but rather whether a person conformed to sex stereotypes.

\*\*\*

The debate over whether female and male leaders are assessed using different yardsticks—whether they're held to different standards—has only become more heated as the proportion of women at the highest echelons of business, politics, and society has grown.

In 2002, the *New York Times* published a story about Carly Fiorina and, more generally, about the trajectory of female corporate leaders. Fiorina had, by that point, led Hewlett-Packard for about three years and was arguably facing her greatest professional challenge since taking on the top job: a high-stakes and extremely public decision on whether to merge with Compaq Computer. The *Times* reported that if Fiorina were to be thwarted, it would be almost inevitable that she would leave the business. If that were to happen, the paper asserted, the big question would be whether Fiorina would be "viewed as simply another risk-embracing chief executive who was driven out when shareholders balked at the company's stock price, or as a poignant symbol of how women still can't quite make it in the cutthroat, male-dominated corporate world."

Fiorina's leadership survived the merger, but in February 2005 she was forced out, unleashing a torrent of scrutiny and forensic analysis of the reasons for her ousting. Some concluded that she was just never up to the job—the wrong personality type, not trustworthy enough. And, to be sure, plenty of criticism relating to her leadership and strategic decisions was rooted in facts with no obvious nods or references to her gender. Indeed, by many metrics her track record in terms of how Hewlett-Packard did under her reign was poor. But others decided—though silently—that Fiorina's exit was simply clear-cut evidence that women, more generally, weren't ready to occupy the top offices of corporate America; they just didn't have it in them.

In a memoir Fiorina published the year after leaving Hewlett-Packard, she points out that in the wake of her departure, six female vice presidents left the company, and she elaborates in some detail on the general way in which women at Hewlett-Packard were treated. "I was alternatively described as 'flashy' or 'glamorous' or 'diamond-studded,' which frequently was translated to mean a superficial 'marketing' type," she writes. "I was usually referred to by my first name. There was much particularly painful commentary that I'd chosen not to have children because I was 'too ambitious.'" she adds. "In the chat rooms around Silicon Valley, from the time I arrived until long after I left HP, I was routinely referred to as either a bimbo or a bitch—too soft, too hard, and presumptuous, besides."

Failures of other women to hold on to jobs at the top of corporations have been pointed to as emblematic of the deficiencies shared by any leader who isn't male. The 2002 *Times* piece noted that several high-profile female executives had, in the preceding years, faltered in their quests to lead companies. Linda Wachner was pushed out from the top slot at textiles and clothing company Warnaco six months after it filed for bankruptcy protection. Diana Brooks resigned as head of auction house Sotheby's and pleaded guilty to price-fixing in 2001. Also in that year, Jill Barad was forced out of toy manufacturing and entertainment company Mattel after an acquisition did not go as planned and corporate earnings reportedly didn't meet projections. The article theorized that there are so few women who make it to the very top of business that, whenever one does, she becomes the representative of every woman, and her failure becomes everyone else's failure too.

Since the early 2000s, female leaders have become less of an anomaly, which has removed some of the scrutiny around individual missteps and failures, but even as recently as 2022, egregious examples have emerged of a corporate development or shortcoming being blamed on a female leader's gender. In May 2022, Amanda Blanc, who two years earlier had become the first female CEO of British insurance giant Aviva, was subjected to a string of blatantly sexist remarks at the company's annual general meeting. Investors said that Blanc was "not the man for the job" and questioned whether she should be "wearing trousers." One investor ostensibly praised the company for its gender diversity and then added: "They [women] are so good at basic housekeeping activities, I'm sure this will be reflected in the direction of the board in future."

"This hectoring is intentionally intimidating. It's designed to diminish and discredit Blanc," Allyson Zimmermann, who at the time worked for the nonprofit women's research organization Catalyst, commented in the days after the meeting. "These tired, hackneyed jibes have no place in the modern world and should not be 'par for the course' for women in senior leadership," she added. But she conceded that what they tragically show is that "gender stereotyping and gender bias is still alive and well."

*\*\**

In 2005, consumed by the question of whether women CEOs and leaders do have a tougher job than their male counterparts, and by a desire to determine whether men or women actually do make better CEOs when success is gauged in terms of a company's stock performance, professors Michelle Ryan and Alexander Haslam of the University of Exeter in the United Kingdom began to investigate. They examined the performance of companies listed on Britain's Financial Times Stock Exchange 100 index before and after the appointment of new board members, with the goal of establishing whether women were habitually brought in as leaders when the likelihood of failure was elevated. Was a woman, they asked themselves, more likely than a man to be appointed as someone who could be spared as an expendable scapegoat?

The pair found that during a period of overall stock-market decline, like during a financial crisis or recession, companies that appointed women to their boards were more likely to have experienced consistently bad performance in the preceding five months than those companies that appointed men. These results, Ryan and Haslam concluded, expose yet another hurdle—and a largely invisible one—that women are forced to overcome in the workplace in order to reach their full professional potential. Namely, that women are more likely to fail—not because of anything related to their skill, competence, or knowledge, but simply on account of the fact that they're more likely to find themselves in power when conditions are tough: They're more likely to be set up to fail.

In 2013, researchers Alison Cook and Christy Glass of Utah State University published research corroborating this theory. Examining

Fortune 500 companies in the United States over a fifteen-year period, they also found that white women, as well as men and women of color, were likelier than white men to be promoted to CEO of firms that had been performing weakly in recent months and years.

Ryan and Haslam termed the phenomenon they researched the "glass cliff." And examples of it are abundant. In 2014, news broke that faulty ignition switches in cars sold by General Motors were putting customers' lives at risk. The company ended up recalling millions of vehicles. GM later admitted that it had known about the problem for years, but it only came to light mere weeks into Mary Barra's term as first-ever female chief executive of GM. She became the face of the company as it grappled with public fury and a barrage of high-profile and even higher-stakes investigations. Other examples include Anne Mulcahy, who served as CEO of Xerox from 2001 to 2009. She was promoted to the top position just as the printer company was teetering on the edge of bankruptcy. By the time she stepped down, however, Xerox was back to being a market leader.

The year Mulcahy left Xerox, Carol Bartz, who had run software company Autodesk, was named CEO of Yahoo! Inc. Still bruised from the 2008 financial crisis, the internet company was struggling in a fiercely competitive market. In 2011, after just two and a half years in the job, Bartz was pushed out—fired, reportedly, over the phone by Yahoo! chairman Roy Bostock. "It is absolutely true that women have a better chance to get a directorship or a senior position if there's trouble," Bartz said in an interview in 2018, reflecting on her time at the helm of Yahoo. She added that it happens for several reasons: "It's mostly because, a lot of times, men don't want a job. And so [members of the board] go for the Tier 1 man on their list, and [he] take[s] a look and say[s], 'I wouldn't touch that with anything.' And then they get to the Tier 2 man. And by the time they get to the Tier 2 man, some woman has finally popped up in their mind. And she's so happy that she has a chance to have a senior position as a director or a CEO that she takes it."

***

In politics, Theresa May is often cited as a textbook case of a woman who found herself facing the glass cliff. She became prime minister of Britain in June 2016, in the wake of the country's referendum decision to leave the European Union, and therefore at a time of severe political and economic instability. Liz Truss, who served as the country's prime minister for fewer than fifty days, stepped down amid a cost-of-living and energy-supply crisis that was plunging thousands of British households into poverty. An even more literal example is that of Sophie Wilmès, who briefly served as Belgium's first-ever female prime minister. She was appointed to the head of the country's temporary caretaker administration in 2019, amid political deadlock that prevented Belgium from forming a government. Wilmès led the European country through the first six months of the COVID-19 pandemic and was then succeeded by a man, Alexander De Croo, when her minority administration was replaced by a majority coalition in October 2020. Wilmès subsequently became Belgium's minister of foreign affairs, making her the first woman to hold that office too.

In the United States, one of the most prominent women whose career is sometimes cited as an example of the glass cliff phenomenon is Janet Yellen. Born in 1946, Yellen graduated summa cum laude from Brown in 1967 and pursued a PhD in economics at Yale. Under the supervision of James Tobin, who would later earn a Nobel Prize in Economics, she wrote her dissertation on employment and studied under Joseph Stiglitz, who eventually became an advisor and close friend (and Nobel Prize winner). Over twenty other economists earned their PhD from Yale at the same time as Yellen. She was the only woman.

She later joined the faculty of Harvard's economics department, where she was one of only two women, and in 1976 she was hired by the Federal Reserve Board of Governors and assigned to research international monetary reform. The following year, she met her future husband, George Akerlof. They married and spent a few years in London before returning to the States, where Yellen accepted a teaching job at UC Berkeley. Bill Clinton's 1994 appointment of Yellen to the Federal

Reserve Board of Governors paved the way for the president in 1997 to appoint her as chair of the White House Council of Economic Advisers. She was only the second woman ever to hold that job, after Laura D'Andrea Tyson did so from 1993 to 1995.

Although the economic backdrop was steady—in fact, the country was in the middle of one of the longest periods of economic growth in history—there were headwinds and complexities to navigate. Reports surfaced that the chair position had initially been offered to Lawrence Summers, who was serving as deputy treasury secretary and who had hoped to be appointed chair of the Council of Economic Advisers back in 1993, when Tyson had made the cut. Summers reportedly declined the position in 1997. Alan Blinder, an academic at Princeton and member of the council, had also been touted as a candidate for the job, but he was reportedly eliminated from consideration because of personal conflicts that he'd had with Summers in the past. And indeed, in the days after Yellen was announced as the new chair, pundits commented that her success would to a large extent depend on her ability to get along with Summers.

A graduate of Massachusetts Institute of Technology and Harvard University, one of the youngest-ever tenured professors in Harvard's history, Summers was known for being pigheaded and obstinate and prone to controversial statements. Years after Yellen's appointment, in 2005, when Summers was president of Harvard University, he provoked a furor by claiming that men were better at math and science than women, simply for biological reasons. In the same speech, he stated that discrimination no longer presented a career barrier for women in academia.

But Yellen seemed undeterred by any ugly character traits and accusations of machismo, choosing instead to focus on Summers's intellectual potential. "He is an extraordinarily fine economist," she said of him at the time of her confirmation, "and I am happy to be on the same team."

***

Yellen's career—her success and prominence—continued, of course, to thrive. In 2004 she was chosen as president and chief executive of the Federal Reserve Bank of San Francisco, overseeing nine states. She was, again, the first woman to hold the role. In her new capacity she issued urgent early warnings about the risk of a market bubble forming, but, like others, she didn't anticipate the extent of the subsequent fallout. By September 2007, Yellen and two other senior Federal Reserve officials noted that the budding crisis in housing and mortgage lending was now threatening the broader economy. In a speech she forecast that the housing decline would likely impose "significant downward pressure" on consumer spending. She urged policymakers to act in order to prevent more systemic damage from occurring, but her alarm failed to register with those at the highest ranks. In the months that followed, the financial system started to creak and then crack. In September 2008, investment bank Lehman Brothers filed for bankruptcy, sending shock waves across the globe, wiping out fortunes and pulverizing livelihoods. Yellen was the first Federal Reserve official to proclaim that the country had entered a recession, and she immediately understood the tools necessary to salvage what was salvageable. She emphatically supported huge stimulus programs that saw the Federal Reserve inject massive sums of cash into the ailing economy. Almost no measure was too unconventional for her, it seemed, and that boldness, informed by the academic brilliance she was increasingly becoming known for, paid off. As corporations and households reeled, as unemployment soared and markets nursed their brutal wounds, Yellen rose.

In 2010, she was nominated by president Barack Obama as vice chairwoman of the Federal Reserve. Three years later, as incumbent chairman Ben Bernanke's second term drew to a close, and as Summers withdrew his bid for the top spot in the face of liberal pressure, Obama nominated her as the next chair. In February 2014, Yellen, dressed in somber black but with a smile plastered ear to ear, was sworn in as the first woman ever to take the reins of America's central bank. In December 2015, she raised interest rates for the first time in eleven years, but the following year in November, when Donald Trump won

Janet Yellen presenting the Monetary Policy Report to the Senate Committee on
Banking, Housing, and Urban Affairs in 2017.

the presidential election, it quickly became apparent that a second term
was unlikely to be on the cards for her. Though he reportedly considered
renominating her, their differences proved irreconcilable. According to
a surreal but not entirely inconceivable article in the *Washington Post*,
the forty-fifth president, who was born just two months before Yellen
and barely twenty miles away from her childhood home, claimed that
the chairwoman, at five feet and three inches, was simply too short to
be able to usher the economy through the next phase of history. In an
exercise of professionalism and civility, Yellen waited until she'd left the
central bank before retaliating, then did so in a fashion that wasted not
a single breath. Asked by a reporter whether she thought the president
had a grasp of macroeconomic policy, she simply responded coolly, "No,
I do not."

Though she was the first Federal Reserve head in almost four
decades not to serve a second term, she's widely considered one of the
most successful, at least from the perspective of labor markets. Over the
course of her term, the national unemployment rate slid to a seventeen-
year low. During every single month of her time in office, the U.S.

economy created jobs. As Jerome Powell took over, Yellen announced she was joining the prestigious Brookings Institution as a distinguished fellow in residence. Her career in politics, however, was far from over. On the last day of November 2020, then-president-elect Joe Biden announced that Yellen would serve as Secretary of the Treasury in his Cabinet. She was confirmed with a Senate vote on January 25, 2021, and was sworn in by newly minted vice president Kamala Harris—the highest-ranking female official in U.S. history—the next day. Neil Irwin of the *New York Times* declared Yellen to be among the "most accomplished people to take over the big office at 1500 Pennsylvania Avenue in the 231-year history of the department." But he also cautioned that her latest gig would be her hardest one yet.

On her first day in the new job, Yellen wrote a letter to all her staff. "Dear colleagues," she addressed them. "My name is Janet Yellen, and a short while ago, I was sworn in as the seventy-eighth Secretary of the Treasury." She outlined her experience in academia and at the Federal Reserve and her thoughts on the economic state of America, the damage wrought by COVID-19, and the work that lay before them all. Then she addressed a question so many people asked her: why she became an economist. "The reason was my father," she wrote. "He was a doctor in a working-class part of Brooklyn. He was also a child of the Depression. He would come home at night, and he would tell us when one of his patients had lost a job or couldn't pay." She went on: "My father had such a visceral reaction to economic hardship. Those moments remain some of the clearest of my early life, and they are likely why, decades later, I still try to see my science—the science of economics—the way my father saw his: as a means to help people."

Even Michelle Ryan and Alexander Haslam, who coined the term, admit that debates are futile over whether or not Yellen has actually found herself teetering on the edge of a glass cliff as she's risen to fifth in line to the U.S. presidency. But in a follow-up paper about the phenomenon that Ryan and Haslam published in collaboration with some other scholars in 2016, they did note that there might be another extremely important piece to the inequality equation that we can't afford to neglect. "If one looks at the data which give rise to the [glass cliff] effect, it is apparent that it is driven as much, if not more, by the fact that men are given preferential access to cushy leadership positions as by the fact that women are appointed to precarious ones," they write. "Perhaps, then, it is the distinctiveness of the leadership positions that men receive that is the real problem. If so, then one important way to get women off the glass cliff may be to start focusing our attention on men's privileged access to the glass cushion."

By the 1980s and 1990s, managers would be sued and sacked for explicitly citing pregnancy or marriage as a reason for not hiring—or even firing—a woman. It would be entirely illegal for a manager to pay a woman less than a man solely on account of her gender. But managers would be much less likely to be sued or sacked for hiring a man over a woman, or for cutting her job instead of a man's, or for staffing a man, rather than a woman, on a high-profile project that is likely to capture the attention of the CEO.

On the surface, this was the era of American female empowerment and representation. Women graced the covers of magazines for reasons other than the beauty of their faces and bodies. Women made decisions about money and diplomacy and education and science that affected the entire country and beyond. But just as appointing a female CEO to the helm of a major company will never automatically remedy a culture of toxic inequality if it permeates an entire organization, so the new women at the top of American business, finance, and politics could not by themselves fix the pervasive prejudice, unconscious bias, and ingrained stereotypes that existed in the culture.

The culture was, in fact, the problem. Notoriously hard to define but undeniably powerful, culture was the reason the FMLA worked in practice but not in spirit. It was the reason Ann Hopkins certainly could have been, but wasn't, a member of Price Waterhouse's partner class of 1983. It was the reason criticism leveled at Carly Fiorina so frequently hinged on her looks and mannerisms, and why so much public commentary has questioned whether Janet Yellen has enough gravitas to head up first the Federal Reserve and then the Treasury.

Culture was also the reason an entire generation, raised on the diet of a twenty-four-hour news cycle, came to believe that objectifying and undermining women was unremarkable, and that a woman claiming to have been victimized might well just be a troublemaker and attention-seeker.

In 1991, all across the country, Americans watched as an entirely white and male Senate committee—chaired by Joe Biden—grilled Anita Hill on the sexual harassment claims she was making against Supreme Court justice nominee Clarence Thomas. Hill, a Black woman, had worked as an advisor to Thomas when he was chair of the Equal Employment Opportunity Commission. The public cringed while the media delighted in Hill's pained testimony that Thomas had forced her to talk to him about sex, about pornographic films, and about rape. Eventually the Senate confirmed Thomas's nomination in a 52–48 vote. Hill received death threats. And despite her many accomplishments, her name remains synonymous with that hearing.

Later in the decade, the same audience binged on sordid news of the Bill Clinton / Monica Lewinsky affair. Lewinsky, just twenty-two at the time, was portrayed alternately as a shameless seductress or a desperate ditz. Journalist Maureen Dowd called Lewinsky "too tubby to be in the high school in-crowd" and "pathetically adolescent." Publicly fat-shaming women—not just in this case—was still common.

Lewinsky's private life was flung into the public domain with the help of the bulky Starr Report to Congress, detailing Clinton and Lewinsky's most intimate exchanges. For years she was a punch line in late-night TV talk shows, not only in America but around the world. "In 1998, I lost my reputation and my dignity," Lewinsky reflected in a 2015 talk delivered in Vancouver. "I lost almost everything. And I almost lost my life." Overnight, she said, she "went from being a completely private person to being a publicly humiliated one worldwide." That derision has endured, conveying the message that it's acceptable to define a woman throughout her life by something that happened when she was barely an adult and in a situation warped by terrifyingly unequal power dynamics.

Plenty of other examples exist that set the tone for what was to come in the decades that followed: the feverishly sensational accounts of Lindsay Lohan's substance addiction and the malicious mocking of Britney Spears's mental health crisis. All provide evidence that, while much had changed in America in terms of women's legal rights and opportunities, in terms of female economic empowerment and professional possibility, some of the most pervasive barriers—the intangible, ill-defined, and unspoken ones—were unshakable. Worse still, the dawn of nonstop news and, later, social media amplified the narratives that cemented the culture of undermining, mocking, and objectifying women, of continuing to reduce them to their appearance or to a single character trait or flaw. More women than ever were now making it to the top, but the unquantifiable cost of being there might actually never have been greater.

## CHAPTER 9

*Promises and Loopholes*

Just being a female in a man's world.
—Witness Cathy Robertson in the 2003 Lilly Ledbetter trial,
in response to being asked why, in her opinion, she as a
female manager was paid less than male managers

Many stories about Lilly Ledbetter begin with a stirring account of that day in March 1998 when she turned up to her shift at the Goodyear Tire and Rubber Company plant in Gadsden, Alabama, and found a note in her mailbox. It was on a torn piece of paper, and the anonymous author had scribbled four names in black ink: Ledbetter's, followed by those of three of her male coworkers. All four had the same seniority at the plant. Next to her name the author had printed a number: $3,727. And even in her state of confusion, Ledbetter immediately recognized it as her monthly salary, accurate down to the dollar. The numbers listed next to the other names ranged from $4,286 to $5,236. The implication was clear, and what happened next is now a famous tale—folklore, even—of equal-pay advocacy in America's history.

But Ledbetter's story, the origins of her discontent, the genesis of her courage to fight big business, and her determination to create a labor market in which any woman could be free of fear, insult, anxiety, and humiliation, goes back much further. Almost twenty years before she received the note that ultimately led to a U.S. Supreme Court case, photo shoots with the Obamas, and the piece of legislation—the first bill signed by Barack Obama after he became president—that bears her name, Ledbetter endured insufferably humiliating and degrading harassment at the hands of the men she worked with.

***

Ledbetter was born Lilly McDaniel in the spring of 1938 in the rural community of Possum Trot, barely a dot on the map of Alabama, at a bend in the road along the southern frontier of the Great Appalachian Valley. The house where Lilly spent her youth had neither running water nor electricity. Her father worked night shifts at a nearby U.S. Army depot, fixing the engines of tanks damaged in Korea and, later, of those returning from Vietnam and the Middle East.

Almost as far back as she can remember, Lilly spent the days when she wasn't at school helping her mother. They would pick beans, okra, and cotton until their limbs and joints screamed. They would hull peas, skin tomatoes, and blanch and can vegetables. In summer, the pair would scour the surrounding woods for huckleberries and blackberries, then make them into jam to last through to the following spring.

While young Lilly never went hungry, she grew up understanding that the prospect of doing without was never far off. Family income was volatile, and the broader economy was fragile. The McDaniels weren't poor, as such, but they also weren't anywhere near as wealthy as Lilly's friend Sandra, who dressed in silk blouses and pretty skirts and didn't have to share a bedroom with her grandmother the way Lilly did. Sandra took fancy vacations to the Gulf Coast and lived in a house that didn't have chickens running around the yard, and her father proudly worked at the Goodyear factory.

Lilly had seen the Goodyear plant many times but couldn't fathom what went on inside. Once a year, when she caught the Greyhound bus to her aunt and uncle's house in Gadsden, she would gaze wistfully at the imposing building as they chugged by. What would life be like, she mused, if her father worked inside that redbrick building, just like Sandra's father.

Lilly first laid eyes on Charles Ledbetter when she was in ninth grade. He was driving the school bus, filling in for his father, who had found more lucrative employment elsewhere. Charles and Lilly married when she was just seventeen and yet to finish high school. The couple knew they wanted to start a family, but Lilly also wanted to earn her own money. Her mother hadn't worked outside the home, but Lilly was the niece of a "Rosie." When the men of Gadsden had gone off to fight in World War II, her Aunt Robbie had taken shifts—incidentally, at Goodyear—and Lilly knew that she was capable of doing the same, wartime or not.

Charles, by that point, had stopped driving the school bus and was working at General Electric. Toward the end of her senior year, Lilly, too, got an offer to join GE's workforce after graduation, welding filaments for television sets and radios for 150 dollars a week. It was far more than what she might have made as a salesperson at Sears or in another job that might have been considered more typical for a woman at the time, but about two years later, she was made redundant as GE sputtered. Not long after, she found out she was pregnant.

Vickie and Phillip were born two years apart, and Lilly was jarred by the unique challenges of early motherhood. Phillip had allergies, and both children were poor sleepers, depriving the young mother of the rest she so desperately needed. Lilly—much like Betty Friedan at around the same time—felt like the walls of her world were closing in on her. A gnawing anxiety she had developed was dramatically exacerbated by money worries when the GE plant shut down and Charles lost his job. He managed to secure part-time work at the Railway Express Agency, a national package delivery service, but every month, unpaid bills stacked up. Proceeds from pies that Lilly baked and sold to neighbors barely helped, and Charles's ventures in growing peanuts and sweet potatoes turned out to be a fine idea but one that failed in practice. After yet another lengthy spate of sleepless nights, Lilly concluded that the only option—the best option, not only for her but for the whole family—was for her to go back to work. Deep down inside, and despite Charles's protestations, it was what she had wanted all along.

\*\*\*

Late in 1968, Lilly passed the H&R Block tax preparation course. In January she was hired and started preparing tax returns at two dollars and ninety cents an hour, the minimum wage, plus a bonus of five dollars for each return she completed. She skipped her paid lunch hour and left the office promptly at four-thirty every day to collect Vickie and Phillip from school. In the evenings, after they'd gone to bed, she'd frequently return to the office to finish up any abandoned forms still sitting on her desk. When she was offered a promotion to full-time office manager the following summer, Lilly accepted on the spot. Charles wasn't thrilled, but it made financial sense for her to climb the career ladder, even if that meant shattering his ideal of what a family should look like.

Soon after, Lilly filled out an application to open her own bank account. It was the simplest way, she reasoned, to demonstrate to Charles just how much of a difference her income was making, the opportunities it was creating for their family. She didn't necessarily identify with the feminist movement that was tentatively fanning out across the nation—even across parts of staunch segregationist George Wallace's rural and conservative Alabama—but she also wasn't willing to take no for an answer. She was determined to stake out her own path, and a salaried job was part of that. Guilt was, of course, an inevitable consequence—working precluded her from being the attentive housewife and stay-at-home mother Charles thought he had married—but it was the lesser evil. It was certainly preferable to poverty.

With time, every member of the Ledbetter family settled into a weekly routine, sharing the burden of household chores in a fashion that was still profoundly unconventional for an American family, particularly in the conservative South. Charles learned not to grumble as he folded the laundry and heated up dinner. They all understood that two incomes made life better than one.

This semblance of equilibrium didn't last, however. Inflation had started to drift higher in the late 1960s, and the oil crisis that ensued triggered a slew of layoffs, against which Lilly wasn't immune. She picked up work wherever she could: a local accounting firm and then a gynecology practice. Briefly, she worked in the financial-aid department of Jacksonville State University before H&R Block hired her back in 1976. A few years later, she happened upon a *Business Week* article about Goodyear. New technology, the feature explained, was transforming the company's production methods, and its management philosophy was morphing too. Teamwork was the new buzzword, and in a display of particularly adventurous experimentation, executives were for the first time actively seeking to recruit women.

Lilly reflected on how, as a child, she was spellbound by Gadsden's Goodyear plant and the mystery of what went on behind those hallowed walls. A vision of Sandra in a pretty twin set dashed through her mind. Then she thought of Vickie's and Phillip's college fees. She was forty-one years old. Life was moving fast. This was her opportunity—perhaps her only remaining opportunity—to do what Aunt Robbie had done before her, to realize her economic and professional potential, or at least to take a decent stab at it. She filed an application and in 1979 stepped through the doors of the Gadsden plant as Goodyear's newest employee and one of only a handful of women.

\*\*\*

Early on, Ledbetter was allocated to a department that conducted trials on tires, and she was frequently assigned to late shifts with one particular colleague. A thirty-year veteran of Goodyear, the man—according to Ledbetter—was brazen, provocative, and unapologetic. He spoke frequently and in sordid detail about his sex life, which would shock Lilly before she got accustomed to it, and he would describe the affair he was having with another woman who also worked at the plant.

Eventually the colleague began telling Ledbetter that he wanted to sleep with her, that she would be his "next woman"—comments that repulsed her and that she tried desperately to ignore. Next, he started spreading rumors around the plant that he was in a relationship with her, bragging that she regularly accompanied him to a strip club, a seedy establishment called the Fuzzy Duck. Ledbetter did her utmost to avoid him, but his incessant advances made her anxious to the extent that she struggled to sleep and even eat or drink. During one particularly harrowing period, Lilly became so dehydrated that she was hospitalized for several days. Her colleague—unperturbed—persisted.

One day in May 1982, he cornered Ledbetter and touched her breast. Not long after that, pushed to the very edge by his constant advances and by his threats to get her fired when she rebuffed him, she summoned the courage to report him to the union division chairman and then to a member of the personnel department. There was simply no way she could go on like this; the anxiety and exhaustion would submerge her.

In the decades that followed, Ledbetter hated even thinking about that man. The prospect of talking about him, of revisiting the torment to which he had subjected her, was too much to handle. But in 2018, as the #MeToo movement, founded by Tarana J. Burke, gathered momentum, Ledbetter felt compelled to share her experience in an article for the *New York Times*. She recalled in that piece how, when she finally complained about her colleague to her human resources representative, she made it clear that she wanted to keep her job at Goodyear but didn't want to be forced to work with the man anymore. She was told to go home and stay there until an internal investigation into the matter had been completed. The representative, a man, informed her that because her colleague had been at the company for decades and because he had a "good track record," there was no reason to make *him* stay away from the plant while the process was ongoing. Ledbetter recoiled. "If he stays, I stay," she insisted.

As far as she was aware, nothing ever came of the investigation, but things shifted markedly for her. As news of her complaint filtered through the plant, colleagues started to ostracize her. She felt like she had to work harder than ever before to protect her reputation and not be regarded as a troublemaker simply for speaking up for herself, for demanding the right to do her job safely and with dignity.

Even before experiencing overt physical harassment, though, being a woman at Goodyear had been difficult. After Ledbetter was appointed as supervisor, she remembers one man announcing, "I already take orders from a bitch at home, and I'm not taking orders from a bitch at work." Other men feared she wouldn't be able to pull her weight on the job. One shift foreman, Ledbetter remembers, referred to her and a Black man who was working on the same team as two "losers" who were likely to "ruin" his performance record. He vowed to get rid of them. "As far as he and some of the others were concerned," Lilly Ledbetter wrote in a memoir published in 2012, "I might as well have been a missionary in a strange land, trying to convert them to a new religion."

Other men on the job constantly commented on her appearance. One called her "Goodyear's mistake," while another once joked to her face about raping her. During a formal performance evaluation in 1981, one of her foremen suggested she sleep with him to get a more favorable review. She walked out of the meeting and a few months later was demoted.

Ledbetter did end up reporting her colleague to the EEOC, which conducted an investigation. News of it again spread rapidly and in hushed tones across the floors of the plant. She heard that people were being told to stay out of the case if they wanted to keep their job. And her reputation, by this point, was in tatters. Colleagues turned their back on her when she walked into the room, and in a particularly searing encounter, one of the only other women working in the department berated her for ruining peoples' careers, for causing such a mess.

While the EEOC got to work combing through evidence relating to her complaint, Ledbetter was reallocated to the quality control department, a lonely posting that kept her away from coworkers, but she never seriously entertained the idea of resigning. She'd supported her two children through college and had household bills that Charles's income alone couldn't cover. She'd grown up teetering on the brink of poverty and had seen how bad things could be, especially in a community so vulnerable to the whims of the global economy. Now, she was determined to keep earning a living.

Eventually the EEOC informed her that she'd won the right to file a lawsuit against Goodyear. But bringing a case, Ledbetter knew, would inevitably become a he-said/she-said scenario with no guarantees. All she was ultimately hoping for was her job back as a supervisor and the ability and right to work without being harassed and intimidated. An attorney she'd hired negotiated an agreement with Goodyear reinstating her as a manager. "I don't mind working hard or even being cussed out," she remembers telling her bosses. "I can put up with a lot, but just don't let anyone harass me."

After the EEOC investigation, Ledbetter returned to her position as a late-night supervisor. She was relieved to be out of quality-control isolation, as she referred to it, and marked her first day back by bringing in a red velvet cake for her coworkers. Baked goods, however, did nothing to sweeten her colleagues' attitudes toward her. The stigma and insults stubbornly endured as she tried to reclaim their respect. And as she assiduously fought inside the plant, the broader economy beyond Gadsden was creating entirely different headwinds. It was the late 1980s, and financial markets were crumbling across global trading hubs, sending shock waves across America's manufacturing hot spots, like Gadsden. Rumors of layoffs reverberated through the plant, and it didn't take long before she, too, was told that her job had been cut.

The layoffs proved temporary, and after a brief stint working at the Tyson chicken plant, Ledbetter was rehired. She agrees that her decision to return to a workplace where she'd experienced so much overt antagonism and hostility might seem counterintuitive—nonsensical, even. But she couldn't resist her sense that Goodyear was home and that her work there was not yet done. "I returned, driven to be recognized for my work and commitment," she wrote in her memoir. "Like a child of an alcoholic who marries an alcoholic, I gravitated to what felt familiar, an environment defined by fear and conflict."

\*\*\*

Given Lilly Ledbetter's history at Goodyear—the abuse and marginalization she endured—it's hardly surprising that when she found that note in her cubby about salary discrepancies on that day in March 1998, she felt like she'd been scalded on the inside and out. It was like someone had tossed a "skillet full of hot grease" on her, she later wrote. She was incandescent with rage and nauseated with anxiety but also acutely aware of the dilemma she now faced, the same dilemma countless women in history had faced before her: do nothing and live with the knowledge that she was being grossly underpaid compared to men doing the same job, or raise the issue and be punished.

The retaliation, she feared, would be far more aggressive and punitive than anything she'd experienced before at Goodyear. With less than a year to go before she was due to retire, she also knew that taking legal action might cost her her pension, but no matter how she considered her options, she couldn't shake a sense of duty that compelled her to not let this one go. The morning after she found the mysterious note, Ledbetter made the sixty-mile drive to Birmingham, accompanied by Charles, to file her second EEOC complaint. This one, she knew, had the potential to truly set something in motion.

For Lilly Ledbetter, the months that followed were defined by deep reflection and self-confrontation. She was off work, recovering from knee surgery. Prompted by Charles, she agreed to see a psychiatrist in Gadsden. After filing the EEOC complaint, she had been gripped by a paralyzing sense of shame. Initially, therapy seemed to wear her down even more, as it peeled away the emotional barriers she'd erected over the years as a means of self-preservation and protection. But eventually she started to see things more vividly, if also more painfully. Over the years, she'd allowed Goodyear to become the family she kept trying to please. She'd allowed the company to distract her from her own real family: her husband, children, and even her grandchildren. Her mother was now dying of cancer. Her father had passed away several years earlier. She wanted desperately to make amends while she still had the chance.

In July 1998, Ledbetter returned to work following medical leave, but a few months later, in the face of fresh economic challenges, employees of the Gadsden plant were urged to take voluntary buyouts. Ledbetter had been at the company for a few months shy of two decades. She knew that if she stayed just a little bit longer, she'd be entitled to a better retirement package, allowing her to pay down the family's debt faster. But it wasn't that easy. For years, she felt she'd clung on against all odds, refusing to follow her husband's and doctor's advice to quit. She'd endured, fueled perhaps by a determination that she would eventually be rewarded with the recognition and appreciation she'd labored for. But instead of appreciation, all she'd gotten was scorn and rebuff, insult and mockery.

In the end, Ledbetter handed in her retirement notice in the fall of 1998. She intended to work until October, but her mother's condition had deteriorated rapidly, and Ledbetter took vacation to stay by her side until she drew her last shaky breath. When she left Goodyear, she recalled, she was left with "an anger as invasive as the cancer I watched destroy my mother's life."

Shortly after Ledbetter's last day working at the plant, a Goodyear attorney contacted her, offering a small sum of money to settle the EEOC complaint she had filed. The prospect of putting the entire ordeal behind her was tempting, but the offer was paltry, so she wrote back with a counter bid: two years of back-dated pay at a level commensurate with that of the next lowest-paid person in the department. According to Ledbetter, Goodyear never responded.

The following year, in October 1999, the EEOC informed her once again that she'd been granted the right to sue, and this time her indignation was unchecked. Ledbetter had recently heard about a young attorney based in Birmingham, Jon Goldfarb, who specialized in employment law and discrimination cases. She immediately got in touch with him, and he agreed to represent her, based—he said in hindsight—on nothing more than intuition. She could afford his services because he got paid only if he won or settled a case; no win, no fee. He also agreed to pay all the associated expenses in the hope that those would end up being reimbursed by winning the case or settling. On November 24, 1999, Goldfarb and Ledbetter filed a lawsuit, toppling the first domino in a chain of events that would last for years and catapult Lilly Ledbetter's name into history books for decades to come.

Charles supported her every step of the way. Despite huge legal expenses, bills had to be paid, and food had to be put on the table, but he understood that this was a cause his wife was not going to let go.

Between meetings with Goldfarb, Ledbetter spent long days at home. She and Charles built birdhouses and chuckled as the squirrels cunningly helped themselves to the birdseed. In the evenings they watched *Law & Order*, fictitious escapism from the real world that ironically echoed so much of what was about to unfold: depositions and affidavits, subpoenas and briefs, exhibit lists and witnesses.

Working with Goldfarb's team, Ledbetter had spent months trying to rally individuals who had worked with her, who knew her, and who were willing to testify on her behalf, but convincing anyone was an uphill battle. The Goodyear plant was a nerve center of the community. During many years it had kept the local economy from fraying at the seams. No one wanted to risk being demonized by a neighbor or friend for taking down the corporate giant that propped up Gadsden or, worse, get fired. Eventually, four individuals agreed. All but one still worked at the plant, and Ledbetter was painfully aware of the risks they were taking to help her.

When it finally came to Ledbetter's own deposition, it was an ordeal that stretched over ten hours. Goodyear's defense attorney pounded her with questions that became increasingly aggressive as the day wore on. Ledbetter's blood pressure spiked. Her heart raced. She felt nauseated, and by the end of the day, she had sweat so much that her elegant blue suit was entirely ruined.

\*\*\*

On January 21, 2003, a bitterly cold morning, the trial in the case of *Lilly M. Ledbetter v. Goodyear Tire and Rubber Company* commenced at the Anniston courthouse, about sixty miles east of Birmingham.

The Ledbetters had drunk an entire pot of coffee, leaving Lilly jittery when she took the stand as the first witness. She glanced up at the wood paneling and vaulted ceilings that called to mind the courthouse scenes in *To Kill a Mockingbird*. That story was set in Alabama in 1936, and in those split seconds before her examination began, Ledbetter mused at how much had changed across the South since then. For one thing, the presiding judge—Judge U. W. Clemon—was the first Black judge in the state of Alabama. At the same time, though, she couldn't help but wonder to what extent attitudes toward gender equality had changed.

That morning, she recounted to the room how a manager who was her supervisor shortly before she retired in 1998 had announced that the plant didn't need women because women caused problems. Supported by evidence in the form of a chart that Goldfarb displayed, she explained that she was paid $18,216.96 a year when she first started working at Goodyear in April 1979. It was the exact same amount as five men earned who were working in comparable roles at the time. Almost twenty years later, Ledbetter's salary had climbed up to $44,724, but it was dwarfed by that of every other person who was working in a similar role. The second lowest-paid worker was a man earning $55,679. One egregious piece of evidence offered up by Goldfarb was that of a young man who had started working in the plant in 1994 and who had replaced Ledbetter when she switched departments. His salary had climbed to over $81,000 by the time Ledbetter left Goodyear.

In one episode during the trial, Goldfarb's partner, Mike Quinn, called a woman named Cathy Robertson, who had been hired by Goodyear in 1976 and who had worked as an area manager for five years from 1993 on, to testify. During the course of questioning, Goldfarb produced an exhibit showing that Robertson had, in fact, earned $2,728 a month as a manager at Goodyear, compared to male managers with similar responsibilities whose salaries at the time ranged from $3,960 to $4,662. After Goldfarb had read out loud all the comparative salaries, he asked Robertson, a single mother with a disabled child, what her understanding of the discrepancy was. She responded, "Just being a female in a man's world."

A woman named Retha Burns also took the stand. Like Robertson, she was a single mother, and she'd worked at Goodyear as a night supervisor in the 1970s until the woman who had been looking after her young child died of cancer, forcing Burns to stay home. She returned in the 1990s as a supervisor and was promised a pay raise, but it never materialized, and she, too, had filed an EEOC complaint.

Ledbetter had expected the trial to last at least a couple of weeks, but on the fourth day she was called into the courtroom. The jury had reached a verdict. On three of the four claims—relating to reasons she was transferred from one department to another—the jury had found Goodyear not guilty, but on the crucial fourth charge, relating to whether Goodyear had paid Ledbetter an unequal salary because of her sex, the jury sided with the plaintiff. Judge Clemon asked the jury what amount of back pay they had decided Lilly Ledbetter was entitled to. "$328,597.93," the foreman read. And to what amount was she entitled on her disparate salary claim? The answer was "$222,776." She was also awarded $4,662 for the mental anguish she had endured, and $3,285,979 for punitive damages, a staggering amount to Ledbetter. "I couldn't have been more shocked than if I'd been sitting on an airplane and the top of the plane peeled off to reveal a blue sky," she recalled. The fight, she thought, was finally over.

Of course, it wasn't. Goodyear appealed with a vengeance. And in any case, by law, punitive damages relating to a case like Ledbetter's and for a company the size of Goodyear, were capped at $300,000. Nonetheless, the verdict hurled the case into the national media. As the appeal wound its way through the legal system, there was nothing for Ledbetter to do but wait. In the fall of 2005, at an appeal hearing in Atlanta, the Eleventh Circuit Court of Appeals reversed the initial verdict, reasoning that Ledbetter's case was filed too late. There was a statutory limit on claims like the ones she had made, and in this case, they had, in effect, timed out.

Goldfarb, collaborating with one of his partners, filed a so-called cert petition requesting that the U.S. Supreme Court review the Court of Appeals's decision. It was a shot in the dark—the Supreme Court considers only a tiny minority of cases it's presented with—but Ledbetter and Goldfarb had come this far, and neither was willing to leave any opportunity untested. Thus, another period of waiting began. At home, meanwhile, a personal tragedy was rapidly unfolding. Charles had been diagnosed with squamous cell carcinoma, an aggressive form of cancer. He was dying, and there was little that could be done.

Several months later, news that the Supreme Court had agreed to hear Ledbetter's case did little to alleviate the heaviness she felt. Nonetheless, she made the trip to Washington just after Thanksgiving in 2006, where she first met with Kevin Russell, an attorney who had clerked for Supreme Court Justice Stephen Breyer and who had agreed to support her legal team. Russell was also backed by the National Women's Law Center and the National Employment Lawyers Association. Both organizations had crafted amicus briefs for the court, legal documents containing expert advice or information relevant to the case.

The hearing at the Supreme Court lasted a single hour. As Russell made his arguments and patiently but purposefully answered the court's questions, Lilly Ledbetter pondered Justice Ruth Bader Ginsburg, the lone woman among the nine individuals sitting at the imposing mahogany bench now looking down at the two warring sides. Ginsburg had been born in 1933, Ledbetter, just five years later. They were of one and the same generation. Ledbetter meditated on the fact that both women had worked for decades in male-dominated domains, often as the only woman in the room. Of course, the legal profession was vastly different from the world of manufacturing, but wasn't it also similar?

The following year, in May, with Charles in the throes of chemotherapy, Mike Quinn called to tell Lilly Ledbetter the calamitous news. They'd lost. The Supreme Court had sided with Goodyear. Jon Goldfarb was at Disney World when he got the call from Quinn. He'd just stepped off the log flume with his kids. A devastating message to receive anywhere, let alone in a place that was—if the marketing slogans were to be believed—the happiest on earth. "It was really, really disappointing," he recalled.

To win, the court wrote, Ledbetter would have had to prove discriminatory intent on the initial discriminatory paycheck twenty years ago, which could not be done: the decision-makers who were responsible at the time were either long gone from the company or dead.

Justice Samuel Alito—who had replaced the only other woman to have served on the Supreme Court, Justice O'Connor—in explaining the decision, reviewed other Title VII Supreme Court cases that supported his reasoning. One such case was *United Air Lines, Inc. v. Evans*, argued and decided in 1977, in which the airline had fired a female flight attendant after she got married, acting on a company rule that stipulated it would not employ married female flight attendants. Later, when the airline changed the rules and rehired her, it refused to credit her for her past employment and treated her as a brand-new employee for seniority purposes. The court ended up siding with United, holding that the company's refusal to give her seniority credit was simply an effect of the airline's past discriminatory policy and did not constitute a "present violation." The court stated at the time: "A discriminatory act which is not made the basis for a timely charge . . . is merely an unfortunate event in history which has no present legal consequences."

That afternoon, an NBC camera crew came to the Ledbetters' home to record an interview. The next day, CNN paid a visit, and then the *New York Times* called. The reporter wanted to know if Ledbetter had heard that Ginsburg had dissented. Ledbetter had not, and, later, when she sat down to read Ginsburg's opinion from start to finish, the justice's strong-willed words soothed her just a little as the world around her appeared to be crumbling.

Ginsburg was joined by three other justices in her dissent: John Paul Stevens, David Souter, and Stephen Breyer. In the published opinion, she particularly took issue with the fact that the court had based its decision on the understanding that each pay decision Goodyear made was treated as a discrete act. An individual annual pay decision would have had to be contested within 180 days or else it would become, as the court stated, grandfathered: it would become a fait accompli that was beyond the province of Title VII ever to repair. But that wasn't the way workplace discrimination manifested itself, Ginsburg noted. "Pay disparities often occur, as they did in Ledbetter's case, in small increments," she wrote. "Cause to suspect that discrimination is at work develops only over time. Comparative pay information, moreover, is often hidden from the employee's view." As a result of this, she concluded, "small initial discrepancies" might not be considered adequate to justify a federal case, "particularly when the employee, trying to succeed in a nontraditional environment, is averse to making waves."

There were many things Lilly Ledbetter couldn't fathom about the outcome, but one thing that became clear to her was the importance of having a woman on the Supreme Court and, for that matter, of having women in positions of power everywhere. Emboldened by this realization, she concluded that the fight was not over. A swath of organizations shared in her fury: the National Women's Law Center, the American Association of University Women, the American Civil Liberties Union, the AFL–CIO, the National Employment Lawyers Association, and the National Council of Jewish Women, to name but a small selection. Furthermore, a sense of obligation propelled her determination; a duty to advocate for her daughter, granddaughter, and the generations that would enter the labor market in their footsteps. She didn't consider pay equity to be a personal problem, and it wasn't a problem that was specific to Alabama, the South, or even to America. Rather, it was an epidemic that had silently spiraled out of control. She now had a chance to remedy that. But it came at a cost.

After that Supreme Court verdict in that May 2007, Ledbetter spent at least two weeks of each month in Washington, meeting congressional staff and telling her story to anyone who would listen. Then she would catch a flight back home to Alabama, where she accompanied Charles to his hospital appointments. She was straddling two worlds, one in which hope was tentatively building, and another in which it was fading fast. The House Democrats had heard the urgency in Justice Ginsburg's opinion, and by June of that year House majority leader Steny Hoyer and Representative George Miller, who chaired the House Committee on Education and the Workforce, had announced that a bill would be passed preventing rulings like Ledbetter's from being repeated. "A key provision of the legislation will make it clear that discrimination occurs not just when the decision to discriminate is made, but also when someone becomes subject to that discriminatory decision, and when they are affected by that discriminatory decision, including each time they are issued a discriminatory paycheck," Miller wrote.

But opposition was fierce, particularly from Republicans like Howard McKeon, a ranking member of the Education and Workforce Committee who charged that the bill would allow any disgruntled individual to sue their employer or former employer years or even decades down the line, when mounting a credible defense would be almost impossible. In April 2008, the bill was defeated by Republicans in the Senate who claimed it would encourage an onslaught of frivolous lawsuits.

Ledbetter and her growing army of supporters endured. She spoke at the 2008 Democratic National Convention in Denver to a crowd of thousands of impassioned allies—some with tears streaming down their face, others chanting with anger at the injustice of pay inequality—after which she endorsed Barack Obama and actively started campaigning for him.

But as momentum around her was building, Charles's condition continued to deteriorate. In December 2008, while Ledbetter was in New York being interviewed by 20/20 about her campaign for pay equity, Charles passed away at their home. It was a week shy of the couple's fifty-third wedding anniversary. In the months that followed, as she mourned, Ledbetter was also wracked with guilt for being away so much during his final years and especially for not being by his side and able to hold his hand at the very end.

Both Hillary Clinton and Barack Obama called her to offer their condolences after the funeral. Michelle Obama telephoned, too. Ledbetter found that grief made her restless and entirely unable to sit still. She accepted an invitation to Washington to attend the inauguration, accompanied by her daughter, grieving the loss of her father. The pair watched as the first African American president was sworn in, and later Lilly Ledbetter attended the Neighborhood Ball as a special guest, where she was asked to dance with the newly minted president. As he gently guided her across the dance floor, Ledbetter was at a loss for words,

Lilly Ledbetter giving remarks at the U.S. Department of Labor's Worker Voice Summit in June 2016.

unable to process what had happened and the person she had become. Perhaps sensing the overwhelming mix of her emotions—acute grief, hope, exhaustion, and sheer disbelief—Obama looked at her intently and offered a kind smile. "We're going to do this," he reassured her quietly. And she knew beyond a shadow of a doubt that he meant it.

In January 2009, the bill was reintroduced in the 111th Congress and passed in the House of Representatives with 250 votes in support and 177 in opposition. Three Republicans—Ed Whitfield of Kentucky, and Leonard Lance and Chris Smith of New Jersey—supported it, while five Democrats—Travis Childers of Mississippi, Dan Boren of Oklahoma, Allen Boyd of Florida, and Parker Griffith and Bobby Bright of Alabama—voted against it. It passed the Senate with sixty-one in favor and thirty-six against. Every Democrat senator supported it apart from Edward Kennedy of Massachusetts, who was absent for health reasons. The bill was also supported by two independents and five Republican senators.

On January 29, nine days after he took office, President Obama signed the Lilly Ledbetter Fair Pay Restoration Act into law, nullifying

*Ledbetter v. Goodyear.* "Lilly Ledbetter did not set out to be a trailblazer or a household name," he said in his address. "She was just a good hard worker who did her job—and did it well—for nearly two decades before discovering that, for years, she was paid less than her male colleagues for the very same work."

Signing the bill, he said, was to send a clear message. A message "that making our economy work means making sure it works for everybody." And describing Ledbetter's motivation and persistence, he said that "she knew it was too late for her—that this bill wouldn't undo the years of injustice she faced or restore the earnings she was denied," but that "this grandmother from Alabama kept on fighting, because she was thinking about the next generation."

\*\*\*

At the heart of Lilly Ledbetter's case was the issue of pay secrecy or, more specifically, the culture of pay secrecy that permeated Goodyear and of which both Ledbetter and Jon Goldfarb frequently spoke when discussing her case. For almost two decades she didn't know she was being discriminated against, because no one talked openly about money—at least, not to her. In fact, to do so was forbidden. As it was when Ledbetter first started working at Goodyear in 1979, pay secrecy today is ubiquitous. During the early 2000s, more than a dozen states as well as the District of Columbia enacted legislation banning pay secrecy policies—workplace rules that explicitly prohibit employees from discussing wages and salaries. The intention of these policies is to prevent companies from being able to discriminate against any worker consciously or unconsciously. Plenty of research shows that a lack of knowledge about who makes what within an organization clearly contributes to pay disparities along gender or other lines. But the policies implemented seem to, so far, have had a limited impact at best.

In January 2021, academics from the Institute for Women's Policy Research, Washington University, and the University of Western Ontario published a policy brief based on a survey of over four thousand full-time employees aged eighteen and over who were not self-employed, which found that a declining share of workers reported workplace policies that formally prohibited discussion of pay. At the same time, however, they discovered that pay secrecy rules appear to have shifted from formal bans to informal discouragement of pay transparency. Private sector and non-unionized workers are especially likely to work under pay secrecy policies, they wrote in the paper, and women continue to be more likely than men to be subject to pay transparency bans.

The researchers concluded that the prevalence of pay secrecy practices may at least in part stem from the loopholes in—and weak enforcement of—the National Labor Relations Act, or NLRA. Congress passed the NLRA in 1935, with the goal of encouraging collective bargaining by protecting workers' freedom of association. It was designed to protect workplace democracy by guaranteeing employees at private sector workplaces the right to seek better working conditions without fear of retaliation.

But much like the Family and Medical Leave Act of 1993, the NLRA has critical inadequacies that have, over time, rendered it wholly inadequate for addressing features of the law that promote inequality. The authors of the policy paper explain that the law permits employers with a "legitimate and substantial business justification" to institute secrecy policies. It also excludes supervisors—an extremely broadly defined term—as well as public sector workers, domestic workers, agricultural workers, and workers employed by railroads or airlines. If an employer is, nonetheless, found to be in violation of the law, that company will usually only be subjected to a minor fine: a slap on the wrist for indirectly depriving a potentially huge proportion of the workforce over any number of years.

By selecting the Lilly Ledbetter Act as his first piece of legislation to sign into law as president, Barack Obama made an implicit promise that he subsequently demonstrated a commitment to fulfilling. Perhaps more than any president who came before him, he prioritized eradicating inequality. Indeed, research by the Council of Economic Advisers credited the Obama presidency for the most aggressive and successful attempt to reduce inequality in fifty years. But despite everything, his efforts only got women so far.

Beyond the Lilly Ledbetter Fair Pay Act, one of Obama's major opportunities to effect marked change for women in the labor market was with the Paycheck Fairness Act. First introduced in Congress in 1997, the PFA promised to remedy a clutch of shortcomings in existing laws and protections. It promised to clarify definitions and provisions and strengthen the remedies available under the Equal Pay Act of 1963, and it also promised to protect employees from retaliation for inquiring about their employer's wage practices or for disclosing their own wages to colleagues.

From the very beginning, though, it failed to gain traction with Republicans. It was passed by the House in both 2007 and 2009, but it died in the Senate. In 2012, that pattern was repeated when Senate Republicans blocked the bill. Obama described it as an "incredibly disappointing" outcome, while Senator Barbara Mikulski, a Democrat from Maryland who authored the bill, spoke of a "sad day" but noted that it was an even "sadder day every day when a paycheck comes and women continue to make less than men. We are sorry," she added, "that this vote occurred strictly on party lines."

As for those who opposed it, their reasons for doing so varied from a purported fear that it would burden small businesses to an ostensible belief that it was entirely unnecessary. "We already have on the books the Equal Pay Act, the Civil Rights Act, and the Lilly Ledbetter Act, which I did support," Susan Collins, a Republican from Maine, told reporters. "I believe that they provide adequate protections." A fourth attempt to pass the bill into law failed in June 2021 on party lines.

\*\*\*

Other efforts by the Obama administration to address pay inequity—and not just between genders—were spectacularly torpedoed by the Trump presidency in well-telegraphed moves that echoed the bigotry and misogyny that underpinned Donald Trump's campaign.

In April 2017, the Center for American Progress policy institute published a briefing paper entitled "100 Days, 100 Ways the Trump Administration Is Harming Women and Families." It detailed how the new administration was endangering women's retirement security, threatening childcare assistance, stalling paid family and medical leave, and stacking the courts with anti-choice judges. It noted that Trump was delaying the Obama administration's overtime rule, under which some 3.2 million women would have been guaranteed the right to pay for working overtime. Single mothers and women of color would have benefited most from this rule.

In March 2009, President Obama signed an executive order creating the White House Council on Women and Girls to coordinate efforts across agencies on issues specifically affecting women and girls, particularly individuals of color and those with disabilities. But under Trump, the Center for American Progress report noted, the council sat dormant. And it underscored the extent to which the Trump administration was hell-bent on banning abortions. In conclusion, the authors wrote, the Trump administration had launched a "comprehensive assault on women's progress." And that was just in the first one hundred days.

Those early months proved to be a grim augury of things to come. In August 2017, the Trump administration announced that it was blocking an Obama-era rule requiring U.S. employers to report detailed pay data, disaggregated by gender and race. The rule had been designed to make discrimination and wage discrepancies easier to identify and stamp out quickly. The White House Office of Management and Budget in a memo, however, said the rule was burdensome to companies and could create privacy and confidentiality issues. Later, Trump nominated Eric Dreiband to be assistant attorney general of the Civil Rights Division of the Department of Justice. According to the National Women's Law Center, Dreiband had systematically "worked to narrow the scope of rights and remedies under crucial sex discrimination laws that provide protection from pay discrimination, pregnancy discrimination, and gender identity discrimination." Dreiband had not only testified against the Lilly Ledbetter Act, but had also defended Bloomberg LP in a high-profile class action case brought by the EEOC. In that case, the EEOC alleged that the media and tech company had engaged in a pattern of pregnancy discrimination and retaliation by demoting and reducing the pay of women after they announced their pregnancies and after they took maternity leave.

In November 2018, the U.S. Department of Health and Human Services finalized rules that expanded religious and moral exemptions for employers, universities, and insurers that objected to providing contraceptive coverage. Other policies implemented by the Trump administration dramatically reduced access to abortion coverage, which indirectly affected women financially. In March 2019, the government finalized a rule prohibiting providers that receive Title X funding from referring patients for abortion services and from providing information or counseling related to abortion.

The Title X program was established as part of the Public Health Service Act in 1970 with the express intent of addressing inequities in access to contraception. But under Trump, federal regulators obstructed this mission in a most aggressive way. The new rule required a physical separation between a facility that provides abortion services and one that provides other health services. Research conducted by the Guttmacher Institute and published in February 2020 showed that the rule—which became known as the domestic "gag rule"—had slashed the Title X national family planning network's patient capacity in half and jeopardized care for some 1.6 million patients across the country. Low-income women, as well as the uninsured and young, had relied disproportionately on Title X and the critical services it had provided them access to. Naturally, these women were most affected by the Trump administration's move.

By the time Joe Biden was sworn in as president in January 2021, women across America were bruised and whiplashed by what had occurred during the preceding four years: a staggering reversal of their fundamental rights to control their own bodies, their own decisions, their own lives. They were livid, enraged at the fact that a brazen misogynist who had been credibly accused of sexual assault by more than a dozen people had proven irrevocably that the patriarchy was thriving. He'd chipped away at the foundations of what the United States professed to stand for: freedom of opportunity for all.

***

A decade and a half after Goodyear's crushing victory over Lilly Ledbetter in the Supreme Court, Jon Goldfarb is still inundated with calls from women just like Ledbetter, who suspect—or know for a fact—that their male counterparts, or even men they supervise, are being paid more than they. "I wish I could tell you [the Fair Pay Act] has changed things," he said, speaking from his office in downtown Birmingham in June 2022. "Yes, Lilly has become the face of equal pay—I mean, when people hear my name, all they associate it with is this famous case I lost years ago," he adds with an ironic smile that thinly veils undeniable lingering disappointment. "But at the end of the day, I don't think that it's made any real impact at all. Cases like Lilly's are still everywhere."

What would really constitute progress for women in the workplace—what would truly help eradicate gender and racial inequality—Goldfarb says, would be if "corporate America were to grow a conscience." But until that happens, he adds, "nothing is going to change." Specifically, what he means is if companies were willing to implement radical pay transparency policies: if every worker could easily and without fear of retribution find out how much they were getting paid in relation to everyone else working at the organization—and not just by happening upon an anonymous note in their cubby. A federal mandate would be the ideal.

Some countries already have such laws in place. The United Kingdom, for example, mandates annual gender pay gap reporting for any company employing more than 250 people. And in certain states across the United States—including New York—companies are now by law required to publish a salary range when advertising a job. The idea is that predetermined ranges will make it harder for employers to be able to decide a worker's pay at will; it will create a standard that could help counteract the influence that bias might have on the size of a salary offered. In some places, salary history bans have also taken effect, preventing hiring managers from being able to ask prospective employees how much they earned in the past. Researchers have found that when employers are able to ask about salary history before making a monetary offer, that enables a form of institutional discrimination and the perpetuation of wage gaps.

In terms of an overarching national pay transparency mandate, though, Goldfarb isn't optimistic. "It's never going to happen," he predicts. "Politicians just won't allow it." For now, Goldfarb says that his hope is that the courts become more ideologically balanced. That, he says, would be the only good start.

# CHAPTER 10

## Cassandra and the Crash

If it had been Lehman Sisters rather than Lehman Brothers, the world might well look a lot different today.

— Christine Lagarde, managing director of the International Monetary Fund, reflecting on the causes of the 2008 financial crisis

Something was bothering Congressman Al Green. It was April 10, 2019, and in Room 2128 of Washington, D.C.'s, Rayburn House, seven stern-faced men had for three hours been answering questions from members of the House Committee on Financial Services. The men had a host of things in common. They were all clad in dark suits with subtle ties. Above clean-shaven white faces, they sported carefully coiffed gray hair or else a bald head. They all made more money in a year than many of their employees would make in their entire lifetimes, and they had all been summoned to Washington on account of their jobs. They were the chief executive officers of America's largest and most powerful banks.

Not coincidentally, this meeting of the millionaires had been arranged around the tenth anniversary of the end of the global financial crisis, a seismic and simultaneous crash in the value of stocks, bonds, and commodities that had decimated livelihoods on every continent. Congress had called the hearing to determine whether these CEOs had internalized the lessons they were meant to have learned: what happens when lending becomes excessive and when complex financial products are indiscriminately flogged to buyers oblivious to the risks, in pursuit of quick profits.

But Al Green was thinking about something else entirely. As Maxine Waters, the chairwoman of the House Financial Services Committee, yielded the floor to the congressman from Texas, it was obvious that he was perturbed. "As I look at the panel . . . the eye would perceive that the seven of you have something in common. You appear to be white men," Green, who himself is Black, observed. "I may be mistaken," he added, before inviting any member of the pack not identifying as white or male to raise his hand. A few of the CEOs shuffled slightly in their seats, avoiding eye contact, patently uncomfortable about where Green was going, but not a single hand moved.

"This is not a pejorative," the congressman asserted swiftly. "You have all sermonized to a certain extent about diversity. If you believe that your likely successor will be a woman or a person of color, would you kindly extend a hand?" A few of the men flinched, pining for the moment to pass. It took a second or two for some of them to even understand what was going on. But again, like schoolboys being pushed to volunteer for a classroom chore, no one raised a hand. The whole episode consumed fewer than two minutes of the more than six-hour hearing that day, and yet the image of Green staring at the CEOs, silently imploring at least one of them to volunteer, was affecting in a way that arguably no other scene that day had been. It underscored the deep-rooted and inconvenient reality that Wall Street's effort to scrub itself of a reputation for being a toxic white men's club was emphatically failing.

In 2012, Lauren Rivera, a professor at Northwestern's Kellogg School of Management, published research on hiring processes at 120 major employers, a third of which were banks. Rivera was raised in Los Angeles by a single mother who survived paycheck to paycheck on a series of minimum-wage jobs. When Rivera was a teenager, her mom was so determined to secure her daughter a good education and not to pass on her own socioeconomic fate that she took a job at an elite private prep school, where children of staff paid no tuition. That proved to be Rivera's leg up to Yale and then into the consulting industry, but her firsthand experiences of privilege and what she calls a particular "pedigree" made such an impression on her that she decided to return to academia and devote her time to studying what can broadly be understood as cultural capital: the reason some people are able to break into the most prestigious, well-paid professions and industries and others fail.

Rivera's research concluded that hiring is "one of those critical gate-keeping moments whereby the judgments we make about people have enduring effects." And therein lies the problem. On the back of her findings, she coined the term "Looking Glass Merit" to describe the unconscious tendency that we as humans have to define merit in a way that is self-validating. "Because these firms leave a lot of discretion to evaluators—'I want you to pick somebody that's driven!'—but they don't tell you what drive looks like, people end up defining it in their own image," she wrote.

The long-term effect of this phenomenon was showcased excruciatingly on that day in April 2019. Michael Corbat of Citigroup, Jamie Dimon of JP Morgan, James Gorman of Morgan Stanley, Brian Moynihan of Bank of America Merrill Lynch, David Solomon of Goldman Sachs, Ronald O'Hanley of State Street, and Charles Scharf of Bank of New York Mellon could easily have passed as relatives or, at the very least, fraternity brothers. Apart from Gorman, who hails from Australia, even their accents were uniform. No woman up until that point had ever led a major American bank, but perhaps even more worrying than that track record was the fact that no one in the group, having just hours earlier extolled the virtues of diversity, found themselves comfortable—even willing—to forecast a woman or person who was not white following in their professional footsteps.

Green's series of questions sent ripples of dismay through parts of the industry as it was broadcast around the world. It was hard for anyone working in finance to deny the reputation that almost all the large banks still battled—that they were elite clubs of well-educated men—but this overt display of homogeneity was, nonetheless, astonishing. Though a bank CEO's potential successor is almost always shrouded in supreme secrecy, the scene that unfolded made it easy to forget about any extenuating industry-specific idiosyncrasies that might have made the bankers' silence look less incriminating. The men's lack of response may well have been a result of years of media training and steely warnings from public-relations executives never to be tricked into providing clues on personnel moves. But the far more obvious interpretation—and the one that was almost impossible not to subscribe to—was that the CEOs were just not prepared to even entertain the prospect of being replaced by someone who didn't resemble them.

Reams of research had at that point already shown that companies with more diverse leaders were not only more economically resilient during times of crisis, but more financially lucrative when conditions were fine. Studies had also proved that having a better gender balance in management enhances overall staff satisfaction, and that senior women are more likely than their male counterparts to embrace employee-friendly policies and initiatives designed to champion racial and gender diversity. Yet women were evidently still not being given the same opportunity as men for making it to the very top of Wall Street's biggest banks, conveying a message—accurate or not—that they simply weren't meant to be there.

As it turned out, Michael Corbat, at least, was wrong that day. In September 2020, the sixty-year-old announced that after almost four decades at Citi and eight years as CEO, he would retire the following February. Jane Fraser, who at the time led the company's consumer banking business, would take his place. She had been at the bank since 2004. Corbat had worked directly with her for many years, and as he announced her new role, he effusively praised her leadership, experience, and values. "I know she will make an outstanding CEO," he said. Less than eighteen months earlier, as Green had posed that revealing question, Fraser had seemingly not merited a place on Corbat's list of potential successors.

*** 

What happened in front of the House Committee on Financial Services that day illustrated the broader lack of diversity across the world of big money. It exemplified Rivera's Looking Glass Merit. It was shocking and—one would hope—embarrassing for the incumbent leaders. But while the hearing did force the CEOs to come face-to-face with the reality of some of the damage wrought by the financial crisis, it stopped short of truly dealing with the topic of gender in anything more than a superficial way. Women, those attending the hearing might have heard, could have played a role in stopping the great financial crisis before it exploded into raging, ruinous enormity. And in a bitter example of irony, it was women who suffered some of the most sustained and bruising damage from the crisis—wounds that would take decades to heal, if they managed to heal at all.

One woman whose story is little known, considering the power she held throughout her career and the role she played in the world of finance, is Brooksley Born. Born grew up in California in the 1940s and 1950s and graduated from Stanford University in 1961, having majored in English literature. She attended Stanford Law School as one of only seven women in her class and was also the first female student ever to be named president of the *Stanford Law Review*. During her first year, she recalled in an interview years later, one man in the class told her that she was "doing a terrible thing" by taking the place of a man who would have to go to Vietnam and might get killed. At the time, men could be drafted if they weren't able to get a deferment. In 1964, Born graduated first in her class, but the school refused to recommend her for a Supreme Court clerkship. When she managed to convince Associate Justice of the Supreme Court Potter Stewart to meet with her, he told her outright that he simply wasn't ready for a female law clerk.

Eventually Born was offered the opportunity to clerk for Judge Henry Edgerton of the U.S. Court of Appeals for the District of Columbia Circuit, paving the way for an associate position at Arnold & Porter, a law firm that today ranks among the largest and most prestigious in the world. Born recalls that she was drawn to the role in Washington, D.C., partly because Arnold & Porter was one of only a handful of firms at the time that had a female partner: Carolyn Agger, who headed up the firm's tax practice. Agger had previously worked in government at the National Labor Relations Board, had served on the Senate subcommittee on education and labor, and in the tax division of the Justice Department.

Born took a leave from Arnold & Porter when her husband—the journalist Jacob C. Landau—received a fellowship from Harvard

University, forcing the couple to relocate to Cambridge. During that time, she worked as a research assistant to Alan Dershowitz, a law professor who would later become best known for representing individuals like O. J. Simpson and Jeffrey Epstein and for joining president Donald Trump's legal team. But when the young lawyer returned to Arnold & Porter, she rose through the ranks swiftly, impressing her superiors and making partner even after temporarily shifting to a three-day workweek to care for her two young children.

Born specialized in institutional and corporate law; complex litigation, mostly in the federal courts; and the regulation of the burgeoning futures market, in which contracts to buy or sell a particular financial asset for delivery at a predetermined time were exchanged. But beyond the global financial system, she also started to foster an interest in the inherent structural inequalities that permeated American society and business and what she, as a lawyer, could do to change that.

In the 1970s, another female lawyer, Marcia Greenberger, was appointed by the Center for Law and Social Policy—a national, nonpartisan group that was advocating for policy solutions to support people with low incomes—to head a new project on women and the law. Greenberger, who had heard about Born, tapped her up to chair an advisory board for the project, and Born proved instrumental in what became known as the National Women's Law Center. While working with the NWLC, Born helped bring one of the first broad-based challenges to how universities were implementing Title IX, the law prohibiting sex-based discrimination in schools and education programs that receive federal funding. An adroit fundraiser, she won grants to pay for the NWLC to hire more lawyers. In 1981, the NWLC spun off from the Center for Law and Social Policy to become an independent organization.

Born also worked as an adjunct professor at Catholic University, where she co-taught one of the first classes ever on women and the law with her friend and fellow lawyer Marna Tucker. She joined the American Bar Association and was appointed the first woman to the ABA's Standing Committee on the Federal Judiciary, evaluating potential federal judges. The committee's job was to advise the president and the Senate Judiciary Committee on the credentials of nominees. In 1981 Born was presented with the Woman Lawyer of the Year Award from the Women's Bar Association of the District of Columbia, an extremely prestigious accolade that in subsequent years was won by Justice Ruth Bader Ginsburg and Associate Justice of the Supreme Court Elena Kagan, as well as Marcia Greenberger.

Born thrived in private practice, but as the daughter of civil servants, she had always dreamed of a government appointment. She felt a desire to give back, to serve her country, to protect and advocate for those less privileged than her. As she gained prominence in legal circles and academia, she'd become acquainted with the Clintons, so when Bill Clinton won the 1992 presidential election, rumors swirled that Born might be his attorney general pick. It was never a hope she voiced publicly, but it certainly would have been a great honor. In February 1993, however, Clinton announced that he'd chosen veteran Miami prosecutor Janet Reno for that post, and in 1996 he awarded Born with what many considered to be a consolation prize: chairmanship of the Commodity Futures Trading Commission, a little-known government agency with a few hundred employees that had been created in 1974 to regulate the market for financial derivatives. Born had admittedly hoped for something a little flashier, but she accepted with gratitude and grace.

Indisputably, she was qualified. During her time at Arnold & Porter, she had represented the London Futures Exchange and had acted on behalf of a Swiss bank in litigation that had stemmed from the Hunt family of Dallas attempting to corner the silver market. That episode had led to a collapse in the price of the commodity on March 27, 1980 — a day that became known as Silver Thursday. She was deeply analytical, staunchly impartial, and blindly devoted to using her position, knowledge, and skill to ensure that the financial system worked to protect American savers. Crucially, she believed in the power of regulation, and she had an unshakable faith in her ability to recognize when regulation was inadequate. "Brooksley had the advantage of knowing the law and understanding the fragility of the system if it weren't regulated,"

Michael Greenberger, who would later serve as her deputy at the CFTC and who was also Marcia Greenberger's husband, said in a magazine interview in 2009. "She could see that the data points, by lack of regulation, were heading the country into a serious set of calamities, each calamity worse than the one before."

Not long after she assumed chairmanship of the CFTC in 1996, Brooksley Born started to feel a lingering sense of unease related to the rapidly expanding market for derivatives. Derivatives allow investors to bet on the trading direction of underlying assets that they "derive" their value from—equities, mortgages, or interest rates, for example—without trading the asset itself. By the mid-1990s, this market was growing at a breakneck pace. Specifically, Born was worried about an explosion in the size of the over-the-counter, or OTC, derivatives market—"the hippopotamus under the rug," as she later came to call it. OTC trades were happening away from public exchanges, quietly and behind closed doors. There was no way of knowing the nature, scope, and true scale of the multi-trillion-dollar market. What had allowed the OTC market to flourish in such an uncontrolled manner was aggressive deregulation that had occurred in the preceding decades.

Two years before Born had been named chair of the CFTC, Bankers Trust had already come within a whisker of blowing up two of its most important clients—Procter & Gamble and Gibson Greeting Cards—after selling them complex derivatives products that, as it later turned out, were falsely valued. A few years before that, it had emerged that a trader at Japanese bank Sumitomo had used derivatives to try to corner the copper market over a decade-long period, leading to billions in losses. The memory of that now haunted Born, and she was also starting to hear rumors that companies were using derivatives to manipulate their quarterly financial statements.

Unfortunately, her fears weren't shared at the highest echelons of government and the Federal Reserve. In March 1998, Born paid a visit to Robert Rubin, who had served as Treasury Secretary since 1995, a period during which the United States had enjoyed remarkable economic growth resulting in near full-employment and a buoyant stock market, coupled with only moderate inflation. A veteran of Goldman Sachs, Rubin had personally overseen the loosening of financial-industry underwriting guidelines that had been in place for more than half a century, and he was confident that deregulation—allowing markets to flow freely and unencumbered—was the key to national economic prosperity.

As such, Rubin wasn't exactly delighted to see her. To him, Born was an inconvenience, and she certainly wasn't in his club. "She had no sense of the smooth collegiality that characterized the top policy-makers of the Clinton administration," journalist Michael Hirsh wrote in his 2010 book, *Capital Offense: How Washington's Wise Men Turned America's Future Over to Wall Street*. "So what if she was running a nominally independent agency? She had no sense of place, no respect for who they were."

A little further down the road, where Alan Greenspan sat atop the Federal Reserve, Born's opinions were just as unpopular. Greenspan, an eccentric and often enigmatic, mostly self-taught economist who ended up presiding over the Fed for more than eighteen years, had begun his career as a worshiper of philosopher and novelist Ayn Rand. He was as devoted to free-market capitalism as Rubin, and Born was an unwelcome voice in his ear.

According to Hirsh's book, Greenspan invited Born to lunch when she first took over at the CFTC, during which she voiced her concerns about the lax regulation in some of the most opaque but sprawling corners of the financial market. "Well, Brooksley, I guess you and I will never agree about fraud," Greenspan reportedly told her, to which Born wondered out loud what, exactly, there was to not agree upon. "Well, you probably will always believe there should be laws against fraud, and I don't think there is any need for it." Greenspan replied, as reported by Hirsh. Born was gobsmacked.

Quoting an unnamed Fed official, Hirsh wrote that staffers under Greenspan privately thought of Born as "a lightweight wacko." Born, for her part, knew that she wasn't, and would never be, one of "them." She was a lawyer, not an economist, and, most obviously, she was a woman. But that didn't dent her resolve to do her job properly, and at that moment she considered that to mean pulling out all the stops to prevent the derivatives market from blowing up in a cataclysmic fashion.

But whatever she said or did, Rubin and Greenspan didn't want to hear about her sleepless nights or her predictions about an impending crisis. They had grown up on Wall Street during an era when braggadocian machismo was a character trait that led to success, and when women never dreamed of expressing an opinion on something as complex as the financial markets. Born headed up an agency that was so obscure, it was housed in a rented space in the commercial district of downtown Washington. As far as they were concerned, she held no real sway in the hallowed halls of government and financial policymaking. They were not about to let her waste their time. With the Asian financial crisis well underway, and contagion a real risk, they had more important matters to deal with, and at least for the time being, it certainly looked like they had America on their side. Greenspan was regularly referred to as the "wizard of monetary policy." In early 1999, *TIME* magazine would run a cover story lauding Rubin, Greenspan, and Lawrence Summers, who was deputy Treasury secretary, as the "Committee to Save the World," heroes of the free market: the "three marketeers."

*\*\*\**

Finally, in the late spring of 1998, Brooksley Born started to act. Under her guidance, the CFTC started preparing what's known as a concept release, an invitation for members of the public to submit comments on the relevance and appropriateness of existing regulation of the OTC derivatives market, which by that time was estimated to have a value of about 29 trillion dollars. A concept release is often a precursor to a formal regulatory proposal, and news that Born was drafting this one shook some of the most influential institutions in Washington to the core. Lawrence Summers reportedly called her in a panicked rage to warn her what would happen if she kept pushing: If Wall Street got too spooked, it would go into meltdown, and it would all be her fault.

The following month Rubin, Greenspan, and Arthur Levitt, the chairman of the Securities and Exchange Commission, came face-to-face with Born on the matter during a meeting of the president's Working Group on Financial Markets, of which they were all members. Rubin cut to the chase. Born was playing a dangerous game, he suggested. If the concept release were to be published, markets might be sent into a tailspin, fueled by uncertainty over what might be about to happen. But quite aside from that, Rubin argued, Born and the CFTC didn't even have jurisdiction to make decisions about this kind of regulation in this particular market. That, Born countered, was ridiculous.

Shortly after the meeting, Greenspan, Rubin, and Levitt published a rare joint statement underscoring their "grave concerns" relating to the CFTC proposal. Summers argued that Born's even so much as drawing attention to the possibility that something needed to change in that particular corner of the market would cast "a shadow of regulatory uncertainty over an otherwise thriving market." They might have thought that grilling her at the Working Group on Financial Markets had served to silence her, but they were wrong. In May, Born circulated the concept release. Rubin was incensed, and Born recalls it triggering a "firestorm of opposition." By some accounts, Rubin never spoke to her again.

The war entered its next battle. One morning and without warning, Born was summoned by staffers for Jim Leach, who chaired the House banking committee, and the chair of the agriculture committee, Richard Lugar, to appear on the Hill, where she was berated yet again for stepping out of line. It was the first of several hearings during which Born tried desperately yet as calmly as possible to explain why she, the chair of a small and relatively toothless agency, was terrified of what might be going on in the derivatives market.

Even in the autumn of that year, as a massive hedge fund, Long-Term Capital Management, which had two Nobel Laureates on its board of directors, almost collapsed under the weight of trillions of dollars of derivative bets gone wrong, no one—it seemed—was prepared to take Born seriously. As Bethany McLean and Joe Nocera write in their 2011 book about the financial crisis, "if there was a moment when Bob Rubin could have used his immense stature to do something about the derivatives problem [. . .] this was it."

It was clear, by this point, that Born had fired all the shots in her arsenal. One last time she pleaded with the House banking committee to do something about "the unknown risks that the over-the-counter derivatives market may pose to the U.S. economy," including credit default swaps. She referenced an "immediate and pressing need to address whether there are unacceptable regulatory gaps." But she was a lone wolf. Not long after, Treasury officials lobbied Congress to pass legislation preventing the CFTC from being able to regulate the OTC derivatives market. Congress responded by barring the commission from enacting any regulation along these lines for six months. In January 1999 Born wrote to President Clinton informing him that she would not be seeking reappointment for a second term atop the CFTC and would be returning to Arnold & Porter instead. Bill Rainer, a long-term friend of President Clinton, succeeded Born. He'd worked as a bond trader before cofounding a trading firm called Greenwich Capital Markets.

***

Born's Cassandra-like warnings, it seemed, were quickly forgotten. Even in 2001, as Enron—which had helped create the global market for energy-based derivatives—was forced to file the largest corporate bankruptcy in American history, regulators didn't change their tune. In fact, as president George W. Bush assumed office, a fresh enthusiasm for Reaganomics and deregulation swept across Washington. Leverage was king.

Several years later, in 2008, Born, who had retired from private practice in 2003, watched from a distance as the unregulated derivatives market that had caused her so many sleepless nights sent the value of financial assets around the world into free fall, bringing economies to their knees and crushing global banks. In the months and years that followed, it became increasingly hard to deny that the multi-trillion-dollar OTC derivative market was the root cause of the great financial crisis.

"It helped foment a mortgage crisis, then a credit crisis, and finally a once-in-a-century systemic financial crisis that, but for huge U.S. taxpayer interventions, would have in the fall of 2008 led the world economy into a devastating Depression," Michael Greenberger stated as he testified at a Financial Crisis Inquiry Commission hearing in June 2010.

Even Alan Greenspan, testifying before a congressional committee in late 2008, admitted that the crisis had exposed a "flaw" in the economic philosophy and ideology that had guided him for years. "I made a mistake in presuming that the self-interests of organizations, specifically banks and others, were such that they were best capable of protecting their own shareholders and their equity in the firms," Greenspan said.

It's impossible not to wonder why no one with the ability and power to make a difference truly took Born's warnings to heart. It's certainly reasonable to conclude that sexism played a part. In a 2009 *Frontline* episode, Arthur Levitt, the former chairman of the SEC and an erstwhile vehement opponent of Born, admitted that the crisis had, for him, catalyzed a change of heart. He felt different now than back when he was pitted against Born during those bitter battles in Washington. "I've come to know her as one of the most capable, dedicated, intelligent, and committed public servants," he said. "I wish I knew her better in Washington," he added. "I could have done much better. I could have made a difference."

Rivera's Looking Glass Merit comes to mind again. Born was distinct. In a sea of economists and politicians in Washington, she was a lawyer. In the President's Working Group on Financial Markets meeting, she was the odd one out, because she sat atop a relatively obscure agency, not the Fed or the Treasury. She didn't grow up on Wall Street, like so many others in government did, and, perhaps most important, she was a woman.

When Alan Greenspan and Robert Rubin and Lawrence Summers batted her concerns aside, they were likely demonstrating confirmation bias: a human instinct or heuristic impulse to seek out and attribute value to evidence that supports our underlying belief about something and to disregard information that might discredit it. As the U.S. economy soared, the powerful trio of men wasn't inclined to entertain the idea that they might be doing something wrong and that the deregulation they had championed for so many years was setting the market up for disaster.

In a blog post published in September 2018, Christine Lagarde, who at the time was managing director of the International Monetary Fund, described the great financial crisis as "a sobering lesson in groupthink." She wrote that in the years since the collapse of Lehman Brothers and other major financial institutions, policy has addressed the flaws in the system that ultimately led to the crisis. Banks, she said, now have much healthier capital and liquidity positions. Regulation has been enhanced, and leverage is lower. Crucially, a big chunk of the over-the-counter derivatives market has been shifted to central clearing, making it more transparent. But there's one thing that's not changed much, she contended, and that's culture.

A necessary element of reform in this regard, Lagarde said, would be more female leadership in finance, and she offered two arguments to support her thesis. "First, greater diversity always sharpens thinking, reducing the potential for groupthink. Second, this diversity also leads to more prudence, with less of the reckless decision-making that provoked the crisis," she wrote. Indeed, research from the IMF and elsewhere has repeatedly shown that a greater share of women on boards of banks and other financial services institutions leads to greater stability. One study by researchers at Cass Business School, now known as Bayes Business School, in London found that banks with more female directors faced lower and less-frequent fines for misconduct, saving those institutions 7.84 million dollars a year, on average. "As I have said many times," Lagarde concluded, "if it had been Lehman Sisters rather than Lehman Brothers, the world might well look a lot different today."

The cruel irony of this, of course, is that women suffered dispro-portionately from the fallout of the 2008 crisis, just as they did in the subsequent economic crisis caused by the COVID-19 pandemic.

As Melanie Long, an assistant professor of economics at the College of Wooster in Ohio, explains, female-headed households went into the 2008 crisis in a much more precarious position than did male-headed ones. Part of the reason for that was what academics have referred to as the feminization of high-cost credit. Because of low-income single women's economic vulnerability and historically limited access to tradi-tional credit products, they were more likely to be targets for predatory subprime lending. Long references research published by academics from the University of British Columbia in 2011 showing that in a 2006 sample of mortgage borrowers, more than half of mortgages owned by Black single women were subprime—or offered at a high interest rate—compared with 28 percent for non-Hispanic white single male borrow-ers. And Long's own research has found that female-headed households experienced a worrying rise in both mortgage debt and educational debt in the lead-up to the crisis, rendering them much more vulnerable when the recession hit.

Research by the Economic Policy Institute, meanwhile, found that although men lost far more jobs than women did during the recession that ensued—over six million, or 8.5 percent of their total December 2007 employment, compared to women who lost about 2.7 million, or 3.5 percent—the gender dynamic reversed in the years that followed. Between February 2010 and June 2014, men gained 5.5 million jobs, while women gained only 3.6 million. Job growth, the EPI found, was more pronounced in industries that disproportionately employ men.

\*\*\*

Whether the Lehman Sisters theory had anything to do with it—or Al Green's dressing down, or the proliferation of research echoing Lauren Rivera's Looking Glass Merit, or even the glass-cliff effect that seems to explain some of the female promotions, particularly in the 1990s and

2000s—we may never know. But in recent years, the world of finance has inched toward greater diversity, albeit at a glacial—in some cases barely perceptible—pace.

Data crunched by consulting firm Oliver Wyman found that in 2021, women made up 20 percent of executive committees and 23 percent of boards at financial services companies globally. That's still a small chunk, but it marks a vast improvement on the 11 percent recorded for both metrics in 2013. As well as the IMF, women have now led the U.S. Treasury, the European Central Bank, a major Wall Street Bank, and the New York Stock Exchange. In February 2021, Teachers Insurance and Annuity Association of America, which at the time managed 1.3 trillion dollars in assets through its retirement accounts and investment funds, named Thasunda Brown Duckett president and chief executive, making her one of Wall Street's most influential executives and one of the most powerful Black bankers in America.

But even a few changes at the very highest level of corporations, sovereign agencies, and nonprofits will never be a panacea for the systemic inequality rife throughout the ranks. A decade after the financial crisis, many of Wall Street's best-known banks boasted workforces that overall were half—or almost half—female, but higher up the seniority spectrum, the proportion of women was tiny. At many of the world's biggest banks, the number of women in the workforce declines by 50 percent or more from graduate level to executive rank. In the United Kingdom, where gender-pay-gap reporting legislation has since 2017 compelled companies to publish their gender pay gap data for each quartile of the company, reported gaps are often negligible for the youngest financiers and yawning for the most senior.

As COVID-19 raged, a survey conducted by professional services firm Accenture found that almost a third of women working in financial services had left their job either permanently or temporarily during the pandemic. More than a third of women who had not quit said that they were considering doing so. One grave finding in that survey was that almost two-thirds of female executives and senior managers, and almost half of entry-level respondents, said that they had become willing to forgo compensation for additional flexibility in the workplace. Gema Zamarro, an economist at the University of Southern California Dornsife Center for Economic and Social Research, told the publication *Institutional Investor* that mothers, especially, were finding themselves at a breaking point in an industry where parenting traditionally had no place at all and where a culture of misogyny has historically run riot. "You're doing three jobs," she said. "Mom, teacher, and your own work."

When women don't have the same access to money as men—in either a professional or personal context—and when they don't enjoy equal opportunities to earn and spend and manage finances, everyone suffers. Research by McKinsey conducted in 2016 found that if women were to participate in the economy identically to men, they could add as much as 28 trillion dollars, or 26 percent, to annual global gross domestic product in 2025. This is approximately equivalent to the size of the U.S. and Chinese economies combined.

A 2017 study by the Institute for Women's Policy Research found that the poverty rate of working women would be halved if women were to earn as much as men. The same research also showed that equal pay in America would add an additional income of 512.6 billion dollars to the national economy even if men's wages stayed the same.

Giving women more economic power and the autonomy to make financial decisions would be universally advantageous too. In Bangladesh, Muhammad Yunus, the Nobel Prize winner who is credited with creating the microcredit phenomenon, has found that women repay loans more often than men do. He also established that, when women control the household budgets, their families were more likely to benefit from the income.

A separate study done in the Philippines has demonstrated that, when women have control over a couple's savings, spending tends to shift toward the purchase of family-targeted durable goods, like washing machines and kitchen appliances, that elevate the whole family's standard of living and well-being.

Viviana Zelizer, professor of sociology at Princeton University, who for years has studied the sociology of money and gender, notes that in 2010 in the aftermath of a devastating earthquake, authorities in Haiti distributed food vouchers only to women. They reasoned that this was because women were more likely than men to ensure that food would be distributed equitably within a household. Similarly, she says, an innovative antipoverty program in Mexico called Oportunidades targeted its cash transfers to mothers, conditional upon their children going to school and the members of their household attending health clinic appointments. Studies found that the cash tended to be spent predominantly on food, children's clothes, and school supplies. Zelizer also references the work of Nicholas Kristof and Sheryl WuDunn. In their 2009 book, *Half the Sky: Turning Oppression into Opportunity for Women Worldwide*, they even go further than Zelizer. "Some of the most wretched suffering," they write, "is caused not just by low incomes, but also by unwise spending—by men."

"The way to understand it is that there's a difference between 'big money' and 'small money,'" Zelizer explains in an interview. The latter, she says, is the money that women are entrusted with to make household purchases: cash for groceries or the school supplies for the children, for example. As a society, we are accustomed to women having control over small money and how to spend it, she says. "These small monies are given great moral dignity, and yet they're not recognized as real contributions, either by public accounting or by private accounting." When it comes to the "big monies," it's a different story.

"Investments, for example, are squarely the domain of men," says Zelizer. "We trust women with the vital day-to-day small expenditures, but above a certain amount it's not for her. Perhaps when it comes to gender, money, and power, that's the greatest paradox of all."

# CHAPTER 11

*The Cost of Silence*

Promises without policies are bullshit.
—Ifeoma Ozoma, whistleblower, advocate, and tech policy consultant

Throughout American history, it's always been the case that great injustices have been able to occur wherever great power has been concentrated.

Look no further than Bernie Madoff, who died in prison in 2021, where he was being held on a 150-year sentence for engineering a decades-long fraud estimated to have been worth as much as 64.8 billion dollars. Madoff's dealings had helped him and his wife amass a combined peak net worth of approximately 825 million dollars. A court found that only a handful of people knew about his Ponzi scheme. Madoff's reputation had been impeccable; he was trusted and endorsed by some of the most important authorities in finance, giving him significant influence, which likely allowed his crime to keep going for so long.

Historian and writer Lord Acton is frequently quoted as saying that "power tends to corrupt, and absolute power corrupts absolutely." And while this may not always be true, there's plenty of evidence that power can lead humans to make decisions that are not as morally conscious or as ethically sound as the decisions they might make otherwise. "Power disinhibits us," organizational psychologist Adam Grant wrote in a 2019 column for the *Washington Post*. "It releases us from the shackles of social pressure," he added. "Gaining influence and authority frees us up to act on our real wishes and show our true colors."

From the 1970s until the early 2000s, the financial services sector was a nexus of wealth, ego, and masculinity where those true colors frequently shone through in all their gaudy glory. Individuals drunk on power made decisions and behaved as if neither the spirit nor the letter of the law applied to them, and as if decency, manners, and respect for others were quaint relics of a bygone time. During Brooksley Born's era of being marginalized for her insights and analyses as chair of the CFTC, as Lilly Ledbetter's historical discrimination case was winding its way through the courts, and as nineties' and early aughts' pop culture normalized the submissiveness of women, a barrage of banks were fighting horrendous allegations.

Morgan Stanley and Merrill Lynch were two of the institutions that paid out multimillion-dollar settlements during that time. A court heard that one branch office of Smith Barney, which was later bought by Morgan Stanley, had a "Boom Boom Room" where male brokers were able to celebrate their birthdays with strippers. Later, a court also heard that women at Smith Barney were paid lower base salaries and were eight times less likely to be promoted to the position of broker, which ultimately resulted in more than two thousand women joining a lawsuit against the firm. Smith Barney ended up paying 150 million dollars in settlements. In her blistering 2022 memoir *Bully Market*, Jamie Fiore Higgins, who worked at Goldman Sachs for seventeen years, documented how she was physically abused, bullied, and discriminated against during that time on account of her gender. Even the bank's human resources department, she explained, was toothless in the face of the toxic masculinity that was so ensconced in the culture.

But even though it certainly didn't stop the misconduct, Lehman Brothers' collapse in September 2008 in some ways marked the start of a new chapter—a shifting of the tides of power from finance into technology. And as the epicenter of power and money palpably migrated in those post-crisis years, so did some the worst elements of corporate culture.

In 2007, as financial markets began to tremble at the prospect of what a crisis in the housing sector could mean, the Federal Reserve started to trim its key policy interest rate from above 5 percent, first to below 4 percent and later much lower. Interest rates are broadly considered one of the Fed's most powerful and reliable tools for controlling the economy. Cutting generally has the effect of encouraging businesses to make new investments because borrowing money becomes more affordable. It can spur savers to buy houses and spend money on renovations, for example, and it can motivate consumers, more generally, to splash cash on durable goods like cars, clothes, appliances, and travel. Traditional economic theory predicts that in a depressed economy in which unemployment is ticking up, the extra spending stimulated by low interest rates will kick-start economic output.

By the time Lehman Brothers collapsed in September 2008, the Fed's key rate was at just 2 percent. A few months later, under the direction of Ben Bernanke, who had succeeded Alan Greenspan in 2006, the central bank was forced to cut the rate to a record low of near zero, while simultaneously announcing that it would print as much money as was needed to breathe life back into credit markets and to counteract what was shaping up to be America's most dramatic economic downturn since the Second World War. "We are running out of the traditional ammunition that's used in a recession, which is to lower interest rates," president-elect Barack Obama said at a press conference at the time, calling on other branches of government to deploy any and all resources available to avert the meltdown that was looking increasingly inevitable.

Views diverge on whether the Fed's approach to the impending crisis was a success. Generally, economists agree that Bernanke's strategy avoided a far more cataclysmic scenario—a replay of the Great Depression of the 1930s. But one indisputable effect of cutting rates to rock bottom, and keeping them there for years, was that cash was historically cheap to borrow. And that cheap money fundamentally transformed the U.S. economy.

Yield-hungry investors speculatively piling into experimental start-ups sent valuations for corporations that few had ever heard of soaring. At the perceived blink of an eye, a company could go from a handful of employees to hundreds without even once showing a profit or generating much revenue to speak of. This exuberance and insatiable appetite for risk—a burning desire to take a bet on what might prove to be the next Amazon or Google—had the effect of creating mind-blowing

wealth distortions and grotesque power asymmetries within corporations: the perfect conditions for rampant inequality and endemic abuse.
And as the technology ecosystem bulged to constitute the lion's share
of the publicly traded stock market in the United States, it became a
bellwether for corporate best practice and culture—for showcasing how
you can treat an employee in the interest of cold, hard, short-term profit.

"Silicon Valley has, in many ways, replaced Wall Street as the country's nexus of money and power," wrote journalist Sheelah Kolhatkar
for *The New Yorker* in 2017. "Many [tech] start-ups begin as a collection of young entrepreneurs in a room, with no clear rules. They rarely
have human-resources departments at first, meaning that there is no
one charged with fielding complaints," she added. "And the emphasis
among venture capitalists on 'growth at any cost' often leads investors
and board members to ignore workplace problems—as well as more
serious violations—so long as a company's valuation is going up."

***

One of the tools that has been used by large corporations liberally over
the last few decades, both as a means of gaining and maintaining power
without fear of real repercussion—even when, in the eyes of the law,
injustice has occurred—is the nondisclosure agreement. Better even
than get-out-of-jail-free cards, NDAs have become never-go-to-jail-in-
the-first-place cards: a means of obscuring much of the misconduct
and behavior that has held women, and other historically disadvantaged
demographic groups, back from reaching their full professional and
economic potential.

It's hard to pin down when NDAs as an invention first came onto
the scene. Michelle Dean, writing in the *Columbia Journalism Review*,
explains that NDAs first got a lease on life in the 1940s in maritime law
but started appearing more frequently several decades later at burgeoning tech firms like IBM. Initially they had nothing to do with discrimination. Instead, they were used to protect trade secrets and important

proprietary algorithms. "Leaks by disloyal employees," Dean writes, "pose very real business risks."

Then, in the 1970s, NDAs started cropping up in a whole host of often-surprising contexts. During an investigation by the House Select Committee on Assassinations into the killings of John F. Kennedy and Martin Luther King Jr., the *Washington Post* reported that individuals working for the committee were forced to sign NDAs ensuring that they wouldn't "indicate, divulge, or acknowledge" that they were even working on the investigation while it was in progress. The terms of the NDA also stipulated that an employee should report to the committee any attempts by journalists to get their hands on information about the investigation.

In the years that followed, a realization of the potential power of NDAs sent their popularity soaring. "It became a de rigueur provision in employment contracts for a certain kind of white-collar job. And perhaps most crucially, it became a regular feature of legal settlement agreements," Dean writes. NDAs became known as "contracts of silence" that prevented corporate scandals and serious misconduct from ever being divulged to the public. They were being used to cover up sex abuse scandals linked to the Catholic Church and to gag plaintiffs who had suffered harm through environmental hazards like toxic-waste leaks.

Global networks of abuse and exploitation, perpetuated by people like movie mogul Harvey Weinstein, were able to go undetected for so long because of the existence of NDAs. The R&B singer R. Kelly, who in 2022 was found guilty on charges relating to child pornography and enticing underage girls to have sex with him, reportedly silenced his victims with NDAs, including the late pop star Aaliyah, who was just fifteen when he married her. Their marriage was later annulled by her parents. Donald Trump was known to have relied on NDAs as a weapon against anyone who spoke out against him or criticized him.

The #MeToo movement in particular added fuel to existing efforts from across an array of industries to ban NDAs. In 2019, former Fox News anchor Gretchen Carlson, who had signed an NDA as part of a

20-million-dollar settlement for sexual harassment by the late Fox CEO Roger Ailes, cofounded a nonprofit with the mission of ending NDAs. In October 2021, California passed the Silenced No More Act. It was cosponsored by Ifeoma Ozoma, a former policy manager at Pinterest who broke the terms of her own NDA to go public with allegations of discrimination at the company in 2020.

Ozoma, the daughter of Nigerian immigrants, told CNN in an interview in 2022 that her dispute with Pinterest began when she found out that she was getting paid less than half of what a white male colleague was getting for doing the same work. Ozoma said that she raised this disparity with her employer and gave them time to address or rectify the issue but that she was let go in March 2020. A few months later—in June—despite having signed an NDA, Ozoma fired off a series of tweets about her experience at Pinterest. Another Black woman, Aerica Shimizu Banks, who left the company at the same time, also spoke out. "The purpose wasn't just, 'let me vent,'" Ozoma told the broadcaster in explaining why she chose to go public. "The purpose was, people need to understand that this is what's happening. And if it happened to me with the public profile that I had within the company and outside of the company, then it can happen to anyone else."

In response, Pinterest hired external counsel to conduct a review of its workplace culture. It also said that it had investigated Ozoma's and Banks's allegations and concluded that they had been "treated fairly." But for Ozoma, the story didn't end there. State law in California, where she had been living and working, at the time provided some protection for employees who broke nondisclosure agreements to speak out against some forms of discrimination, but those protections did not include racial discrimination.

Ozoma later started a campaign to educate employees on their rights and to encourage tech companies to reconsider strict NDA policies that were in place. She also reached out to lawmakers and eventually started cooperating with State Senator Connie Leyva on a law that prevents NDAs from being implemented when employees speak out on any type of workplace discrimination, including racial.

Her efforts culminated in California governor Gavin Newsom in October 2021 signing the Silenced No More bill into law. "California workers should absolutely be able to speak out—if they so wish—when they are a victim of any type of harassment or discrimination in the workplace," Senator Leyva said in a statement at the time. "It is unconscionable that an employer would ever want or seek to silence the voices of survivors that have been subjected to racist, sexist, homophobic, or other attacks at work."

In an interview, Ozoma said that the law, of course, represents progress. It's something that she's immensely proud of. Indeed, in the house in which she now lives in Santa Fe, New Mexico, she has a framed copy of the act hanging on the wall next to a copy of an op-ed she wrote for the *New York Times* when the bill was first introduced. But it's also only an incremental step, and so much more still needs to be done to create even something akin to absolute equality of opportunity across corporate America.

One problem, Ozoma says, is that business leaders commit to changing culture. "But the term 'culture,'" she says, "is a screen for changing actual policies and codifying protections that workers actually need. Culture obscures," she adds. "Culture is promises, and promises without policies are bullshit when they're coming from organizations."

As of the end of 2022, more than a dozen states had passed restrictions on private sector employers imposing contracts preventing employees from speaking out about certain types of sexual harassment, assault, and discrimination. But there are loopholes aplenty. For one thing, many of the organizations that are committing the most heinous offenses are huge, with a sprawling employee base across different states and sometimes even different countries. Only employees with contracts in the states in which laws have passed are offered the protections afforded by those laws.

"So much more work is needed. And every tiny bit of progress relies on the efforts and advocacy of many," Ozoma says. "When people ask me what's next for me, I usually turn the question around and ask them what they're doing to further the cause. Everyone has to step up.

Progress is certainly not going to come out of the goodness of the power-ful corporations that have so much control."

And academics have also cautioned that even categorically banning NDAs would not be enough to end the cycles of persistent unethical and abusive behavior, frequently directed at women and other company minorities in certain workplaces.

Research conducted by scholars in Canada and the United States and published in 2019 refers to "networks of complicity" that are cen-tral to explaining the persistence of sexual, and other types of, harass-ment in organizations. "By using power and manipulating information, perpetrators [built] networks that protected them from sanction and enabled their behavior to continue unchecked," they wrote of the organi-zations they studied. "Networks of complicity metastasized and caused lasting harm to victims, other employees, and the organization as a whole." Perhaps the most unsettling conclusion they drew based on their research was that these networks can survive and thrive even if the original perpetrator is removed. "Leaders must proactively work to identify and disband the network of complicity," the academics noted. Also important, they added, "the organizational culture must be trans-formed, which is typically a long-term endeavor, but it can be done."

For now, such networks of complicity seem to be thriving in the tech sector—an industry that, on account of its sheer size, in many ways sets the tone for corporate behavior in America more broadly. In 2015, a group of female tech investors and executives conducted a survey of over two hundred women working in Silicon Valley who had at least a decade of experience. The respondents included companies' chief executive officers, chief marketing officers, and chief technology officers but also individuals working at venture capital firms—the key financial backers of virtually all technology companies—as well as founders and entrepreneurs. The resulting report, entitled "The Elephant in the Val-ley," described a culture of discrimination that was brutally pervasive but often subtle enough for it to go unchecked and unacknowledged for years. Some 84 percent of the respondents indicated that they had been told they were "too aggressive" in the office, and 66 percent said that they had been excluded from important events on account of their gender. Sixty percent said that they had experienced unwanted sexual advances in the workplace, many from an individual who was senior to them.

A third of all women questioned said that they had at some point, in a work context, been concerned for their own safety. When asked why they didn't report particular incidents of inappropriate or threatening behavior, many women said that they were afraid of retaliation. A significant proportion who did raise concerns reported being "blown off" by their boss or human resources department.

*** 

One of the first high-profile discrimination cases in Silicon Valley was Ellen Pao's 2012 suit against the venture capital firm Kleiner Perkins Caufield & Byers, known for being an early investor in Amazon, Google, and Twitter. Pao, who accused her former employer of gender discrimination and retaliation, lost the case, but, due to the size of the damages she sought—16 million dollars—and the nature of the claims, it garnered a huge amount of media attention.

Pao never signed an NDA. This enabled her to speak candidly about her experience and even publish a book documenting in her own words what had happened. It also, arguably, paved the way for other women and minorities, in some cases very publicly, to take legal action for their suffering at the hands of their employers. In 2015, Chia Hong filed a suit against Facebook, in which she made eleven separate legal claims. Hong alleged that, while at the company, she suffered discrimination and harassment based on her gender, race, and nationality and that she was retaliated against after she complained. She also said that she was ultimately unlawfully fired from the company. Hong dropped the case in the fall of 2015. Neither side commented on whether or not a settlement had been reached.

That same year, Tina Huang filed a class-action lawsuit against Twitter on behalf of herself and other women who had worked at the company, claiming that its promotion practices discriminated against women. "Promotion into Twitter's senior technical positions is based on subjective judgments, by committees that are comprised of and dependent on upper management at Twitter, and predominantly male," her allegations read. "These judgments are tainted with conscious or unconscious prejudices and gender-based stereotypes, which explains why so few women employees at Twitter advance to senior and leadership positions." Huang's case was ultimately denied class-action status.

The pace of major lawsuits being brought has barely slackened since. In 2018, Uber agreed to pay 10 million dollars to women and people of color working for the company after a state-level pay equity suit. In December 2020, just months after Ozoma and Banks spoke out, Pinterest agreed to pay 22.5 million dollars to settle a gender discrimination and retaliation lawsuit brought by its former chief operating officer, and in June 2022, Google announced that it would pay 118 million dollars to settle a class-action lawsuit that accused it of consistently paying women less than men. The tech giant stopped short, however, of admitting any guilt whatsoever in the matter. Google's parent company, Alphabet, generated revenue of about 257 billion dollars during the prior year.

The steep rise in the number of women in tech publicly speaking out against sexism, mistreatment, and discrimination in the wake of Ellen Pao's trial has been so striking, in fact, that some have dubbed it the "Pao Effect." But for everyone who does find the resources and courage to act, countless others are unable to. As is evidenced by forums and reports like "The Elephant in the Valley," a terrifyingly large number of women face assault, abuse, and discrimination on a daily basis in the tech industry but can't fight it in a meaningful way. That may be for any number of reasons: fear of retaliation, economic insecurity, a lack of understanding of the legal system, or simply the existence of overbearing networks of complicity that ensure that bad behaviors are so unmeshed in corporate culture that they're entirely unremarkable.

Speaking to women who work or have worked in the tech industry, it's apparent that sexism is an intrinsic—even foundational—characteristic of huge swaths of the sector. In 2019, women in the United States held only a quarter of jobs in computing and left the technology and engineering sectors at twice the rate of men. Female managers were a vanishingly small minority in the field, and in the years since, little has changed. Those who do stay in the sector speak—almost entirely on condition of anonymity—of the multi-pronged challenge they have to master in order to reach their full professional potential and earn even close to what they're worth. They must excel technically at the tasks that constitute their job, but they must also navigate the sexism they encounter with grace and dignity, avoiding the temptation to snap and be branded hysterical or deemed not a good team player.

Susan Wu, an entrepreneur and investor, spoke in an interview with the *Atlantic* of "the countless times I've had to move a man's hand from my thigh (or back or shoulder or hair or arm) during a meeting (or networking event or professional lunch or brainstorming session or pitch meeting) without seeming confrontational (or bitchy or rejecting or demanding or aggressive)." Many women interviewed on the agreement that they would not be identified said that the greatest challenge a woman in tech—or even a woman in other industries, particularly in companies that were new or growing rapidly—faced was that every single day you were tasked with the impossible: be assertive but not aggressive, feminine but not emotional, intelligent but not nerdy, one of the guys but undeniably still a woman. They spoke of the constant push and pull that can drive you to the brink of sanity. And on top of everything else, you also have to do your job exceptionally well—ideally, better than any man—in order to be treated and compensated just as well as a man would be.

*\*\*\**

The gender pay gap is one metric for gauging inequality in Silicon Valley, but the gender equity gap is perhaps the less understood yet even more pertinent. While salaries can make you wealthy, it's more often than not equity ownership that renders you fabulously rich: having the privilege of being in possession of a small sliver of a company that has the potential to grow exponentially. Shares in a company can constitute a substantial chunk of a compensation package, and equity ownership is rarely—almost never, in fact—reflected in gender pay gap reports. Gender pay gap reporting is becoming more common across many industries, as a function of both cultural pressure and legislation, but these reports shed light on only a single gauge of inequality—a gauge that is rarely the most indicative of the true extent of the uneven playing field.

In 2015, April Underwood, the former chief product officer of Slack who had also worked at Google and Twitter, cofounded what she described as an investing collective with some of her former colleagues. They set themselves a dual mandate of investing in female founders but also pushing for more transparency around who owns start-ups. "It started from a shared desire we had to angel invest," Underwood told the *Financial Times* in 2020, referring to the act of being an early buyer of equity in a recently founded company. "Frankly, we wanted to be like our male peers who were getting involved in some of the most successful companies in the community."

In 2018, the collective—referring to itself as the #Angels—published research, which they conducted in collaboration with the software company Carta, showing that women at the time made up 35 percent of equity-holding employees at start-ups but held only 20 percent of the equity. In other words, the average woman who held stock in a particular company owned a stake that was worth much less in dollar terms than a man who owned stock in it. An even more shocking statistic that emerged: While women accounted for 13 percent of all start-up founders in the samples that they examined—a sample that consisted of 6,000 companies with a combined total equity value of nearly 45 billion dollars—they held just 6 percent of all founder equity.

The members of Underwood's collective pored over the data and determined that there were several possible explanations for the stark divide. Because of the culture, female founders might be less likely to stand their ground in negotiations, making them more likely than male founders to be forced to give up more of their own equity in return for investor cash, they suggested. One overarching explanation that they landed on, though, was bias: Investors might simply treat female founders differently, "from biased responses to their pitches to discrimination in the perceived capabilities and barriers to success for female founders." Indeed, a study published in the *Harvard Business Review* in 2017 found that both female and male venture capitalists—individuals who tend to be important early investors in new companies—posed different types of questions to male and female founders. While they tended to ask men questions about the potential for gains, women were more frequently grilled on the potential for losses.

In a hypercompetitive environment, in which dozens of founders are vying for a chunk of cash to stay afloat, entrepreneurs must convince prospective investors of their start-ups' "home run" potential, the academics wrote, adding that it's not enough to simply demonstrate that they're unlikely to lose investors' money. After controlling for all other factors, the researchers concluded, this explained the funding gap between male and female founders in its entirety. And, all said, that gap was substantial: Men, according to the study, received seven times more funding than women.

In the years since this research was published, and since the research by Underwood and her colleagues was conducted, progress has been elusive. U.S. start-ups founded by women alone raised nearly 6.4 billion dollars of venture funding in 2021, representing an impressive 83 percent rise on the previous year's figure, according to data group PitchBook. But a closer look at the figures is damning. Despite that sizable jump, companies founded solely by women garnered just 2 percent of all dollars invested in venture-capitalist-backed start-ups in the United States.

\*\*\*

Just like the employees who work in organizations where misogyny thrives, the female founders who have raised money—or tried to—and have experienced their gender as a barrier are often terrified of speaking out. Word travels fast in investment communities, and being deemed a troublemaker is a certain way of ensuring that cash becomes even more challenging to come by. No cash means no business, and no business frequently means no livelihood. The irony is that it is because of this inevitable, unavoidable culture of silence that sexism and abuse have been as rampant in pitch meetings as they have in other corners of the tech industry and beyond.

Some women founders speak of relatively subtle but infuriating signs of disrespect: One mentioned a male VC partner who incessantly asked her about her husband's career in a conversation that should have centered around the potential of her business—a business in which her husband played absolutely no role. "It was framed as innocent chitchat— just small talk—but anyone with any common sense would've been able to recognize his ulterior motive," she said, speaking on the condition of anonymity. "He wanted to know if my husband was rich and smart enough to bail me out if I screwed up."

Next on the spectrum, countless women, also unwilling to be associated by name with their anecdotes, mention the family-related questions that are piled upon them in an ostensibly casual way: from the seemingly innocent "Do you have kids?" to the more probing "Do you have plans to start a family?"

"Can you imagine a male founder being asked whether he's planning on having children anytime soon?" a second female founder said. "I think on one level every investor knows that it's not appropriate, but when it comes to the decision of who should get their cash, what horse to bet on, appropriateness and even just good old-fashioned manners fly out the window."

And then there are the unwanted advances and even assaults that female founders have to endure in their impossible quest to achieve the same degree of respect and acceptance as their male counterparts. Anywhere there are female founders and VC money, there are whispered stories of women being touched inappropriately, propositioned, and maligned and insulted when a sexual advance is rebuffed.

For many, the pressure to raise capital to sustain a business becomes intolerable when overlaid with a culture of rampant misogyny. Entrepreneurialism is enshrined in the American Dream. It's a core tenet of the structures of capitalism that are supposed to have made the United States a global and timeless economic superpower. But the American way, it seems, is also to look away from painful realities when it's convenient to do so, to ignore the fact that it's often impossible for a founder to reach their professional potential if they don't happen to be of a certain gender.

"The most cynical way of looking at this is to consider the proportion of funding allocated to female founders to be a gauge of the respect that women in this world are afforded," a third female founder said in an interview. "Single digits at best, in terms of that investment allocation, and I don't see that changing anytime soon. Perhaps we need to stop thinking about the land of opportunity," she added. "The land of male opportunity—depressing as it sounds—is probably more accurate."

# CHAPTER 12

## The American Fever Dream

When an hour in the pediatrician's office is as valuable as an hour in the boardroom, that's when things truly change and no sooner than that.

—Eve Rodsky, author and activist

In a bookshop on New York City's affluent Upper West Side, the covers of children's board books do their best to capture the attention of a tiny restless customer dragged to the store by a parent now browsing in the "New Nonfiction" section. The kids' books collectively proclaim the message that you can be anything you want to be. They pay homage to Kamala Harris, Marie Curie, Sally Ride, Megan Rapinoe, and Billie Jean King. From notebooks, pins, and tote bags, Ruth Bader Ginsburg's stern face stares at the small patron. A pencil case announces that "time is on the side of change."

If the reality projected inside the bookstore reflected the reality beyond its walls, we'd be living in a feminist utopia: a true meritocracy, a world in which it's entirely unspectacular for a woman to run one of the world's biggest companies, fly into space, win a Nobel Prize, or preside over a huge economy. Thanks to the civil rights and equality laws in that meritocracy, to its gender parity in education, and to its flock of brazen trailblazers, any girl from any neighborhood in America would have the potential to change the world. She would be able to soar in the slipstream of Mae Krier and millions of Rosie the Riveters who demonstrated unequivocally that they were just as capable at propping up the labor market as men were. She would be able to follow in the footsteps of Katharine Dexter McCormick and Pauli Murray and Shirley Chisholm and Alice Paul and Muriel Siebert. She wouldn't have to endure the shame and fear that Lillian Garland suffered when she lost her job for taking a few months off to recover from a harrowing cesarean delivery of her baby girl. And she would not have to deal with being marginalized, insulted, threatened, and gaslit the way that Ann Hopkins, Lilly Ledbetter, Brooksley Born, and Ellen Pao so flagrantly were, just for doing their job.

And yet in America today, she does have to endure those indignities.

Every year, thousands of gender discrimination claims are filed, but the cases that enter the system are a mere tip of a hulking iceberg. Many women don't comprehend until years after an incident has happened that they've been the victim of discrimination, or worse. The law is like a fishing net with gaping holes: It has been cast wide, but only the biggest creatures—the most egregious offenses, from which no one could reasonably look away—get ensnared in it. Microaggressions, especially directed at women of color, are ubiquitous. Edith Cooper, a CEO, founder, and board member, wrote in a 2021 column for the *New York Times* about a conversation she'd had with a sixty-something white man in which he'd lamented that the board opportunities he had been expecting were now unlikely to materialize. "There's no chance now, for the next twenty years," she quoted him as saying. "All they want are women. Edith, you must be in great demand—as a Black woman."

Cooper went on to write that this exchange perfectly illustrates what holds women and people of color back in the workplace. On the one hand, it's the suggestion that race and gender are the necessary credentials for being appointed to a board position. But on the other hand, and even more galling, she wrote, "was his implied complaint about the injustice of it all: How can a well-respected white man with solid experience lose out to women or people of color?" As for solid experience, Cooper could have by that point legitimately boasted about a more than thirty-five-year career working in financial services, during which time she had become the first Black woman to be named partner at Goldman Sachs.

In September 2018, Lenore Blum, a distinguished professor who had helped found the Association for Women in Mathematics, resigned from her position at Carnegie Mellon University. In an interview, she explained that sexism was one of the dominant reasons she chose to quit. "Subtle biases and microaggressions pile up, few of which on their own rise to the level of 'let's take action,' but [they] are insidious nonetheless. Speak up, and you're labeled 'difficult,'" she said. Sexual harassment and sexism are two very different things, Blum acknowledged. She cautioned that while sexual harassment has rightly been a prominent topic of public conversation over the last few years, especially in the wake of the #MeToo movement, "we can't whitewash the more pervasive and no less damaging effect of sexism in the workplace—not only by individuals but enabled by systems incorporated in the workplace." One study, conducted by nonprofit Catalyst in 2022, showed that more than 60 percent of employees from marginalized racial and ethnic groups experienced being "on guard" to protect against bias due to race, ethnicity, or gender in the workplace. "The emotional tax people from marginalized racial and ethnic groups experience in the workplace is persistent, pervasive, and global," said Lorraine Hariton, president and CEO of Catalyst.

The subtlety of microaggressions is what makes them so pernicious, but also what makes their impact so hard to quantify. Even if all of history's greatest advocates for women's equality in the workplace were to join forces to try to collectively come up with a way to categorically combat microaggressions, they'd be unlikely to succeed. But in the process of conducting research for her book, *The End of Bias: A Beginning*, journalist Jessica Nordell aimed to at least shed light on the ubiquity of the problem. She partnered up with a computer science professor and a graduate student at the University at Buffalo to design and create a computer simulation of a workplace she called "NormCorp."

NormCorp is the type of company in which many Americans toil. People complete projects, sometimes alone and sometimes in pairs. If a project fails, the individual or individuals working on that project will suffer a decline in their "promotability" score. Every six months employees go through performance reviews. The highest scorers in these reviews are rewarded with a promotion to the next level of seniority.

NormCorp's workplace culture is shaped by the types of behaviors that crop up in thousands of businesses just like it, Nordell explains, and thus NormCorp employees are affected by the kinds of gender bias that are endemic in the U.S. workplace.

Because of these gender biases, if a woman is working alone on a particular project, her accomplishments—on average—are attributed slightly less value than if a man is working alone on a project. If a woman and a man are collaborating on a project, her contributions accrue less credit than his. When a woman fails at something, the consequences are slightly more serious than when a man fails. Women's potential is under-recognized and underappreciated. Women have to have chalked up more successes than men in order to be assigned to so-called "stretch" projects, for which the potential for reward is outsized. And, mirroring reality, a tiny number of women voice their discontent and speak out against the unfairness of the system. Those who do suffer consequences. They're penalized and accused of self-promoting. Just like in real life, some women leave, while those who are left behind experience even more stereotyping.

Nordell simulated ten years of life at NormCorp—every project, every promotion cycle—and learned what countless women across America had known, or at least suspected, for decades. Being female makes it tougher and more time-consuming to reach the highest echelons of a company. A woman's career path to the top is more demanding than a man's; she needs to be able to claim more successes than a man, and even when she's able to do that, it still takes longer. Writing about her research for the *New York Times*, Nordell spotlights two fictional workers at NormCorp: a woman called Jenelle and a man named William.

Jenelle joins the company in an entry-level role and progresses to executive level. It takes her seventeen performance review cycles—so, more than eight years—and she needs to be able to claim credit for more than two hundred projects. William starts at the same level as Jenelle, but he reaches executive level after eight performance review cycles, having worked on just half as many successful projects as she. Jenelle's journey to the top was likely slowed down by seemingly inconsequential, innocuous behaviors, attitudes, and decisions made by those she's working alongside and for. Her managers didn't necessarily commit a flagrant act of lawbreaking discrimination that caused her career to trail William's. Instead, she simply suffered the consequences of being a woman trying to do well in a large corporation in America.

"So, what's to be done?" Nordell asks. Many companies mandate diversity training for all employees, but frequently this proves to be no more effective than a Band-Aid. Sociologists Frank Dobbin at Harvard and Alexandra Kalev at Tel Aviv University concluded from their research that even after mandatory diversity training sessions, the likelihood of women and men of color becoming managers either stayed the same or decreased. Writing for the *Harvard Business Review*, the pair note that "while people are easily taught to respond correctly to a questionnaire about bias, they soon forget the right answers." They conclude: "The positive effects of diversity training rarely last beyond a day or two, and a number of studies suggest that it can activate bias or spark a backlash."

A more effective approach to stamping out inequity, Dobbin and Kalev's research has shown, is to abide by three principles in the workplace: engage managers in solving a particular problem, expose them to people from different groups, and encourage social accountability for change.

The engagement part, they explain, is critical, because when a person's beliefs and behaviors are out of sync, they tend to experience what psychologists describe as cognitive dissonance. This inner conflict is stressful, and much research has shown that humans have a tendency to correct it by changing either their behavior or their beliefs to achieve alignment between the two. That means that if you encourage people to act in a certain way, their opinions are more likely to begin to correspond to that behavior. One example Dobbin and Kalev cite: Ask a staunch opponent of the death penalty to write an essay defending it, and you may just get that person to change their mind or at least recognize some cracks in the soundness of their original argument.

Similarly, if you persuade a manager to advocate for women and people of color in the workplace, they might just find themselves becoming a true champion for diversity. The simple act of behaving like a diversity champion might just turn them into one: a twist on the classic adage of "fake it till you make it."

To explain the second principle—exposure to people from different groups—they cite an example from World War II. The U.S. Army was segregated: Individuals had to be white to serve in a combat role. As casualties rose, General Dwight Eisenhower appealed for Black volunteers for combat duty. Samuel Stouffer, a Harvard sociologist, later surveyed troops on their racial attitudes and found that white men whose companies had been joined by Black platoons were less racist and more willing to work in desegregated companies than those whose units had remained segregated. White soldiers who were working alongside Black soldiers, Stouffer explained, were more likely to recognize what they had in common than what differentiated them. They were more likely to think of themselves as working toward a common goal as equals. In workplaces, "working side-by-side breaks down stereotypes, which leads to more equitable hiring and promotion," Dobbin and Kalev write.

The final principle is social accountability. To explain this, the pair draws on an experiment conducted in Israel during which trainee teachers were tasked with grading identical compositions attributed to Jewish students with either Ashkenazic names—names of Central or Eastern European heritage—or Sephardic names—names of Iberian, African, or Asian heritage. Sephardic students in Israel generally tend to come from lower-income families and perform worse in school. In the experiment, teacher trainees gave the Ashkenazic essays an average of a B grade and the Sephardic essays an average of grade D. But when the trainees were told that they would have to discuss the grades with their peers, the grade difference between the two groups vanished. The prospect of having to explain and defend their decisions encouraged the trainees to assess the work purely by the quality of the composition and on its merit, not by the name of the student who supposedly did the work.

This is the rationale behind pay transparency legislation and gender-pay-gap reporting mandates: an ethos of what gets measured gets done, and that accountability fuels change. In many cases, it's too early to say whether these efforts are paying off in a notable way, and surely there are loopholes and shortcomings that the laws and policies aren't addressing—bonuses, for example, aren't taken into account in many gender-pay-gap reporting laws—but they are, of course, a step in the right direction, a step toward eradicating the mostly invisible organizational tics that can make work so frustrating for people who are not male and not white.

\*\*\*

By the time someone like Janelle reaches the level of executive at a company like NormCorp, she might have become accustomed to some of the barriers that she has to confront in order to be seen, heard, recognized, and rewarded. But there's one barrier that will likely catch her off guard, no matter how much grit and resilience she thinks she's accumulated throughout her career.

It might start with a hot flash. Janelle might notice a subtle change in her mood and energy level. She might start finding it tougher to concentrate on tasks she previously sailed through effortlessly. Soon she'll acknowledge that she's probably joined the 25 percent of the U.S. workforce who are generating a significant economic impact but who are also menopause-age women.

In addition to hot flashes and night sweats, menopause—which begins when a woman has gone twelve months without a menstrual period—can lead to loss of sleep, erratic moods, and a reduced ability to concentrate. Some women experience only mild or no issues at all, but for others the symptoms can be debilitating and interfere with every part of their life. A research paper based on a survey of over four thousand menopause-age women and published in 2022 estimated that over 60 percent of them believe that menopause symptoms significantly impact their work performance. Some admit to menopause being the reason they abandon their careers altogether. It's a reality that's not being addressed, a fact that is, for the most part, being entirely glossed over in the workforce.

Writing for *Fast Company* in 2022, Terry Weber, the CEO of healthcare company Biote, notes that despite the huge chunk of the labor force struggling with menopause symptoms at any given time, few companies have established guidelines or protocols on how to support those affected.

"As a female CEO in male-dominated industries for most of my career, I can almost see the eye-rolling," she writes. "How can this be a severe issue"—she quotes her male counterparts as wondering—"when you've never heard anyone say menopause was their reason for ending employment?" Huge numbers of women don't talk about it, she elaborates, because when women do seek medical care, they are often misdiagnosed or told to "wait it out." Neither of those options helps someone manage distracting symptoms in the workplace. She adds that an "alarming number of health care providers are uncomfortable treating menopause or [are] unfamiliar with the variety of symptoms that hormonal imbalances can cause." The majority of medical schools and residency programs in the United States don't teach physicians in training about menopause. One relatively small study led by academics at Johns Hopkins found that fewer than one in five medical students receive formal training in menopause medicine.

Women aged fifty-five and older represent the single fastest-growing segment of the American labor force. Many of the pioneers of women's economic rights are now aging into that demographic bracket. According to one estimate, in the decade to the end of 2026, that group alone is expected to have accounted for more than a third of all workers entering the labor market: about 3.6 million individuals. The age at which women tend to enter menopause—about forty-five to fifty-five—is typically also the age at which women have gained enough professional and life experience to enter the most senior and lucrative jobs in the labor market. The economic firepower of these people—if they're afforded the opportunity and support to reach their full professional potential—would be enormous. But in many ways, the parameters of the workday don't allow for this to happen. Menopausal women would benefit from being able to work flexibly or part-time—for example, job sharing—so that they can fulfill their professional potential and ambition while also responding to their own health and well-being needs. These types of arrangements are still too rarely available, and, if they are available, women can be disparaged or discredited for taking advantage of them. In short, our economy is failing menopausal women.

Of course, if a woman is being discriminated against or harassed at work because she is menopausal—or because she is menstruating, for that matter—she is technically protected under federal and state employment laws. But as always, proving that certain behaviors or actions constitute discrimination can be extremely difficult. Separately, the social stigma surrounding menopause means that many women who are experiencing it will go to great lengths not to draw attention to their own personal challenges. Filing a lawsuit may well be a surefire way of achieving precisely the opposite.

\*\*\*

And then there are the forces keeping women from having access to money and from having power over their own lives and careers that don't exist despite the law; they exist because of it.

On June 24, 2022, the Supreme Court of the United States overturned its 1973 *Roe v. Wade* decision, eliminating the constitutional right to abortion and immediately leading to outright bans on ending pregnancies in about half of the country's states. The court also reversed *Planned Parenthood v. Casey*, a decision from 1992 that reaffirmed *Roe*. The three Supreme Court Justices who had been appointed by Donald Trump during his presidency helped form the majority in the six-to-three ruling, which led the anti-choice movement to erupt into a days-long celebration. "I think it's a miracle," Representative Marjorie Taylor Greene of Georgia said in a video recording of her standing in front of the Supreme Court. "I'm so thrilled. I've cried about this. We've prayed about this. Everybody here is celebrating." The three liberal justices who dissented—Stephen Breyer, Sonia Sotomayor, and Elena Kagan—wrote of the ruling that it "eliminates a fifty-year-old constitutional right that safeguards women's freedom and equal station" and "places in jeopardy other rights, from contraception to same-sex intimacy and marriage." Finally, they said, it undermines the Supreme Court's legitimacy. "With sorrow—for this Court, but more, for the many millions of American women who have today lost a fundamental constitutional protection— we dissent," they wrote.

The launch of the contraceptive pill in 1960 and the *Roe* decision of 1973 were unequivocally two of the most consequential developments for female economic empowerment in the twentieth century, and economists were quick to point out that the overturn of *Roe* would no doubt reverse that empowerment, at least to a degree.

Stanford economist Luigi Pistaferri explained in an interview shortly after the decision that, while the legalization of abortion that took place across the United States during the 1970s, culminating in the 1973 decision, led to an approximately 5 percent reduction in the aggregate birth rate, the reversal of *Roe* would be unlikely to increase the birthrate by as much. Primarily, that's because of the availability of new medical technologies, abortion medication, and birth control methods like IUDs. Nonetheless, he noted that he did expect the overturn to result in an increase in the proportion of women who are single mothers. "Being a single mother is a strong predictor of ending up poor," he explained, adding that children born in one-parent households are more likely to perform poorly in school and have greater odds of poor adult outcomes. He noted that, more broadly, women with either intended or unintended children tend to experience less favorable wage outcomes than those without—the "motherhood penalty," as it's frequently described—which, he said, "may weaken their 'bargaining' position within a marriage or cohabiting relationship, increasing intra-household inequality."

Wage inequality, Pistaferri added, is likely to increase for all women and within individual states the disparities between low- and high-income women. "How large these effects are going to be, it is hard to say—but while one may be uncertain about the magnitude, it is easier to predict the direction of the changes," he said.

Alicia Sasser Modestino, associate professor of public policy and urban affairs and economics at Northeastern University, described the Supreme Court's decision as an "unfunded mandate," a mandate that requires citizens to do something—in this case, not terminate their pregnancies—without providing any financial support that would enable them to do that. "We have no paid maternity leave. We lack any formal paid leave, and so 80 percent of workers don't even have paid formal leave through their employer," she said in an interview. "We know that childcare costs, on average, 15,000 dollars a year for an infant at this point, and that assumes that you can find childcare."

Perhaps the most compelling argument for the dire economic consequences of overturning *Roe v. Wade*, however, came in the form of an amicus brief filed by 150 researchers and economists in September 2021, well before the decision was made to abandon *Roe*. "Abortion remains a critical component of women's reproductive healthcare and decision-making," the authors of the brief wrote. "For significant segments of the population, reliable and affordable contraception remains out of reach. And for many women, affordable childcare is as illusory as employment policies that accommodate working parents."

They noted that, even though women experience unintended pregnancies and seek abortions at varying stages of life, one common thread is that many women who are seeking abortions are already facing difficult financial circumstances. They cited research showing that almost half of all women in the United States who seek an abortion are poor, three-quarters are low income, 59 percent already have children, and 55 percent recently endured a disruptive life event such as the death of a close friend or family member, the loss of a job, the termination of a relationship with a partner, or overdue rent or mortgage obligations. They concluded that if *Roe* were to be overturned, women of every demographic group would be affected, but reduced abortion access would have the greatest effect on young women and women of color. In the first year alone, they predicted, over one hundred thousand women seeking to end a pregnancy would likely be unable to reach an abortion provider.

In the most tragic cases, the inability to access an abortion provider could lead—and, indeed, is leading—to death. In October 2012, Savita Halappanavar, a thirty-one-year-old Indian-born dentist, died in the Irish city of Galway after doctors refused to offer her an abortion that could have saved her life. Medical staff cited the country's strict antiabortion laws for their decision, even though an official report subsequently concluded that there had been no chance of the baby surviving: A miscarriage had been inevitable. Halappanavar's death sent shock waves through the traditionally conservative and predominantly Roman Catholic country and ignited a pro-choice movement that culminated in a 2018 referendum that legalized the ending of pregnancies. In the United States in the wake of the 2022 decision to overturn *Roe*, many women have come forward with accounts of how they almost died because they had to struggle to get swift access to an abortion that was necessary to save their life.

\*\*\*

Many proponents of *Roe v. Wade*, including the authors of the amicus brief and Alicia Sasser Modestino of Northeastern University, point to America's childcare crisis as one of the principal reasons a woman's right to choose should be irrevocably enshrined in law. It is a crisis that's raging across all fifty states—an epidemic that's paralyzed some regional economies entirely—and yet there's no palpable sign of a real remedy.

To understand the root cause of the crisis, one must appreciate America's historical attitude toward childcare itself. As journalist Alisha Haridasani Gupta writes in the *New York Times*, unlike every other developed country in the world, the United States has never, apart from during World War II, treated childcare as an essential service. The most obvious illustration of this: In December 1971, President Richard Nixon vetoed a bipartisan effort to establish a national system of comprehensive child development and day care. The proposal, he said, was characterized by "fiscal irresponsibility, administrative unworkability, and family weakening implications," adding, "Neither the immediate need nor the desirability of a national child development program of this character has been demonstrated."

Gupta notes that these foundational American attitudes toward childcare—that it's not a matter for the government, but rather a personal matter, a mother's matter—led to the springing up of "a fragmented and sprawling patchwork of day-care options, essentially small businesses, that are simultaneously expensive for parents [. . .] and yet persistently low-paying for their predominantly female workers." At the time of her writing, the median hourly wage for childcare workers was just over eleven dollars.

These two factors mean that the entire U.S. childcare system is constantly precariously balanced on the precipice of failure. A significant proportion of childcare centers benefit from public funding, but the vast majority of cash comes from tuition fees. Government subsidies are generally only available to families in the lowest income brackets. And although public schools receive funding from the government for every student who is enrolled, Gupta points out that day-care centers only receive government support when a child is in attendance. If a child is out sick, for example, that income is lost.

The crisis in childcare was already harrowing before COVID-19, but the pandemic brought the system to the brink of collapse. In August 2020, the Center for American Progress published a report based on data on infant and toddler childcare availability in nineteen states and the District of Columbia, a sample that, in total, represented close to 40 percent of the U.S. population.

The report found that there were more than four children under the age of three per licensed childcare slot: enough licensed childcare to serve less than a quarter of infants and toddlers. The Center for American Progress uses the term "childcare deserts" to describe places where there are three or more children for each licensed childcare slot.

According to this definition, more than 80 percent of the counties in this study would be classified as an infant and toddler childcare desert.

In households with young children and two adults, the burden of care for infants or toddlers usually falls on the adult who brings in a smaller proportion of total income. Because of the gender pay gap, women—if earning money outside the home—frequently give up opportunities in the labor market if and when a childcare crunch occurs. It's the financially rational decision, and it's also the reason female labor force participation seems to have hit a ceiling and why the gender pay gap just won't go away.

What makes the reality of the childcare crisis in America particularly crushing is that plenty of international examples illustrate that it doesn't have to be this way. Sweden, for example, offers parents 480 days of paid parental leave per child that two parents are entitled to share. Each parent can transfer part of their leave to the other, but ninety days have to be reserved specifically for each parent. From 2008 until 2017, as an incentive for fathers to take more time off, families were entitled to a monetary bonus determined by the number of days divided equally between parents. The policy seems to be working: One study in 2019 showed that approximately 90 percent of eligible Swedish fathers claim paternity leave and that, on average, they take 96 percent of the total amount of leave time allotted to them. Sweden is also a leader among advanced economies in terms of female labor market participation, according to the Organization for Economic Co-operation and Development (OECD). In 2021, its rate was at 80 percent compared to just 68 percent in the United States.

Women in the United States make up the majority—almost two-thirds—of part-time workers. Mothers with a child younger than six are more likely to work part-time than mothers of older children. But fathers, regardless of how old their children are, are less likely than mothers to be in part-time work. In other words, because of the systems, beliefs, and biases ingrained in the way we work and live, mothers are still much more likely than fathers to step in when alternative childcare is inaccessible, unaffordable, or just unreliable.

In 2018, researchers from the Federal Reserve Bank of San Francisco set out to understand why labor force participation among U.S. men and women aged between twenty-four and fifty-four had been declining over the preceding twenty years, and they looked to Canada—where the participation rate over the same period had been rising—for answers.

They established that three-quarters of the difference between the two countries could be attributed to the growing gap in labor force attachment of women. "A key factor is the extensive parental leave policies in Canada," they wrote. Generous parental leave policies are one way of markedly easing pressure on a country's childcare system. Canadian parents get thirty-five weeks of shared paid benefits, paid at 55 percent of regular pay, in addition to which fathers get five exclusive weeks of leave. The United States, meanwhile, is famously the only rich nation in the world that doesn't guarantee maternity leave. "If the United States could reverse the trend in participation of prime-age women to match Canada," the researchers from the Federal Reserve Bank of San Francisco concluded, "it would see five million additional prime-age workers join the labor force."

*\*\**

The American Dream, the guiding principle that has enticed so many women and minorities to "go for it," to "lean in," and to grasp with both hands for the highest rung on the ladder, may just be the most elaborate myth of our time. In reality, there are certain dogged characteristics of American culture and society that shackle an individual's potential, that keep a woman's earning power in check, and, in most cases, there's very little we can do about it.

Over the last eighty years, the country's collective attitude toward the professional responsibilities, the societal roles, and the rights of women has oscillated. During the Second World War, we had no choice but to welcome women into the paid labor market. If we hadn't, the economy would have faltered, and the war could have been lost. During the 1960s, the Civil Rights Movement became a springboard for feminism and for legislation designed to afford women the same standing as men in work and society. But in later decades, the limits of the law as a mechanism for enshrining gender equality have become increasingly apparent. It sometimes seems that we're applauding female economic empowerment one day and bemoaning it the next, celebrating a woman's career progress in one breath and questioning whether her professional ambition might be curtailing her ability to be a good mother the next.

From the way in which female corporate executives are scrutinized by the media, to the way in which women bear the brunt of responsibility when childcare facilities aren't available, there's evidence everywhere that gender inequality is rife. The majority of mothers who work outside the home face a second shift of unpaid housework and caregiving after their day of earning money in the paid labor market ends. When paid work, household labor, and childcare are combined, working mothers spend more time working than fathers, though fathers—across the board—earn more.

This inequality in unpaid care work, as one paper by the OECD puts it, is the missing link that influences gender gaps in labor outcomes. "Every minute more that a woman spends on unpaid care work," the paper asserts, "represents one minute less that she could be potentially spending on market-related activities or investing in her educational and vocational skills." Perhaps because it's still so frequently the domain of women, the societal and economic importance of unpaid labor is critically downplayed. Not a single widely used measure of a country's or community's economic value or productivity even attempts to account for the worth of unpaid labor. In 2021, Bank of America tried to put a number on the unpaid global labor market, estimating that 16.4 billion hours are spent by men and women on unpaid care work every day. At minimum wage levels, that would amount to 9 percent of global gross domestic product, or 11 trillion dollars per year, the bank found, and it calculated that women perform about three-quarters of all unpaid care work of the total hours provided.

In January 2020, author, activist, researcher, and Harvard Law graduate Eve Rodsky spoke on a panel at the World Economic Forum in Davos, Switzerland. Because of unpaid labor, she cautioned, America was "one crisis away from losing thirty to forty years of women's economic participation in the workforce." The scenario she foreshadowed came to pass, exposing the tragedy that the progress toward gender inequality that we'd achieved by that point was so fragile. As Rodsky, along with billions of other people around the world, experienced and observed the effects of the pandemic, her resolve to change our collective attitude toward unpaid labor and, by extension, toward the economic value of women, hardened.

Two years into the pandemic, in April 2022, she launched "Unpaid Work in the GDP by 2030," a campaign aimed at getting this often-invisible labor recognized in national statistics. "What I realized," Rodsky explains, "is that there's a fundamental assumption that organizes how economists do their work that is actually sexist, and that assumption is that people can optimize their time." Women simply can't. In every country around the world, they are forced—to a greater or lesser extent—to be the social security net that supports a functioning society. The idea that time choice exists for women and particularly for mothers is a myth, Rodsky, who was raised by a single mom, says. "As a society, we still view the time that a man has in the day as protected, finite, and precious—as precious as diamonds," she explains. "A woman's time is infinite and unprotected. She's always available to pick up childcare, do a chore, deal with a problem, or give herself to other unpaid labor. No meaningful progress is going to be made toward gender equality until women's time is also viewed as diamonds." Of course there are exceptions, cases where a father is a primary caregiver or in which he might not work in the paid labor market at all. And there are cases in which, in a heterosexual couple, parents split childcare duties completely equally. The data, however, provides evidence that a clear default still remains.

Evidence of the disparity between how we value men's time and how we value women's time was provided in 2009 in the findings of a study conducted by Asaf Levanon, Paula England, and Paul Allison and published in the journal *Social Forces*. Using U.S. Census data from 1950 to 2000, the academics found that, when controlling for education, work experience, skills, race, and geography, industries dominated by women on average paid less than those dominated by men. But when women moved into a particular sector in large numbers, the research found, jobs in that field started to pay less even when controlling for all those factors.

As a result of the systemic inequity that has shaped our society for centuries, women have internalized a belief that their time is worth less than a man's. "Women have started telling themselves that they do the housework and childcare because their husband makes more money, or because they're better at multitasking than their husband, or because it's just more efficient and that, in the time it would take to explain to their husband what needs to be done, they might as well just do it themselves. So many women I speak to tell me that being available all the time has become part of their identity," Rodsky says. "But this is crazy, and it's depriving women of time-choice," she adds. "When we lose time-choice, we lose freedom, and when we lose freedom, we lose power."

## CHAPTER 13

*Hope, or Something Like It*

It's perhaps hard to speak of outright hope amid everything that's going on, but I definitely think there are reasons to be optimistic.

—Ashley All, reproductive rights advocate

On Sunday, May 31, 2009, George Tiller was murdered by a single bullet to the head. Tiller had been standing in the foyer of his local church—Wichita's Reformation Lutheran Church in Kansas—handing out the church bulletin. He was sixty-seven years old and a grandfather of ten.

Tiller was also a doctor, one of only a handful of physicians in the country who performed late-stage abortions. This had earned him the moniker "Saint George" in some reproductive rights advocacy circles. His motto had been "Trust women," and his commitment to providing care had remained steadfast even after his clinic was firebombed and he'd been shot at several times.

The man who fired the gun that eventually killed him was Scott Roeder, an antiabortion extremist. Roeder was convicted of first-degree murder in 2010 and sentenced to life in prison with a "hard fifty"—no chance of parole for fifty years.

Tiller had been in the crosshairs of protestors for decades. In July and August of 1991—a period that would become known as the "Summer of Mercy"—antiabortion activists had thronged clinics in Wichita as part of a national campaign by the antiabortion movement to shut down what they described as the "baby-killing industry." Kansas at the time had no restrictions on abortion, and the movement's ire was directed at three clinics, but mostly at George Tiller's.

Protestors blocked his clinic's gates while, nearby, leaders of what was called "Operation Rescue" orated passionately to crowds, distributed pamphlets and bumper stickers, and did their utmost to recruit locals not only to join their ranks, but also to run for office. Over the course of six weeks, thousands were arrested, but the activists persevered, and political strategists began to use the "Summer of Mercy" as a rallying cry for conservative Christians across the state to get involved in politics. The result was that Republicans established a sixty-six-seat majority in the House and a ten-seat majority in the Senate, enabling them to strengthen antiabortion legislation considerably, for example, by changing the definition of fetal viability to earlier in the pregnancy.

As reporters for the *Kansas City Star* put it, "the 46-day Summer of Mercy campaign had pushed abortion opponents out of the pews, into the streets, then into the political arena. And in the process, it became a catalyst for antiabortion activism in Kansas." Over the course of a few years, the state went from having some of the most liberal laws on abortion to some of the most restrictive nationwide. By the mid-1990s, Kansas was an anti-choice stronghold. In August 1993, an extremist named Shelley Shannon attempted to kill George Tiller by firing six shots at him as he left his clinic in his car. The bullets hit both of his arms, but he was back at work the next day.

Antiabortion extremists spent fifteen years trying to finish the job Shannon started. Activists in the movement spent decades fighting to ban abortion procedures through legislative and legal means. But in 2019, in a legal battle resulting from an abortion restriction, Kansas's highest court ruled that access to abortion is a protected matter of bodily autonomy under the state constitution. This set off a firestorm in Republican political circles and calls for changes to the Kansas Bill of Rights. By January 2021, hard-right lawmakers in the legislature had passed an amendment to strip the right to abortion from the constitution. They planned to put it before the voters of Kansas in August 2022.

"We were in a social protest movement that was geared to create political firepower that resulted in abortion being illegal in Kansas," Randall Terry, who's credited with founding Operation Rescue, said shortly before that vote, reflecting on what happened in 1991. "And we're almost on the cusp of that dream being fulfilled."

Ashley All had other plans. The sixth-generation Kansan and mother of five had grown up close to where George Tiller had operated his clinic and not far from the church where he was murdered. Issues around reproductive health and the divisive impact that abortion had on local communities were always "in the ether," she recalls. They weren't something she paid conscious attention to, but she was always aware of them.

After attending the University of Kansas, she spent two decades working in politics and public policy in her home state. She served as communications director for the Kansas Attorney General and then worked for Governor Laura Kelly.

One of the first campaigns All worked on was a 2006 campaign against the former attorney general, Phill Kline, an antiabortionist who had crusaded viciously against Tiller and other care providers. Kline had gained national prominence for subpoenaing women's medical records. The campaign All helped run against Kline didn't once mention the word "abortion," but it emphasized every citizen's right to medical privacy, Kline's attempts to obtain medical records, and the risks associated with that right being violated. Kline lost.

In January 2022, All became director of communications for a bipartisan coalition of reproductive rights advocates, Kansans for Constitutional Freedom. That meant she became the public face of the pro-choice effort to block the antiabortion amendment. Along with her colleagues, she took on much of the responsibility of spearheading the effort to persuade Kansans to vote no on the constitutional amendment that Randall Terry and others had hoped would cement the state's status as a stronghold of America's antiabortion movement.

The task at hand was daunting. In a deeply red state, her team had to craft a campaign message and strategy that would make it clear that abortion didn't have to be a partisan issue. They argued that Kansans deserved the right to make their own private medical decisions free from government interference. And that the antiabortion amendment would "mandate government control over our private medical decisions and pave the way for a total ban on abortion," she says.

Just forty days before the August vote, the U.S. Supreme Court overturned *Roe v. Wade*, making Kansas the first state in the nation to vote on abortion rights following the fall of *Roe*. A draft of that Supreme Court opinion had leaked in May. The stakes of the vote were higher than ever. Pro-choice advocates in Kansas worked tirelessly to persuade and turn out voters. All was overwhelmed by national media requests and attention.

She remembers that she wasn't initially sure whether to bring her three young daughters—at the time aged between seven and twelve—to the watch party on election night. Despite her eight-month crusade to secure abortion access for Kansans, the potential for crushing disappointment was considerable. But in the end, she decided they had to be there. History would be written either way that night, and if the worst came to pass, the girls could distract themselves with television and snacks in the hotel room.

As it turned out, that wasn't necessary. Shortly after 10:30 P.M., the race was called: 59 percent of voters had rejected the amendment—a sizable margin and a stinging defeat for the antiabortion movement that had been emboldened by the Supreme Court's June opinion.

Media outlets from around the world marveled at the fact that conservative Kansas—a state in which registered Republicans at the time outnumbered Democrats by a ratio of almost two-to-one—had mastered a, at one time unthinkable, U-turn. "This vote makes clear what we know: The majority of Americans agree that women should have access to abortion and should have the right to make their own healthcare decisions," Joe Biden said in a statement. Kansans for Constitutional Freedom called the victory "huge and decisive."

One of the most striking images featured in local network coverage that night was that of All embracing one of her daughters; the young girl's arms and legs are flung around her mother. For All, this was as much a personal victory as it was a professional one. When the Supreme Court decision that led to the overturning of *Roe* had leaked in May, All had not been able to stop thinking about the prospect of her children having fewer constitutional rights growing up than she did. So, when the decision officially came down in June, it triggered a relentless determination in her to do whatever it took to protect her children's rights and personal freedoms, including the right to abortion access. "They might move away, but they're going to grow up in Kansas, and they need to have the right to make decisions for themselves about their bodies, about what their future holds," she said in an interview with *Rolling Stone* magazine. "And they, as women, deserve to have equal rights just like everyone else."

About nine months after the Kansas vote, the glow of victory is still evident when Ashley All talks about the campaign that made her something of a local celebrity—a local hero, in some circles—and that changed the course of Kansas history. Abortion access is not only a basic human right, she says, but also a critical determinant of a woman's economic independence and power to make her own, autonomous, personal, and professional life choices. Of course, what happened in Kansas doesn't diminish the tragedy of the fall of *Roe*, but it does inspire a semblance of hope that trajectories can change, she says, even in places where political ideologies seem entrenched and uncompromisable.

"Kansas and everything that's happened here is complicated," All says in an interview. She is careful in responding to the narrative peddled by some that if reproductive rights can be protected in Kansas, they can be protected anywhere. "It's certainly not that simple. It's much more nuanced than that," she asserts. But she does think that what she helped achieve can contribute to galvanizing the movement to making this country a better place and can refuel the sometimes tired and ineffectual efforts to achieve gender equality. "It's perhaps hard to speak of outright hope amid everything that's going on, but I definitely think there are reasons to be optimistic."

\*\*\*

In May 2023, in another sign that reproductive rights are not vanishing altogether, external advisors to the Food and Drug Administration unanimously endorsed making a birth control pill available without a prescription. The recommendation to offer a medication called Opill over-the-counter (OTC) overrode concerns raised by the FDA about whether it would and could be used in a safe and effective manner without the direct oversight of a physician. "I think this represents a landmark in our history of women's health," Margery Gass, a member of the advisory committee and an emerita professor at the University of Cincinnati College of Medicine, said, according to the *Washington Post*, after the seventeen-to-zero vote.

Other commentators noted that if the FDA were to go ahead and approve sales of the pill without a prescription—which it did a few months later—it would significantly expand access to contraception for some of the most medically underserved communities: low-income individuals, people of color, immigrants, and those living in rural communities who might be unable to see a doctor because of the cost and logistical challenges associated with travel. "I think Opill has the potential to have a huge positive public health impact," one advisory committee member, Kathryn Curtis, a health scientist with the Centers for Disease Control and Prevention's division of reproductive health, was quoted as saying in the *New York Times*.

America has been a laggard on reproductive healthcare, but this could be a sign that it's tentatively readying itself to catch up with the rest of the Western world. According to research done by the campaign Free the Pill in 2023, OTC medical contraceptives were at the time already available in over one hundred countries, predominantly in Latin America, Africa, and across Europe. One 2011 survey of a nationally representative sample of more than two thousand U.S. women between the ages of eighteen and forty-four found that 62 percent of respondents said they were "strongly or somewhat in favor" of oral contraceptives being made available OTC.

There's other evidence that a groundswell of support for reproductive rights is becoming harder to ignore and will eventually impact the economies of individual states and their ability to attract labor and talent. In the spring of 2023, the Institute for Women's Policy Research (IWPR) commissioned a poll that found that about three-quarters of young people in the Northeast of the United States—the demographic that's most likely to pursue a college education outside their home state—said that they did not want to attend college in a state in which abortion is restricted. A similar proportion of the parents polled said they'd prefer their child to attend school in a state without restrictions.

"Abortion bans are affecting where students feel comfortable living and learning," said Daisy Chin-Lor, president and chief executive of IWPR. "They do not want to go to states that restrict their reproductive health choices, and their parents do not want to support states that limit women's freedom. This dynamic has serious implications for colleges and universities, particularly those in abortion ban states that traditionally have a lot of out-of-state students."

Previous research done by the Center on the Economics of Reproductive Health—which is part of the IWPR—found that abortion bans and targeted restrictions on abortion providers cost state and local economies 105 billion dollars annually, because they reduce labor force participation and earnings among women. Any move toward reproductive rights and freedoms—like the Kansas decision or an approval to offer the contraceptive pill without a prescription—is also a move toward female economic empowerment.

*** 

Decisive progress toward gender equality—in any guise—depends on a mix of factors. Legal rights, such as reproductive rights, are indispensable, but so are the more abstract dynamics, those discussed in this book, that can't as easily be measured: those related to culture.

In late 2022, a survey of more than 14,000 individuals around the world showed that trust in women leaders had fallen markedly over the last year. Across the G-7 nations, which include Canada, France, Germany, Italy, Japan, the United Kingdom, and the United States, fewer than half of respondents—47 percent—said that they were "'very comfortable" having a woman as CEO of a major company in their country, down from 54 percent a year earlier. Men were significantly more likely than women to be critical of a female leader, and one in ten respondents said that they would explicitly not be comfortable with a female CEO. When asked about female political leaders, responses followed a similar pattern: just 45 percent of those questioned in the G-7 said that they were "very comfortable" with a woman at the head of their government, down from 52 percent in 2021.

Explanations for diminishing trust in female CEOs vary, but many follow common themes. Some experts argue that institutional misogyny and distrust on account of gender has been supercharged by both the political landscape and the pandemic. "If you're going to have a national conversation about whether women should even be allowed to take control of their own healthcare, then what do you expect?" said Michelle Harrison, global CEO of Kantar Public, the company that gathered the data, referring to the recent *Roe* decision.

Another piece of the puzzle relates to women leaving the paid labor market and picking up the bulk of childcare and other domestic chores during the COVID-19 pandemic. This likely resulted in a "hardening of old traditional assumptions" about the role of women at work and in the home, Danna Greenberg, a professor of organizational behavior at Babson College in Massachusetts, said in an interview. And then there's the fact that during times of uncertainty—be that political, economic, social, or other—humans have a natural tendency to seek out the familiar. Greenberg was speaking at the end of 2022. The war in Ukraine was raging, and the U.S. economy—along with other major economies around the world—was teetering on the brink of an economic recession. "Recessions generally equate to periods of fear," Greenberg said. "Fear ignites us to move toward what we've traditionally been taught is safe and secure," she added. "And when it comes to leadership, that, unfortunately, still means men being in charge."

In addition, more women than ever before are now in corporate and political leadership positions and the share of women who earn as much as—or significantly more than—their husbands has roughly

tripled over the past fifty years. That departure from the status quo—
a status quo in which men always called the shots—has triggered
something.

Perhaps the best way to understand the inherent distrust of women
is through the lens of the gender authority gap: the mother of all gender
gaps, as Mary Ann Sieghart, author of a book called *The Authority Gap*,
describes it. In that book, Sieghart tells the story of how, some years
earlier, she was sitting next to a banker at a dinner when he turned to
her and asked her what she did for a living. She reeled off a list of her
professional achievements, which included working as a political col-
umnist chairing a think tank, sitting on several boards, and producing
some radio shows. "Wow," he countered when she'd finished, "you're a
busy little girl." Sieghart, at the time, was fifty years old.

It was a prime example of a microaggression in the wild—
one of those insidious, evil little phrases or comments that's easily
overlooked—but it's more than that, too. It's an example of one of the
countless ways in which "women are belittled, undermined, questioned, mocked, talked over, and generally not taken seriously in public
and professional life," journalist Stephanie Merritt wrote in her review
of Sieghart's book, adding that one of the most depressing things about
the authority gap is that, just as Michelle Harrison of Kantar Public
observed, "women can be just as guilty" of perpetuating it as men. "It
is ingrained from what we see modeled to us in our own families and
the prevailing culture from childhood."

Evidence of the authority gap is everywhere. Referencing data
collected by an app called Woman Interrupted, which detects when a
female voice is interrupted by a male voice, women are interrupted 1.43
times a minute in the United States and about 1.67 times a minute in the
United Kingdom. In Nigeria and Pakistan, that number rises to a shocking 6.66 times and 7.22 times respectively. Sieghart draws on research
conducted in Australia by academics from the United Kingdom and the
United States that discredits the popular narrative that women are less
likely than men to ask for a pay raise. Women are actually just as likely,

the research found, but they are less successful at getting a pay raise or promotion because they, unlike men, are rewarded—consciously or unconsciously—for being likable and are punished for being assertive or confident.

Sieghart cites studies showing that a female applicant is 30 percent less likely to be offered a job interview than an equally qualified man, and that male students generally rate other male students as smarter than female ones, even if the women are better-performing. Other research she references shows that men are four times more likely to read a book by a man than by a woman, while women read books by both women and men roughly equally, and that a man who's hiring an employee is five times more likely to say that he does not want to work with a woman who tries to negotiate on pay than with a man who tries.

Sieghart also tells the story of the late Stanford neuroscientist Ben Barres, who, in the 1990s, transitioned from female to male. Barres was in his mid-forties at the time and was dumbstruck by the changes in his professional life that occurred after he transitioned. He was considered more credible, and his ideas were consistently taken more seriously. He described in amazement the unfamiliar experience of being able to utter an entire sentence without being interrupted by a man. And then there was a colleague who hadn't known that Barres was transgender and went so far as to praise his work as much better than his sister's.

Individually, each of these facts is depressing, but taken together, they paint a profoundly tragic picture of the extent to which we, as a human race, have stagnated; the extent to which we've allowed our development to be curtailed by systemic bias, antiquated cultural stereotypes, and a pernicious internalized myth that there is a "weaker" sex.

Under the reigning system of capitalism, credibility and trust are the basic building blocks of personal success. That success is what leads to money and wealth, which is necessary for being able to enjoy the opportunity of choice and—ultimately—freedom. Even in the United States, one of the most developed countries on the planet, women widely have an image and credibility problem that is so entrenched that it is hard to imagine it ever being fixed.

But here, too, it doesn't have to be this way. The more we cast a light on the trust problem and the authority gap, the more likely it is that we'll be able to alter the bleak trajectory of the past few years. And this awareness-raising can take on any number of forms. Ashley All of Kansas talks about being careful not to frame issues as an "us versus them" story, which might serve to entrench certain views that people have. It might serve to make people who doubt the existence of gender gaps even more determined to think of them as bogus, for example. Instead, we should tap into common values. In other words, we should focus on ways in which treating all genders equally and calling out injustice can benefit everyone in any number of ways.

In the spring of 2023, investment bank Goldman Sachs announced, in a joint statement with lawyers acting on behalf of 2,800 plaintiffs, that it was paying 215 million dollars to end a years-long class-action lawsuit accusing it of systemically underpaying women. The settlement deal, it explained, covered associates and vice presidents employed in the bank's investment banking, investment management, and securities divisions. A trial had been scheduled to kick off the following month. The suit had garnered a huge amount of attention on account of the number of women involved. Originally, it was filed in 2010 by three former employees, but it was granted class-action status in 2018.

One of the named plaintiffs, Allison Gamba, expressed satisfaction at the outcome. "My goal in this case has always been to support strong women on Wall Street. I am proud that the result we achieved here will advance gender equity," she said. Another, Shanna Orlich, shared her sentiment: "As one of the original plaintiffs, I have been proud to support this case without hesitation over the last nearly thirteen years and believe this settlement will help the women I had in mind when I filed the case."

But outside commentators weren't convinced that this necessarily constituted justice. The New York Times pointed out that the individual payout amount itself was lower than the top-line figure might suggest.

Subtracting legal fees, it reported, it equated to about 47,000 dollars per plaintiff. Goldman at the time, for context, had an approximate market capitalization of about 108 billion dollars. Its CEO, David Solomon, had during the previous year pocketed pay of about 25 million dollars.

Yes, this might be framed as a large powerful institution using its financial and legal resources and prowess to make problems go away. And there are good arguments to be made that the amount was inadequate. Nonetheless, a large headline-grabbing settlement can be a terrible look, a reputational wrecking ball, and an inconvenience that no bank would willingly risk having to navigate.

Just one day after news of the Goldman settlement came out, a jury in New York City determined that former president Donald Trump must pay five million dollars in damages for sexually abusing magazine writer E. Jean Carroll back in the 1990s, defaming her by calling her a liar, and accusing her of making everything up in order to sell books. "Today, the world finally knows the truth," Carroll said in a statement released through her lawyer. "This victory is not just for me but for every woman who has suffered because she was not believed." The same narrative applies here as in the Goldman case. On the one hand, five million dollars is—objectively—a considerable sum of money. On the other hand, it's impossible to make an argument for being able to determine the monetary price or value of heinous abuse and its lingering consequences and repercussions.

The nature of the systems upon which the United States is built means that wealthy individuals and massive corporations will continue to be able to throw their weight around and not ever adequately pay for their crimes and missteps. That's unlikely to change anytime soon. But it's certainly heartening that there are examples of even the most boisterous millionaires and megalomaniacs, and even the most powerful corporate behemoths, being held to account in one way or another. Incremental progress is still progress.

Cultural mores, stereotypes, and conventions change at a glacial pace, but they do change. As the constructs of the societies in which we live evolve, so, too, will the perceptions of—and trust we place

President Joe Biden and Associate Supreme Court nominee Ketanji Brown Jackson watch as the U.S. Senate votes on her confirmation to the Supreme Court in April 2022.

in—women. Today, the typical CEO of a Fortune 500 company is a white, cisgender man, but every person who isn't a white, cisgender man and who manages to rise to the highest echelons of business and politics is chipping away at a convention. Eventually that won't be remarkable. Eventually that won't trigger a backlash.

In June 2022, Ketanji Brown Jackson replaced Justice Stephen Breyer to become the first Black woman to serve on the U.S. Supreme Court. In the same year, Claudine Gay, the daughter of Haitian immigrants, was announced as Harvard's thirtieth president. Gay, in 2023, became the second woman ever to preside over the university and the second Black woman to lead an Ivy League school, after former Brown University president Ruth J. Simmons. Also in 2023, Nemat "Minouche" Shafik, an economist who has served as president of the London School of Economics since 2017, and as deputy governor of the Bank of England before that, replaced Lee Bollinger to become the first woman to preside over Columbia University. Other firsts are noteworthy, even if predominantly for their symbolism. In January 2023, for the first time in the Fortune 500 list's sixty-eight-year history, more than 10 percent of companies in the prestigious index were led by women: 53 of them, or 10.6 percent, to be precise.

In the 1940s, '50s, '60s, and '70s, signs of progress were blatant because there was so much that needed to be done—so much low-hanging fruit. Laws could be changed with tremendous impact. Institutional decisions, like whether to become a coeducational college, or whether to allow women to become traders, or whether to provide any sort of parental benefits—had repercussions far beyond the confines of companies, industries, or corners of society.

The trajectory is much shallower now, and progress is not as obvious. But it does exist. From pay transparency legislation that's passing in many states to gender-based quotas and goals for corporate boards and executive teams, the conversation around the importance of gender equality, and equality of opportunity in leadership and elsewhere, has never been louder or more prominent. In December 2022, President Biden signed the PUMP for Nursing Mothers Act into law, expanding employees' rights to break time and facilities to be able to pump milk while at work without fear of repercussion.

In 2010, Congress had already included a provision in the Affordable Care Act requiring employers to provide those nursing with "reasonable break time" and a private space "other than a bathroom" for one year after their child's birth. But that provision proved riddled with loopholes and shortcomings. It didn't apply to workers who were exempt from overtime pay, for example, which the Department of Labor defines extremely liberally as people who have managerial duties; who work in certain industries, like transportation or agriculture; or who work on a commission basis, among other things.

In essence, approximately nine million workers of childbearing age did not qualify for protections to pump breastmilk while at work. The new PUMP Act—which covers almost all employees—is, therefore, noteworthy in that it implicitly addresses the shortcomings of a previous policy. And, more fundamentally, of course it acknowledges some of the more challenging realities of what it's like to be a woman in the workplace, realities that for so long went unmentioned because they were just too awkward, too inconvenient, or considered peripheral because they didn't relate to the default, male worker. If we can begin to talk about breastfeeding in the workplace, perhaps conversations around menstruation or menopause will someday become more commonplace too.

Despite lingering stigma, women are also finding the courage and platforms to speak out against discrimination and abuse; they're finding the means to advocate for themselves and for others. In the summer of 2020, more than seventy people in the gaming industry—a sector that is perhaps more male-dominated and more frequently accused of harboring a culture of sexism and toxic masculinity than any other— spoke out with allegations of gender-based discrimination, harassment, and even sexual assault. An industry that at one time never looked like it would have a #MeToo moment experienced just that.

In a 2023 book, academics Amy Diehl and Leanne M. Dzubinski argue that one of the first things we need to do to make progress and reset the trajectory is to stop oversimplifying the barriers that women face by framing the problem through the concept of a simple "glass ceiling." It's much more complex than that. We need to consider the glass walls that surround women on every side, they contend. "No matter which way a woman turns, the ever-present but invisible barriers impede her," Diehl and Dzubinski write. To even have a chance at eradicating these walls, we need to make them visible and call them out. And again, each of us has a responsibility to speak out and publicly object, be it to a microaggression, an oversight that disenfranchises, marginalizes, or ignores someone, or a blatant act of discrimination. Part of that responsibility is also to point out the shared benefits of ensuring that gender isn't a barrier to anything, reminding those around us of the trillions of dollars in collective wealth that we'd all be able to take advantage of if the gender pay gap were a relic of the past. Every person— regardless of gender—must take on that responsibility by learning to recognize and understand how to address, challenge, and, ideally, rectify structural inequities.

Of course, institutions and the ever-evolving legal structures by which we live still have a considerable role to play. They always will. But we can't rely on them to effect change alone. Every one of us must check our own preconceptions and be cognizant of the impact that the decisions we make have on others. Hope can feel elusive at times. Part of our collective duty is not to lose it.

In late 2022, I wrote an article for the BBC's website about the waning trust in female business and political leaders. The piece was based on the data collected and crunched by Kantar Public, and it called out the reasons referenced in the last chapter for why we, as a society, still have such a tough time trusting women. I quoted several academics, people who had spent their professional lives trying to figure out why humans think the way they do. I also spoke to economists and statisticians who weren't explicitly referred to by name in the published article but whose expert opinions I was interested in as a means of testing my theses.

The piece was read widely and sparked a flurry of debate on social media. Readers from around the world reached out to thank me for shedding light on such a pernicious yet still underreported problem. Then there were people who reached out not to offer praise or thanks, but to volunteer their judgement of me, as a person, and of my fitness to write for a media outlet as prestigious as the BBC. One reader wrote to tell me that he was horrified by my reporting, that the piece was "bad on so many levels," and that the data I referenced was clearly made up, because—in the process of trying to fact-check it—he had not been able to find it elsewhere online. Information, I would have told him if I had chosen to respond, is often newsworthy precisely because it's not widely available. My critic didn't explicitly use the words, but what he did say left me with little doubt: He didn't trust me. Based on scant information about me, beyond my female-sounding name and a profile picture I use for social media, he had determined that I was not qualified to be writing about such an important matter.

This interaction is, of course, a relatively harmless and trivial example of how biases and stereotypes shape the world we live in, but it is indicative of so much more. Gender-based bias is everywhere. It's online and in person, it's in offices and homes, stores, restaurants, and bars. It's in hospitals and academic institutions. It's in culture and religion and, of course, it's in the media. The internet has simply placed a magnifying glass over what might otherwise be mostly hidden attitudes and beliefs.

The fact that I have the means to write a book that documents women's battles for economic empowerment and equality is, all by itself, evidence of the freedoms I enjoy. I'm healthy and financially stable. I have a good education. I am a white woman living in a dual-income household. We can afford childcare for our daughter and graduate school for me. My husband and I have a pension and health insurance. We take vacations and buy nice things. I'm not stigmatized on account of my sexuality, faith, or heritage.

And yet, even I have come up against the limitations of opportunity on account of my gender. When I was offered my first newsroom job with managing duties, the thrill of the task at hand and the responsibility I was being handed made up for the salary that I knew was below market rate. It was only a year after I signed the contract that I realized I was being paid less than a number of the men who were reporting to me. I should feel privileged, was the message that was conveyed to me upon challenging the company, to have the opportunity to manage such talented and knowledgeable men.

From that day on, the word "privileged" has haunted me. Women are taught that our positions in the economy and in society—the positions that all the greats who came before us fought for—should be considered privileges rather than the basic rights they are. Being able to rise through the ranks of a Fortune 500 company and occupy an office that could have belonged to a man? A privilege. Being able to run a political campaign, win an election, and run a country? A privilege. Being able to earn the same amount as a man for doing the same job despite being a woman? An absolute privilege.

For centuries, women have been assigned roles that are consistent with the way that we've been portrayed in history. We've been caregivers, we've been the nurturers who support the breadwinners, and we've been the person who picks up the pieces behind the scenes to keep the show running. We've been property, arm candy, and objects of desire. Intellectually, we've moved on, but intuitively, we often haven't.

To change that, we can't afford to be shy or to be cowed by expectation. We can't dismiss even the slightest hint of sexism in a throwaway comment or in absent-minded behavior. We can't feed harmful stereotypes in any way, and we must scrutinize our own behavior and biases and those of the people around us with radical honesty. Like the employees of Goldman Sachs who fought their class-action lawsuit for so long, and like E. Jean Carroll and Lilly Ledbetter and Ann Hopkins and so many others whose stories I've told and whose stories never will be told, we must hold the most powerful to account in whatever way we can. We must trust that our courage to object to something that seems wrong will in some way promote justice, even if we don't win every case. Even the act of digging our heels in a little bit—the act of saying "I disagree" or "This doesn't seem fair" or even "Wait, can we discuss this again?"—can raise awareness or at least spark a conversation about something that would otherwise simply pass. We must seize every opportunity to educate those who can't see the inequality that's still everywhere, but we must do so in a way that does not entrench the differences between us. We must do it so that it shines a light on how fixing inequality can lead to gains for all, in a way that everyone can see what's in it for them personally.

So often, polarization is the enemy of progress. In our collective quest for fairness, we must, therefore, always seek common ground. When we experience the impulse to scream in the face of someone who disagrees with us—or to denounce someone we believe to be enforcing or endorsing structures or rules that we think exacerbate inequality as stupid or bigoted—we must consider what truly is most likely to change that person's mind and behavior. Usually, the answer is considered conversation. At work, this might mean taking the time to explain to a manager that you, as a mother, can't physically come to the office every day because you need to accommodate a babysitter's, or nanny's, or daycare's, or school's schedule, but that you're still willing and able to put in the same hours as any other employee. In a relationship with a domestic partner, this might involve a frank but measured conversation about personal and professional ambition, about the concept that Eve Rodsky describes as time choice. A conversation in which everyone's interests are respected and considered is likely to be a conversation that yields some kind of agreement, even if not everyone's demands can be met simultaneously. A shared understanding and acknowledgment that unpaid domestic labor is as important as paid labor is critical to a functioning household. Ashley All in Kansas demonstrated brilliantly what can be achieved if human connection is sought and fostered and if conversations are built on a foundation of common values—values like personal freedom, independence, and trust.

Perhaps the greatest impact we can have lies in what we teach our children. Research from 2017 shows that gendered notions of "brilliance" develop in children who are barely old enough to read. Girls as young as six are less likely than boys to believe that members of their own gender are "really, really smart." Our duty as parents is to make sure that no child's potential is hamstrung by a misguided generalization, by an untruth that has encumbered so many generations of their predecessors. We have to encourage our daughters to risk failure and setback exactly as we'd encourage our sons to do so. It's something that cuts every way: All children deserve the opportunity to develop the traits, characteristics, preferences, and ambitions they choose, unencumbered by what someone else might expect of them on account of the gender they were assigned at birth. As parents, we must constantly question our own beliefs and attitudes about our offspring and the world. And we should never underestimate our power as role models.

My hope is that this book illuminates the tragedy of ubiquitous gender gaps and enduring power gaps and the degree to which money is a crude, but also often accurate and insightful, gauge of the value we attribute to—and the respect we afford—women. We underpay women and deny them professional opportunities for precisely the same reasons we don't believe them, don't trust them, and don't consider them as capable, skilled, or knowledgeable as men. The best way we can honor the women whose stories I've told, and the people who have dedicated their lives to fighting for change, is to ensure that their efforts weren't in vain—that this moment in history is a mere blip in humanity's slow and steady journey toward a fairer and more equitable future.

## ACKNOWLEDGMENTS

It takes a village to write a book. My village was both populous and wildly generous.

First off, I owe a huge thanks to the individuals who believed in this project and supported it when it was barely more than the essence of an idea. My teacher and mentor, Samuel Freedman, saw my potential as an author long before I even dared to dream of publication day. My agent, Dan Mandel, helped me shape my abstract thoughts and unfocused ambitions into something that would translate into the real world. My editor, Jamison Stoltz, gave me the courage to explore unfamiliar territory. Jamison's scrutiny and criticism were the "tough love" I needed to do this subject matter justice. A huge thanks to Sarah Robbins, too. The critical eye and fresh perspective these professionals brought to the editing process were invaluable.

Thank you to the members of the 2020/2021 Knight-Bagehot Fellowship class at Columbia Journalism School, as well as the students in Professor Freedman's spring 2021 book seminar who provided feedback on early drafts of the proposal that would ultimately become the foundation of this book. Thank you to the staff and faculty at Columbia Journalism School and Columbia Business School.

Many friends, colleagues, and acquaintances provided feedback on ideas, concepts, drafts of excerpts, and even on the full manuscript. I owe a debt of gratitude to Julia Kete, Kathy Kete, Juliet Brooks, Stephanie Crouch, Andy Whitehouse, Adam Shelepak, Jonathan Eig, David Enrich, Jon Goldfarb, Neale Godfrey, Ashley All, Rebecca Kelliher, Andrea Kaman, Holly Baxter, Julia Love, David Filipov, Viviana Zelizer, Viktoria Dendrinou, and Christy Wise. I am especially grateful to Julia Kete for accompanying me on reporting trips, for celebrating every win with me, and for talking me off the metaphorical ledge on more than one occasion.

Thank you to everyone who sent me research, bravely shared anecdotes and experiences, contributed ideas, and made introductions in the interest of enriching the stories this book tells. Thank you, also, to Meredith Turits and Leah Carroll—my editors at the BBC—whose ideas and instincts inspired and enriched this book immeasurably. Thank you to Francesca Donner for constantly reminding me of the urgent need for these stories to be told.

Thank you to Alena Tomka, and to the Saleh and Gürel families for your unwavering support, and especially to Stefanie and Kazim Gürel, who generously made their house available to me on several occasions when the intensity of New York City became too much. Writing and editing are much easier when they're done with views over the rolling hills of Vermont.

Thank you to the Mizels—for being our family away from home—and to Wilma Romano, who alleviated the worry of childcare during long days of researching, writing, rewriting, editing, and doing all of that over and over again. Thank you to Marketa Winfield for providing clarity, perspective, and encouragement during times of self-doubt and exhaustion.

None of this would have been possible without David, Zuzana, and Meghan Cox. From an early age, my parents and sister have encouraged me to pursue my passions fiercely and fearlessly. The prospect of failure, they taught me, is never a good reason not to do something. If they hadn't instilled this lesson in me, this book would never have been anything more than a pipe dream.

Finally, thank you to Karim—my partner in everything—whose limitless patience, support, encouragement, humor, and love didn't only make this book possible, but also make me the person I am and want to be.

# NOTES

## Prologue

4    **has hardly budged:** Carolina Aragão, "Gender Pay Gap in U.S. Hasn't Changed Much in Two Decades," Pew Research Center. March 1, 2023. https://www.pewresearch.org/fact-tank/2023/03/01/gender-pay-gap-facts.

## Chapter 1: Was Rosie the Riveter Robbed?

8    **Anna Mae Burkett was born:** Based on interviews with Anna Mae Krier (née Burkett) conducted in September and October 2021.

9    **By 1930, farmers:** Section 1: The Great Depression | North Dakota Studies. Accessed October 1, 2021. https://www.ndstudies.gov/gr8/content/unit-iv-modern-north-dakota-1921-present/lesson-2-making-living/topic-2-great-depression-drought-ccc-wpa/section-1-great-depression.

9    **forty-one dollars per acre:** Ibid.

11    **"They had no rights":** Catherine Allgor, "Coverture: The Word You Probably Don't Know but Should." National Women's History Museum, September 4, 2012. https://www.womenshistory.org/articles/coverture-word-you-probably-dont-know-should.

12    **"His total mastery":** Ibid.

12    **By one estimate:** Jennifer Wright, *Madame Restell: The Life, Death, and Resurrection of Old New York's Most Fabulous, Fearless, and Infamous Abortionist* (New York: Hachette Books, Hachette Book Group, 2023), p. 18.

12    **The daughter of abolitionist:** "The Gilder Lehrman Institute of American History Advanced Placement United States History Study Guide." The struggle for married women's rights, circa 1880s | AP US History Study Guide from The Gilder Lehrman Institute of American History, July 16, 2014. https://ap.gilderlehrman.org/resources/struggle-for-married-women%C3%A2%E2%82%AC%E2%84%A2s-rights-circa-1880s.

13    **By the turn of the century:** "Women's Suffrage in the Progressive Era," The Library of Congress. Accessed March 17, 2023. https://www.loc.gov/classroom-materials/united-states-history-primary-source-timeline/progressive-era-to-new-era-1900-1929/womens-suffrage-in-progressive-era.

13    **"It is perhaps true":** Lee Boomer, "Women without a Country," Women & the American Story, July 9, 2022. https://wams.nyhistory.org/modernizing-america/xenophobia-and-racism/women-without-a-country.

13    **four million had husbands:** Lee Boomer, "Married Women and Work." Women & the American Story, July 7, 2022. https://wams.nyhistory.org/confidence-and-crises/great-depression/married-women-and-work.

13    **a similar poll reported:** Ibid.

14  **Credit institutions in many cases:** Rose Eveleth, "Forty Years Ago, Women Had a Hard Time Getting Credit Cards." Smithsonian.com. Smithsonian Institution, January 8, 2014. https://www.smithsonianmag.com/smart-news/forty-years-ago-women-had-a-hard-time-getting-credit-cards-180949289.

14  **it took another decade and a half:** "Policy Guidance on Current Issues of Sexual Harassment," US EEOC. Accessed March 9, 2023. https://www.eeoc.gov/laws/guidance/policy-guidance-current-issues-sexual-harassment.

15  **An estimated 600,000 African American women:** "The Rosies: United States." National Association of Black Military Women. Accessed April 4, 2023. https://www.nabmw.org/the-rosies.

15  **geared toward wartime production:** Arthur Herman, *Freedom's Forge: How American Business Produced Victory in World War II* (New York: Random House Trade Paperbacks, 2013), p. 283.

15  **only 1.9 billion dollars had been spent:** Michael G. Carew, *Becoming the Arsenal: The American Industrial Mobilization for World War II, 1938–1942.* Lanham, MD: University Press of America, 2010), p. 166.

15  **by the summer of 1944:** Evan K. Rose, "The Rise and Fall of Female Labor Force Participation during World War II in the United States." *Journal of Economic History* 78, no. 3 (2018), pp. 673–711. https://doi.org/10.1017/s0022050718000323.

15  **"nimble fingers":** "Women in Defense: National Archives and Records Administration." Internet Archive, January 1, 1970. https://archive.org/details/gov.archives.arc.38686.

16  **At a conference of Allied leaders:** "The Last Act: The Atomic Bomb and the End of World War II." Accessed June 2, 2023. https://files.eric.ed.gov/fulltext/ED401218.pdf.

16  **women held one-third:** Rose, "The Rise and Fall of Female Labor Force Participation during World War II in the United States."

16  **For fourteen- to nineteen-year-olds:** Claudia Goldin, *Understanding the Gender Gap: An Economic History of American Women* (New York: Oxford University Press, 1990).

16  **largest proportional rise:** "Women and Post-WWII Wages." National Bureau of Economic Research. Accessed June 2, 2023. https://www.nber.org/digest/nov02/women-and-post-wwii-wages.

16  **something that was true:** Ruth Milkman, "Redefining 'Women's Work': The Sexual Division of Labor in the Auto Industry during World War II." *Feminist Studies* 8, no. 2 (1982), pp. 336–72.

19  **while sitting for a portrait:** "Franklin D. Roosevelt Portrait." White House Historical Association. Accessed June 2, 2023. https://www.whitehousehistory.org/photos/franklin-d-roosevelt-portrait-1.

19  **"The armies and fleets":** Arthur Knock, "President Roosevelt Is Dead," *New York Times*, April 12, 1945. https://archive.nytimes.com/www.nytimes.com/learning/general/onthisday/big/0412.html.

19  **About four months later:** "The President's News Conference." The President's News Conference | Harry S. Truman, August 14, 1945. https://www.trumanlibrary.gov/library/public-papers/100/presidents-news-conference.

20  **Mary Doyle Keefe:** Rosemary Counter, "Why You Keep Reading Obituaries for Rosie the Riveter." *Vanity Fair*, May 7, 2015. https://www.vanityfair.com/culture/2015/05/why-you-keep-reading-obituaries-rosie-riveter.

21  **a wealthy Long Island heiress:** Heidi A. Strobel, "Rosie the Riveter (fl. 1920), Iconic Figure of the Women Who Worked in Defense Industries during World War II," American

National Biography online, 2009. https://doi.org/10.1093/anb/9780198606697
.article.2001920.

21  **an avid cellist:** Timothy Williams, "Geraldine Doyle, Iconic Face of World War II, Dies
at 86," *New York Times*, December 30, 2010. https://www.nytimes.com/2010/12/30/us
/30doyle.html.

21  **never been mastered before:** Elizabeth Cook-Stuntz, "The Daughters of Rosie the
Riveter," December 14, 2015. https://scholar.harvard.edu/files/cook-stuntz/files/cook
-stuntz_job_market_paper_december.pdf.

21  **Still today:** James Kimble and Lester Olson, "Visual Rhetoric Representing Rosie the
Riveter: Myth and Misconception in J. Howard Miller's 'We Can Do It!' Poster." *Rhetoric & Public Affairs* 9, no. 4 (Winter 2006), pp. 533–69.

22  **Some historians argue:** "Ronnie the Bren Gun Girl." YouTube, October 6, 2012. https://
www.youtube.com/watch?v=-E0KvWve-9g.

22  **drilling 900 lap joint holes:** Hank Pellissier, "Rosie the Riveter Memorial," *New York
Times*, January 16, 2011. https://www.nytimes.com/2011/01/16/us/16bcintel.html.

23  **particularly in industries:** Based on an interview with Evan K. Rose conducted in September 2021.

24  **"bumped" as veterans returned:** Ibid.

24  **housewives who had entered the labor force:** Cook-Stuntz, p. 7.

26  **published an article:** Nancy A. Nichols, "Whatever Happened to Rosie the Riveter?"
*Harvard Business Review*, August 1, 2014. https://hbr.org/1993/07/whatever-happened
-to-rosie-the-riveter.

26  **Ford's huge River Rouge plant:** Sherrie A. Kossoudji and Laura J. Dresser, "Working
Class Rosies: Women Industrial Workers during World War II." *Journal of Economic
History* 52, no. 2 (1992), pp. 431–46. https://doi.org/10.1017/s0022050700010846.

27  **gender-counter-stereotypical role models:** Maria Olsson and Sarah E. Martiny, "Does
Exposure to Counterstereotypical Role Models Influence Girls' and Women's Gender
Stereotypes and Career Choices? A Review of Social Psychological Research." *Frontiers
in Psychology* 9 (2018). https://doi.org/10.3389/fpsyg.2018.02264.

28  **"that liberty is subject":** *Muller v. Oregon*, 208 U.S. 412 (1908), Justia Law. Accessed
June 2, 2023. https://supreme.justia.com/cases/federal/us/208/412.

28  **setting the minimum hourly wage:** Jonathan Grossman, "Fair Labor Standards Act of
1938: Maximum Struggle for a Minimum Wage." DOL. Accessed June 2, 2023. https://
www.dol.gov/general/aboutdol/history/flsa1938.

28  **lower wages than men:** "The Equal Pay Act of 1963." US EEOC. Accessed June 2, 2023.
https://www.eeoc.gov/statutes/equal-pay-act-1963.

28  **although women were needed:** Cook-Stuntz, p. 8.

29  **model of citizenship and responsibility:** Maureen Honey, *Creating Rosie the Riveter:
Class, Gender, and Propaganda During World War II* (Amherst: University of Massachusetts Press, 1984), p. 211.

30  **no correlation between:** R. Fernández, A. Fogli, and C. Olivetti, "Mothers and Sons:
Preference Formation and Female Labor Force Dynamics." *Quarterly Journal of Economics* 119, no. 4 (2004), pp. 1249–99. https://doi.org/10.1162/0033553042476224.

30  **A separate study:** Melinda Sandler Morrill and Thayer Morrill, "Intergenerational
Links in Female Labor Force Participation." *Labour Economics* 20 (2013), pp. 38–47.
https://doi.org/10.1016/j.labeco.2012.10.002.

30  **women born in the 1940s:** Statista Research Department, "Percentage of the U.S. Population with a College Degree by Gender 1940–2021," Statista, June 2, 2023. https://

www.statista.com/statistics/184272/educational-attainment-of-college-diploma-or
-higher-by-gender.

Chapter 2: Wonderful Things in Small Packets

33 **Samantha Bee in November 2010:** Vanessa Grigoriadis, "Waking Up From the Pill," *New York* magazine, November 24, 2010. https://nymag.com/news/features/69789.]

33 **In May 1946:** Landon Jones, *Great Expectations, America and the Baby Boom Generation* (New York: Ballantine Books, 1981), p. 10.

33 **they faced prejudice and discrimination:** "Servicemen's Readjustment Act (1944)," National Archives and Records Administration. Accessed May 22, 2023. https://www.archives.gov/milestone-documents/servicemens-readjustment-act.

34 **the median age of marriage:** "Figure MS-2 Median Age at First Marriage: 1890 to Present." Accessed November 29, 2021. https://www.census.gov/content/dam/Census/library/visualizations/time-series/demo/families-and-households/ms-2.pdf.

34 **Almost 2.3 million couples:** "Marriage Rates in the United States, 1900–2018." Centers for Disease Control and Prevention, April 29, 2020. https://www.cdc.gov/nchs/data/hestat/marriage_rate_2018/marriage_rate_2018.htm.

34 **By 1960:** Average number of children per U.S. family (historic). Accessed June 2, 2023. https://populationeducation.org/wp-content/uploads/2020/04/average-number-children-per-us-family-historic-infographic.pdf.

34 **But then in peacetime it had promptly returned:** Mary M. Schweitzer, "World War II and Female Labor Force Participation Rates," *Journal of Economic History* 40, no. 1 (1980), pp. 89–95. http://www.jstor.org/stable/2120427.

35 **So-called little Comstock laws:** Helen Lefkowitz Horowitz, *Attitudes Toward Sex in Antebellum America: A Brief History with Documents* (New York: Palgrave Macmillan, 2006).

35 **"It seems unreasonable":** *United States v. One Package*, 86 F.2d 737 (2d Cir. 1936). Justia Law. Accessed November 22, 2021. https://law.justia.com/cases/federal/appellate-courts/F2/86/737/1567252.

36 **The most popular brand:** Nicole Pasulka, "When Women Used Lysol as Birth Control," *Mother Jones*, March 8, 2012. https://www.motherjones.com/media/2012/03/when-women-used-lysol-birth-control.

36 **the timing of which:** Ilise L. Feitshans, "Job Security for Pregnant Employees: The Model Employment Termination Act." *Annals of the American Academy of Political and Social Science* 536, no. 1 (1994), pp. 119–34. https://doi.org/10.1177/0002716294536001010.

36 **Stanley, his youngest son:** Miriam Kleiman, "Rich, Famous, and Questionably Sane," National Archives and Records Administration, Summer 2007. https://www.archives.gov/publications/prologue/2007/summer/mccormick.html.

37 **Other branches of the sprawling family:** Ibid.

37 **Shortly after her brother's funeral:** Armond Fields, *Katharine Dexter McCormick: Pioneer for Women's Rights* (Westport, CT: Praeger, 2003), p. 23.

39 **eventually she acknowledged:** Genevieve Wanucha, "A Mind of Her Own," *MIT Technology Review*, February 11, 2020. https://www.technologyreview.com/2011/02/22/196980/a-mind-of-her-own.

39 **what would have passed:** Fields, p. 61.

39 **sought explanations in the textbooks:** "Katherine McCormick," Carrie Chapman Catt

Center for Women and Politics. Accessed June 2, 2023. https://awpc.cattcenter.iastate.edu/directory/katherine-mccormick.

40 **According to one medical report:** Kleiman, 2007.

40 **His regular treatment:** Fields, p. 85.

40 **But nothing at all:** Michael Redmon, "Montecito's Riven Rock," *Santa Barbara Independent*, December 21, 2016. https://www.independent.com/2016/12/21/montecitos-riven-rock.

40 **Katharine McCormick would nonetheless:** Jonathan Eig, *The Birth of the Pill: How Four Crusaders Reinvented Sex and Launched a Revolution* (London: Pan Books, 2016), p. 93.

41 **wear hats in science labs:** Genevieve Wanucha, "A Mind of Her Own." MIT Technology Review, February 11, 2020. https://www.technologyreview.com/2011/02/22/196980/a-mind-of-her-own.

42 **"the brunt of unwilling motherhood":** Margaret Sanger, "Voluntary Motherhood," Teaching American History, July 8, 2022. https://teachingamericanhistory.org/document/voluntary-motherhood.

44 **the short time that its doors were open:** "The Embryo Project Encyclopedia," First American Birth Control Clinic (The Brownsville Clinic), 1916. Accessed June 2, 2023. https://embryo.asu.edu/pages/first-american-birth-control-clinic-brownsville-clinic-1916.

45 **It had three governing principles:** Sanger, Margaret. The Pivot of Civilization. Accessed June 2, 2023. https://www.gutenberg.org/files/1689/1689-h/1689-h.htm.

45 **In January 1923:** "Birth Control Organizations—Birth Control Clinical Research Bureau." The Margaret Sanger Papers Project. Accessed July 15, 2023. https://sanger.hosting.nyu.edu/aboutms/organization_bccrb.

46 **adored French fashion:** Fields, p. 182.

47 **Diaphragms were hidden in cosmetics cases:** Fields, p. 186.

47 **a powerful earthquake:** Scott Harrison, "From the Archives: The 1925 Santa Barbara Earthquake," *Los Angeles Times*, June 28, 2019. https://www.latimes.com/visuals/photography/la-me-fw-archives-the-1925-santa-barbara-earthquake-20190626-htmlstory.html.

48 **Instead, she had decided:** "The History of the Birth Control Pill, Part 4: Margaret Sanger's 'Magic Pill,'" advocatesaz.org, December 9, 2013. http://advocatesaz.org/2013/04/09/the-history-of-the-birth-control-pill-part-4-margaret-sangers-magic-pill.

48 **Even though the relevant sections:** Caitlin Knowles Myers, "Confidential and Legal Access to Abortion and Contraception in the USA, 1960–2020." *Journal of Population Economics* 35, no. 4 (2022), pp. 1385–1441. https://doi.org/10.1007/s00148-022-00902-4.

49 **One night in 1950:** Christian R. Johnson, "Feminism, Philanthropy and Science in the Development of the Oral Contraceptive Pill." *Pharmacy in History* 19, no. 2 (1977), pp. 63–78. http://www.jstor.org/stable/41109030.

49 **The press, in articles:** "Science: Pincogenesis," *TIME* magazine, November 13, 1939. https://content.time.com/time/subscriber/article/0,33009,789596,00.html.

50 **"I think so":** Eig, p. 6.

51 **"It's pretty trying":** Fields, p. 256.

51 **On June 8, 1953:** Eig, p. 141.

52 **Later that night:** Ibid.

52 **"If it had not been":** Eig, p. 155.

52 **He was interested in:** Drew Pendergrass and Michelle Raji, "The Bitter Pill: Harvard

and the Dark History of Birth Control: Magazine: The Harvard Crimson." Magazine | The Harvard Crimson, September 28, 2017. https://www.thecrimson.com/article /2017/9/28/the-bitter-pill.

53 **As an island:** "The Birth Control Pill: A History." Planned Parenthood. Accessed June 2, 2023. https://www.plannedparenthood.org/files/1514/3518/7100/Pill_History _FactSheet.pdf.

53 **In 1937, the United States had imposed:** "Sterilization Abuse: The Policies Behind the Practice: National Women's Health Network." National Women's Health Network, April 30, 2021. https://nwhn.org/sterilization-abuse-the-policies-behind-the -practice.

54 **In Puerto Rico:** Margaret S. Marsh and Wanda Ronner, *The Fertility Doctor: John Rock and the Reproductive Revolution* (Baltimore: Johns Hopkins University Press, 2008), p. 151.

54 **She started calling it:** Marsh and Ronner, p. 225.

55 **For a year or two:** Bernard Asbell, *The Pill: A Biography of the Drug That Changed the World* (New York: Random House, 1995).

55 **The data submitted:** Lara Marks, *Sexual Chemistry: A History of the Contraceptive Pill* (New Haven, CT: Yale University Press, 2010), p. 111.

55 **Searle assumed the application:** Edward T. Tyler, "Oral Contraception and Venous Thrombosis," *JAMA: The Journal of the American Medical Association* 185, no. 2 (1963), p. 131. https://doi.org/10.1001/jama.1963.03060020091034.

56 **DeFelice opened the meeting:** Fields, p. 290.

56 **Finally, on May 9, 1960:** "U.S. Approves Pill for Birth Control," *New York Times*, May 10, 1960. https://www.nytimes.com/1960/05/10/archives/us-approves-pill-for -birth-control.html.

57 **On August 22, 1967:** "Dr. Pincus, Developer of Birth-Control Pill, Dies; Worcester Foundation Chief Worked with Chang and Rock on Contraceptive," *New York Times*, August 23, 1967. https://www.nytimes.com/1967/08/23/archives/dr -pincus-developer-of-birthcontrol-pill-dies-worcester-foundation.html?searchResult Position=1.

57 **Margaret Sanger had passed away:** "Margaret Sanger Is Dead at 82; Led Campaign for Birth Control; Mrs. Margaret Sanger, Pioneer in Birth Control, Is Dead at 82," *New York Times*, September 7, 1966. https://www.nytimes.com/1966/09/07/archives /margaret-sanger-is-dead-at-82-led-campaign-for-birth-control-mrs.html.

58 **To advance the birth control movement:** Samantha Schmidt, "Planned Parenthood to Remove Margaret Sanger's Name from N.Y. Clinic over Views on Eugenics," *Washington Post*, July 21, 2020. https://www.washingtonpost.com/history/2020/07/21 /margaret-sanger-planned-parenthood-eugenics.

58 **In 1947, the Nuremberg Code:** Ravindra B. Ghooi, "The Nuremberg Code—A Critique," Perspectives in Clinical Research, U.S. National Library of Medicine, April 2011. https://www.ncbi.nlm.nih.gov/pmc/articles/PMC3121268.

58 **The Kefauver-Harris Drug Amendments:** "The Belmont Report," HHS.gov.Office for Human Research Protections (OHRP), October 17, 2022. https://www.hhs.gov/ohrp /regulations-and-policy/belmont-report/index.html.

58 **Some have compared the trials:** Theresa Vargas, "Guinea Pigs or Pioneers? How Puerto Rican Women Were Used to Test the Birth Control Pill," *Washington Post*, October 28, 2021. https://www.washingtonpost.com/news/retropolis/wp/2017/05 /09/guinea-pigs-or-pioneers-how-puerto-rican-women-were-used-to-test-the-birth -control-pill.

58  **In a biography of Rock:** Ibid.

59  **almost all women in the United States today:** "Current Contraceptive Status Among Women Aged 15–49: United States, 2017–2019." Centers for Disease Control and Prevention, October 20, 2020. https://www.cdc.gov/nchs/products/databriefs/db388 .htm.

59  **As Armond Fields notes:** Fields, p. 306.

60  **Loretta McLaughlin, in her book:** Loretta McLaughlin, *The Pill, John Rock, and the Church: The Biography of a Revolution* (Boston: Little, Brown, 1982).

60  **encouraged by a considerable price cut:** Megan Gibson, "Birth Control Pill Enovid 55 Year Anniversary," *TIME* magazine, June 23, 2015. https://time.com/3929971/enovid -the-pill/

60  **Two years later:** Asbell, 1995.

62  **women who planned to have children:** Kevin Stange, "A Longitudinal Analysis of the Relationship between Fertility Timing and Schooling," *Demography* 48, no. 3 (2011), pp. 931–56. https://doi.org/10.1007/s13524-011-0050-3.

62  **there were 1.60 men:** David R. Francis, "Why Do Women Outnumber Men in College?" NBER, January 2007. Accessed February 27, 2023. https://www.nber.org/digest/jan07 /why-do-women-outnumber-men-college.

62  **graduation rates surged:** Oksana Leukhina and Amy Smaldone, "Why Do Women Outnumber Men in College Enrollment?" Federal Reserve Bank of St. Louis, January 3, 2023. https://www.stlouisfed.org/on-the-economy/2022/mar/why-women-outnumber -men-college-enrollment.

62  **challenging the "Mrs. degree" label:** C. Goldin, L. F. Katz, and I. Kuziemko, "The Homecoming of American College Women: The Reversal of the Gender Gap in College." *Journal of Economic Perspectives*, 2006.

62  **In a 2002 paper:** Claudia Goldin and Lawrence F. Katz, "The Power of the Pill: Oral Contraceptives and Women's Career and Marriage Decisions," *Journal of Political Economy* 110, no. 4 (2002), pp. 730–70. https://doi.org/10.1086/340778.

62  **delaying motherhood leads to:** Amalia Rebecca Miller, *The Effects of Motherhood Timing on Career Path*, Job Market Paper, Department of Economics, Stanford University, Stanford, CA, July 2005.

63  **In many cases:** Martha J. Bailey et al., "The Opt-in Revolution? Contraception and the Gender Gap in Wages." *American Economic Journal. Applied Economics,* July 2012. https://www.ncbi.nlm.nih.gov/pmc/articles/PMC3684076.

Chapter 3: Giving the Problem a Name

64  **It was meant to be:** Betty Friedan, *Life So Far* (New York: Simon & Schuster Paperbacks, 2006), p. 102.

64  **She'd then spent a year:** Friedan, *Life So Far*, p. 52.

65  **Bettye wrote for her school newspaper:** Friedan, *Life So Far*, p. 23.

65  **She was spirited:** Friedan, *Life So Far*, p. 27.

65  **She read Virginia Woolf:** Friedan, *Life So Far*, p. 35.

66  **After graduating:** Friedan, *Life So Far*, p. 57.

66  **Betty broke off her relationship:** Friedan, *Life So Far*, p. 62.

66  **She started working for:** Friedan, *Life So Far*, p. 64.

66  **She crafted a safety net:** "This Month in Business History: Frances Perkins Became the First Female Cabinet Member," Research Guides. Accessed November 18, 2021. https://guides.loc.gov/this-month-in-business-history/march/frances-perkins.

67 **Many women concealed their marital status:** Claudia Goldin, "Marriage Bars: Discrimination Against Married Women Workers, 1920s to 1950s," 1988. https://doi.org/10.3386/w2747.

67 **they're less likely to get pregnant:** "The Marriage Bar, 23 Aug 1946," *Spectator*. Archive, accessed November 16, 2021. http://archive.spectator.co.uk/article/23rd-august-1946/2/the-marriage-bar.

67 **On their first date:** Friedan, *Life So Far*, p. 68.

68 **Betty was fired:** Friedan, *Life So Far*, p. 79.

68 **It wasn't until 1978:** "The Pregnancy Discrimination Act of 1978." U.S. Equal Employment Opportunity Commission. Accessed November 16, 2021. https://www.eeoc.gov/statutes/pregnancy-discrimination-act-1978.

68 **One evening in 1956:** Friedan, *Life So Far*, pp. 83–85.

69 **In 1947, Marynia Farnham and Ferdinand Lundberg:** Marynia Farnham and Ferdinand Lundberg, *Modern Woman: The Lost Sex* (New York: Harper & Brothers Publishers, 1947).

70 **Education was not the root:** Friedan, *Life So Far*, p. 97.

70 **Several of the questions:** Friedan, *Life So Far*, pp. 99–101.

71 **Others already knew:** Friedan, *Life So Far*, p. 102.

71 **"Are Women Wasting Their Time":** Peter Dreier, "Betty Friedan's Radical Century." Public Seminar, March 4, 2021. https://publicseminar.org/essays/betty-friedans-radical-century.

72 **"off her rocker":** Friedan, *Life So Far*, p. 103.

72 **"It's almost like":** Friedan, *Life So Far*, p. 104.

72 **We're onto something:** Friedan, *Life So Far*, p. 105.

73 **Brockway agreed instantly:** Friedan, *Life So Far*, p. 107.

75 **Miltown, a tranquilizer pill:** Andrea Tone, *The Age of Anxiety: A History of America's Turbulent Affair with Tranquilizers* (New York: Basic Books, 2012).

75 **One of Friedan's former classmates:** Betty Friedan, *The Feminine Mystique* (New York: W.W. Norton & Company, 1963), p. 28.

75 **In the prologue:** Friedan, *The Feminine Mystique*, p. 22.

77 **One of Kennedy's closest allies:** "Esther Eggertsen Peterson: AFL-CIO." AFL. Accessed July 17, 2023. https://aflcio.org/about/history/labor-history-people/esther-peterson.

78 **Chaired by Eleanor Roosevelt:** "Statement by the President on the Establishment of the President's Commission on the Status of Women." The American Presidency Project, December 14, 1961. https://www.presidency.ucsb.edu/documents/statement-the-president-the-establishment-the-presidents-commission-the-status-women.

79 **At its inaugural meeting in 1962:** Cynthia Ellen Harrison, *On Account of Sex: The Politics of Women's Issues, 1945–1968* (Berkeley: University of California Press, 1988), p. 94.

79 **Citing an industrial study on absenteeism:** Equal Pay Act: Hearings Before the Special Subcommittee on Labor of the Committee on Education and Labor, House of Representatives, Eighty-eighth Congress, First Session on H.R. 3861 and Related Bills.

80 **By some accounts:** Jane Sherron De Hart, *Ruth Bader Ginsburg: A Life* (New York: Vintage Books, 2021), p. 105

80 **He acknowledged that:** "Remarks upon Signing the Equal Pay Act." Remarks Upon Signing the Equal Pay Act | The American Presidency Project, June 10, 1963. https://www.presidency.ucsb.edu/documents/remarks-upon-signing-the-equal-pay-act.

80 **Between 1949 and 1959:** Tony Schwartz and Jules Feiffer. "Hope for America: Performers, Politics and Pop Culture Television and Politics." Library of Congress,

July 11, 2010. https://www.loc.gov/exhibits/hope-for-america/television-and-politics .html.

82  **It was around that time:** Friedan, *Life So Far*, p. 162.

82  **Friedan had been reading:** Ibid.

83  **Under the headline:** Edith Evans Asbury, "Protest Proposed on Women's Jobs; Yale Professor Says It May Be Needed to Obtain Rights," *New York Times*, October 13, 1965. https://www.nytimes.com/1965/10/13/archives/protest-proposed-on-womens-jobs -yale-professor-says-it-may-be.html.

83  **In a 2005 book:** Susan Ware and Stacy Lorraine Braukman, *Notable American Women: A Biographical Dictionary, Completing the Twentieth Century* (Cambridge, MA: Belknap, 2005), p. xxix.

83  **Anna Pauline Murray was born:** "Who Is Pauli Murray?" Pauli Murray Center. Accessed July 17, 2023. https://www.paulimurraycenter.com/who-is-pauli.

84  **After her mother's death:** Kathryn Schulz, "The Many Lives of Pauli Murray," *The New Yorker*, April 10, 2017. https://www.newyorker.com/magazine/2017/04/17/the-many -lives-of-pauli-murray.

84  **In 1926, at age fifteen:** Pauli Murray. *Song in a Weary Throat* (New York: Harper & Row, 1987), p. 82.

84  **As young as fifteen:** Rosalind Rosenberg, *Jane Crow: The Life of Pauli Murray* (New York: Oxford University Press, 2017), p. 38.

85  **"her strategies of negotiation and survival":** Brittney C. Cooper, *Beyond Respectability: The Intellectual Thought of Race Women* (Urbana: University of Illinois Press, 2017).

86  **The university administration:** Gail Collins, *When Everything Changed: The Amazing Journey of American Women from 1960 to the Present: A Keepsake Journal* (New York: Little, Brown and Company, 2014), p. 75.

87  **Murray wrote in a letter:** Tina Lu, "Pauli Murray, in the Now," *Yale Daily News*, September 5, 2017. https://yaledailynews.com/blog/2017/09/05/lu-pauli-murray-in-the -now.

87  **she published a tome:** Pauli Murray, *States' Laws on Race and Color: And Appendices Containing International Documents, Federal Laws and Regulations, Local Ordinances and Charts* (Cincinnati: Women's Division of Christian Service, Board of Missions and Church Extension, The Methodist Church, 1952).

87  **Thurgood Marshall dubbed it:** Murray, *Song in a Weary Throat*.

88  **In a 2017 interview:** Steve Rose, "'How Is Pauli Murray Not a Household Name?' The Extraordinary Life of the US's Most Radical Activist," *Guardian*. Guardian News and Media, September 17, 2021. https://www.theguardian.com/film/2021/sep/17/how-is -pauli-murray-not-a-household-name-the-extraordinary-life-of-the-uss-most-radical -activist.

88  **That case concerned:** *Reed v. Reed*, 404 U.S. 71 (1971), Justia Law. Accessed June 3, 2023. https://supreme.justia.com/cases/federal/us/404/71.

89  **On November 22, 1971:** "Supreme Court Decisions & Women's Rights: Breaking New Ground—*Reed v. Reed*: Schs Classroom Resources." Supreme Court Historical Society, April 27, 2022. https://supremecourthistory.org/classroom-resources-teachers -students/decisions-womens-rights-reed-v-reed.

89  **In one letter:** Jeanne Theoharis, "How Women's Voices Were Excluded from the March," NBC News.com, September 5, 2013. https://www.nbcnews.com/id /wbna52919737.

89  **When on July 2, 1964:** "Jane Crow & the Story of Pauli Murray." National Museum of

African American History and Culture, April 25, 2023. https://nmaahc.si.edu/explore
/stories/jane-crow-story-pauli-murray.

90 **NOW's mission:** "Statement of Purpose," National Organization for Women, March 31,
2017. https://now.org/about/history/statement-of-purpose.

91 **Pauli Murray kept diaries:** Murray, *Song in a Weary Throat.*

91 **In one diary entry:** "The Trailblazing, Multifaceted Activism of Lawyer-Turned-Priest
Pauli Murray." Smithsonian.com, October 19, 2021. https://www.smithsonianmag
.com/history/the-trailblazing-multifaceted-activism-of-lawyer-turned-priest-pauli
-murray-180978890.

91 **As Kathryn Schulz wrote:** Kathryn Schulz, "The Many Lives of Pauli Murray," *The New
Yorker,* April 10, 2017. https://www.newyorker.com/magazine/2017/04/17/the-many
-lives-of-pauli-murray.

92 **The *Reed v. Reed* decision:** "*Reed v. Reed* at 40: A Landmark Decision." NWLC, November 30. https://nwlc.org/blog/reed-v-reed-40-landmark-decision.

92 **With women entering the workforce:** "Teaching Center - Supreme Court Decisions
& Women's Rights - Milestones to Equality - Breaking New Ground - Reed v. Reed,
404 U.S. 71 (1971)." The Supreme Court Historical Society, June 23, 2021. https://
supremecourthistory.org/learning-center/text-books-supreme-court-decisions
-womens-rights-milestones-to-equality/breaking-new-ground-reed-v-reed-404-u-s
-71-1971.

92 **In its entry:** "Pauli Murray," The Episcopal Diocese of North Carolina. Accessed
November 10, 2021. https://www.episdionc.org/pauli-murray.

92 **In a 1963 letter to Friedan:** Linda K. Kerber, Jane Sherron De Hart, Cornelia Hughes
Dayton, and Karissa Haugeberg, *Women's America: Refocusing the Past* (New York:
Oxford University Press, 2020).

93 **She was in pain:** Irin Carmon. "'The Firebrand and the First Lady,' by Patricia Bell-
Scott," *New York Times,* February 19, 2016. https://www.nytimes.com/2016/02/21
/books/review/the-firebrand-and-the-first-lady-by-patricia-bell-scott.html.

93 **Years later, in 1970:** Rosenberg, p. 5.

93 **In 2021 in the United States:** "Five Facts about the State of the Gender Pay Gap," U.S.
Department of Labor Blog. Accessed June 2, 2023. https://blog.dol.gov/2021/03/19
/5-facts-about-the-state-of-the-gender-pay-gap.

94 **They concluded that,** Friedan, *Life So Far,* p. 105.

95 **Respondents indicated that they experienced:** Jaime M. Grant, Lisa A. Mottet, Justin Tanis, Jack Harrison, Jody L. Herman, and Mara Keisling, "Injustice at Every
Turn: A Report of the National Transgender Discrimination Survey" (Washington:
National Center for Transgender Equality and National Gay and Lesbian Task Force,
2011).

Chapter 4: Progress in Failure

95 **In a 1974 interview:** "About Alice Paul." Alice Paul Institute. Accessed January 3, 2022.
https://www.alicepaul.org/about-alice-paul.

96 **Throughout her life:** Debra Michals, "Lucretia Mott," National Women's History Museum. Accessed May 26, 2023. https://www.womenshistory.org/education
-resources/biographies/lucretia-mott.

96 **Paul went to a Quaker school:** "1975 Alice Paul '05 and the Women's Center," A Brief
History: Swarthmore College, September 26, 2018. https://www.swarthmore.edu
/a-brief-history/1975-alice-paul-05-and-womens-center.

96   **a mathematics professor named Susan Cunningham:** Peter L. Duren, Richard Askey, Uta Merzbach, and Harold M. Edwards, *A Century of Mathematics in America* (Providence, RI: American Mathematical Society, 1989), p. 382.

97   **"The agitation has brought England":** "About Alice Paul." Alice Paul Institute. Accessed December 3, 2021. https://www.alicepaul.org/about-alice-paul.

98   **"We shall fight":** Belinda A. Stillion Southard, *Militant Citizenship: Rhetorical Strategies of the National Woman's Party, 1913–1920* (College Station: Texas A&M University Press, 2011).

99   **Paul ended up being moved:** "About Alice Paul." Alice Paul Institute. Accessed December 3, 2021. https://www.alicepaul.org/about-alice-paul.

100  **Wilson met with members of Congress:** Melissa De Witt, "How World War I Strengthened Women's Suffrage," *Stanford News*, May 4, 2022. https://news.stanford.edu/2020/08/12/world-war-strengthened-womens-suffrage.

100  **he ripped off the red rose:** Katie Mettler, "A Mother's Letter, a Son's Choice and the Incredible Moment Women Won the Vote," *Washington Post*, August 10, 2020. https://www.washingtonpost.com/graphics/2020/local/history/tennessee-19-amendment-letter-harry-burn-mother-febb.

101  **The amendment called for:** "Alice Paul." Radcliffe Institute for Advanced Study at Harvard University. Accessed July 17, 2023. https://www.radcliffe.harvard.edu/schlesinger-library/collections/alice-paul.

101  **The new version stated:** "The Equal Rights Amendment Explained." Brennan Center for Justice, October 9, 2019. https://www.brennancenter.org/our-work/research-reports/equal-rights-amendment-explained.

101  **Congresswoman Martha Griffiths:** "Why the Equal Rights Amendment Is Still Not Part of the Constitution." Smithsonian.com. Smithsonian Institution. Accessed April 17, 2023. https://www.smithsonianmag.com/history/equal-rights-amendment-96-years-old-and-still-not-part-constitution-heres-why-180973548.

102  **"Male dominance is so deeply":** Daniel Patrick Moynihan, *Daniel Patrick Moynihan: A Portrait in Letters of an American Visionary* (New York: PublicAffairs, 2010), p. 201.

102  **Nixon did eventually:** "Letter to the Senate Minority Leader about the Proposed Constitutional Amendment on Equal Rights for Men and Women." | The American Presidency Project, March 18, 1972. https://www.presidency.ucsb.edu/documents/letter-the-senate-minority-leader-about-the-proposed-constitutional-amendment-equal-rights.

102  **Ford stormed out of the convention:** Zoë Barth-Werb, "Former First Lady and Women's Rights Advocate: Betty Ford." American Civil Liberties Union, April 26, 2015. https://www.aclu.org/blog/immigrants-rights/former-first-lady-and-womens-rights-advocate-betty-ford.

102  **In a speech in 1970:** "Shirley Chisholm, 'for the Equal Rights Amendment,'" Speech Text, Voices of Democracy, June 17, 2016. https://voicesofdemocracy.umd.edu/chisholm-for-the-equal-rights-amendment-speech-text.

104  **"It is time to sweep away these relics":** Ibid.

104  **In January of that year:** *Shultz v. Wheaton Glass Co.*, 319 F. Supp. 229 (D.N.J. 1970). Justia Law. Accessed December 8, 2021. https://law.justia.com/cases/federal/district-courts/FSupp/319/229/2135028.

104  **A witness in a federal legislation:** "National Public Policy Primer." NAWBO Greater Detroit. Accessed December 8, 2021. https://nawbogdc.org/content.php?page=News_From_National.

105  **Ginsburg argued that Paula:** *Weinberger v. Wiesenfeld*, 420 US 636 (1975). Justia Law. Accessed December 8, 2021. https://supreme.justia.com/cases/federal/us/420/636.

105 **in the face of entrenched norms:** Fred Strebeigh, *Equal: Women Reshape American Law* (New York: W. W. Norton, 2009).

105 **about half of all single women:** Janet L. Yellen, "The History of Women's Work and Wages and How It Has Created Success for Us All." Brookings, January 6, 2021. https://www.brookings.edu/essay/the-history-of-womens-work-and-wages-and-how-it-has-created-success-for-us-all.

105 **Harry T. Burn had cast:** "History of Women in the U.S. Congress." Center for American Women and Politics. Accessed December 5, 2022. https://cawp.rutgers.edu/facts/levels-office/congress/history-women-us-congress.

105 **It had been seven years:** Pay Equity Information. Accessed December 9, 2021. https://www.pay-equity.org/info-time.html.

106 **In no state was marital rape:** David Cotter, Joan M. Hermsen, and Reeve Vanneman, "The End of the Gender Revolution? Gender Role Attitudes from 1977 to 2008," *American Journal of Sociology* 117, no. 1 (2011), pp. 259–89. https://doi.org/10.1086/658853.

106 **Their demands included:** David M. Dismore, "Today in Feminist History: *Ladies' Home Journal* Employees Stage a Sit-In (March 18, 1970)," *Ms.* magazine, March 16, 2020. https://msmagazine.com/2020/03/18/today-in-feminist-history-ladies-home-journal-employees-stage-a-sit-in-march-18-1970.

106 **"we ought to have some sort of women's strike":** Judy Klemesrud, "Coming Wednesday," *New York Times*, August 23, 1970. https://www.nytimes.com/1970/08/23/archives/coming-wednesday-a-herstorymaking-event-demonstrations-and-parades.html.

107 **resembled a cross section:** "It Was a Great Day for Women on the March," *New York Times*, August 30, 1970. https://timesmachine.nytimes.com/timesmachine/1970/08/30/355766892.pdf.

107 **To that end:** Sarah Seidman, "Reconsidering Feminist Waves through the Strike for Women's Equality March." Museum of the City of New York. Accessed July 17, 2023. https://www.mcny.org/story/reconsidering-feminist-waves-through-strike-womens-equality-march.

107 **Eleanor Holmes Norton:** Lynn Povich, *The Good Girls Revolt: How the Women of Newsweek Sued Their Bosses and Changed the Workplace* (New York: PublicAffairs, 2016).

108 **Countless housewives turned their backs:** "Women Strike for Equality," Women & the American Story, June 25, 2021. https://wams.nyhistory.org/growth-and-turmoil/feminism-and-the-backlash/women-strike-for-equality/#.

108 **In the weeks and months:** Maggie Doherty, "Feminist Factions United and Filled the Streets for This Historic March," *New York Times*, August 26, 2020. https://www.nytimes.com/2020/08/26/us/womens-strike-for-equality.html.

109 **Within a year of the ERA passing:** Howard Kurtz, "Rehnquist Argued ERA Would Harm the Family," *Washington Post*, September 10, 1986. https://www.washingtonpost.com/archive/politics/1986/09/10/rehnquist-argued-era-would-harm-the-family/40344438-1ad8-48ca-9d8d-334dfaf79e8e.

109 **"We tried to convey to them":** Herma Hill Kay, "Ruth Bader Ginsburg, Professor of Law," *Columbia Law Review* 104, no. 1 (2004). https://doi.org/10.2307/4099343.

110 **Between 1956 and 1964:** Carol Felsenthal, *The Sweetheart of the Silent Majority: The Biography of Phyllis Schlafly* (Garden City, NY: Doubleday, 1981).

111 **The amendment's death:** "June 30, 1982: The Day the Era Dies." UPI. UPI, June 30, 1982. https://www.upi.com/Archives/1982/06/30/June-30-1982-The-Day-the-ERA-Dies/6826394257600.

Chapter 5: Winds of Legal Change

112 **In January 1971:** *Phillips v. Martin Marietta Corp.*, 400 US 542 (1971). Justia Law. Accessed December 10, 2021. https://supreme.justia.com/cases/federal/us/400/542.

113 **That extended to most schools:** "Title IX and Sex Discrimination." Home. US Department of Education (ED), August 20, 2021. https://www2.ed.gov/about/offices/list/ocr/docs/tix_dis.html.

113 **"Men and women depend":** Clare Cushman, *Supreme Court Decisions and Women's Rights* (Washington, D.C.: CQ Press, 2011), p. 46.

114 **"I ask no favor for my sex":** Arguments Transcripts: *Frontiero v. Laird (1973)*. Supreme Court of the United States. Accessed June 3, 2023. https://www.supremecourt.gov/oral_arguments/argument_transcript.aspx.

114 **"That's when it dawned on me":** "ACLU News & Commentary." American Civil Liberties Union. Accessed December 10, 2021. https://www.aclu.org/news/civil-liberties/in-memory-of-justice-ruth-bader-ginsburg-1933-2020.

114 **Boggs—born Marie Corinne Claiborne:** Lindy Boggs and Katherine Hatch, *Washington Through a Purple Veil: Memoirs of a Southern Woman* (Anstey, Leicestershire: Niagara, 1995).

115 **Also during the 1970s:** *Bell v. Burson.* Legal research tools from Casetext, May 24, 1971. https://casetext.com/case/bell-v-burson.

115 **Significantly, in 1972:** "Equal Employment Opportunity Commission." Legal Information Institute. Accessed May 28, 2023. https://www.law.cornell.edu/wex/equal_employment_opportunity_commission.

115 **the U.S. Military Academy at West Point:** "45th Anniversary of Women Admitted to West Point." GovInfo, March 9, 2022. https://www.govinfo.gov/features/anniversary-women-west-point.

116 **In January 1973:** *Roe v. Wade*, 410 U.S. 113 (1973). Justia Law. Accessed March 8, 2023. https://supreme.justia.com/cases/federal/us/410/113.

116 **"To label family planning":** Shirley Chisholm, *Unbought and Unbossed* (Washington, D.C.: Take Root Media, 2010), p. 130.

117 **They also compared changes:** Caitlin Knowles Myers and Morgan Welch, "What Can Economic Research Tell Us About the Effect of Abortion Access on Women's Lives?" Brookings, November 30, 2021. https://www.brookings.edu/research/what-can-economic-research-tell-us-about-the-effect-of-abortion-access-on-womens-lives.

117 **nearly three times greater:** P. B. Levine, D. Staiger, T. J. Kane, and D. J. Zimmerman, "Roe v. Wade and American Fertility," *American Journal of Public Health* 89, no. 2 (1999), pp. 199–203. https://doi.org/10.2105/ajph.89.2.199.

117 **Other studies have found:** J. Gruber, P. Levine, and D. Staiger, "Abortion Legalization and Child Living Circumstances: Who Is the 'Marginal Child'?" *Quarterly Journal of Economics* 114, no. 1 (1999), pp. 263–91. https://doi.org/10.1162/003355399556007; Elizabeth Oltmans Ananat et al., "Abortion and Selection," *Review of Economics and Statistics* 91, no. 1 (February 2009), pp. 124–36.

118 **Its failure to be ratified:** "Why We Need the Equal Rights Amendment." Equal Rights Amendment. Accessed December 17, 2021. https://www.equalrightsamendment.org/why.

118 **"laws like the Equal Pay Act":** "Why We Need the Equal Rights Amendment," *New York Times*, January 22, 2020. https://www.nytimes.com/2020/01/22/opinion/letters/equal-rights-amendment.html.

118    **In March 2017:** Colin Dwyer and Carrie Kaufman, "Nevada Ratifies the Equal Rights Amendment . . . 35 Years after the Deadline." NPR, March 21, 2017. https://www.npr .org/sections/thetwo-way/2017/03/21/520962541/nevada-on-cusp-of-ratifying-equal -rights-amendment-35-years-after-deadline.

119    **Of all those questioned:** "American Women: Topical Essays: The Long Road to Equality: What Women Won from the ERA Ratification Effort." Research Guides. Accessed January 3, 2022. https://guides.loc.gov/american-women-essays/era-ratification-effort #note_33.

119    **The cover article:** "Women of the Year: Great Changes, New Chances, Tough Choices," *TIME*, January 5, 1976. http://content.time.com/time/magazine/article /0,9171,947597,00.html.

120    **In the two decades following 1970:** Clyde Wilcox and Sue Thomas, *Women and Elective Office: Past, Present, and Future* (New York: Oxford University Press, 2014), p. 62.

120    **Between 1973 and 1993:** "The Long Road to Equality: What Women Won from the ERA Ratification Effort." Library of Congress. Research Guides. Accessed July 18, 2023. https://guides.loc.gov/american-women-essays/era-ratification-effort.

120    **The increase in female political:** "Women Political Leaders: The Impact of Gender on Democracy." Women Political Leaders: The Impact of Gender on Democracy | Global Institute for Women's Leadership | King's College London. Accessed January 3, 2022. https://www.kcl.ac.uk/giwl/research/women-political-leaders-the-impact-of-gender -on-democracy.

121    **The echoes of her advocacy:** "Kamala Harris Enters 2020 Bid with Tribute to Woman Who Broke Barriers," *The Guardian*. Guardian News and Media, January 21, 2019. https://www.theguardian.com/us-news/2019/jan/21/kamala-harris-2020-presidential -bid--logo-tribute-shirley-chisholm.

121    **Of Chisholm, she said:** DeNeen L. Brown, "Shirley Chisholm Blazed the Way for Kamala Harris to Be Biden's VP Pick," *Washington Post*, August 11, 2020. https://www .washingtonpost.com/history/2020/08/01/shirley-chisholm-black-women-biden-vp.

121    **The United Nations General Assembly:** "Gender Equality." United Nations. Accessed January 3, 2022. https://www.un.org/en/global-issues/gender-equality.

121    **Back in the United States:** Pay equity information. Accessed July 18, 2023. https://www .pay-equity.org/info-time.html.

122    **Alice Paul died in 1977:** Dena Kleiman, "Alice Paul, a Leader for Suffrage and Women's Rights, Dies at 92," *New York Times*, July 10, 1977. https://www.nytimes.com /1977/07/10/archives/alice-paul-a-leader-for-suffrage-and-womens-rights-dies-at-92 .html.

122    **Chisholm turned her back:** Jane Perlez, "Rep. Chisholm's Angry Farewell," *New York Times*, October 12, 1982. https://www.nytimes.com/1982/10/12/us/rep-chisholm -s-angry-farewell.html.


Chapter 6: 1,365 Men and Me

123    **In 1981, a magazine article:** Gail Collins, *When Everything Changed: The Amazing Journey of American Women from 1960 to the Present* (London: Little, Brown and Company, 2010), p. 293.

123    **Around the same time:** Ibid.

123    **more than half a century:** Moira Macdonald, "Women Who Ran Seattle: Bertha Knight Landes, First Female Mayor of a Major US City, Demanded Equal Treatment," *Seattle*

*Times*, March 1, 2022. https://www.seattletimes.com/life/women-who-ran-seattle
-bertha-knight-landes-was-the-first-female-mayor-of-a-major-u-s-city.

123  **almost a hundred years:** "Susanna Madora Salter First Woman Mayor," Kansas Historical Society. Accessed April 11, 2022. https://www.kshs.org/p/kansas-historical
-quarterly-susanna-madora-salter/13106.

123  **the trajectory by 1980:** "The Data on Women Leaders," Pew Research Center's Social & Demographic Trends Project. Pew Research Center, February 25, 2021. https://www
.pewresearch.org/social-trends/fact-sheet/the-data-on-women-leaders.

124  **the first television drama:** Julie D'Acci, "Defining Women: Television and the Case of Cagney and Lacey." *Choice Reviews Online* 32, no. 2 (1994). https://doi.org/10.5860
/choice.32-0721.

124  **Gallup asked Americans:** Clare Malone, "From 1937 to Hillary Clinton, How Americans Have Felt About a Woman President," FiveThirtyEight. FiveThirtyEight, June 9, 2016. https://fivethirtyeight.com/features/from-1937-to-hillary-clinton-how-americans-have
-felt-about-a-female-president.

124  **In the seven years:** "The Number of Women Attending Law Schools Has More . . ." UPI. UPI, February 28, 1982. https://www.upi.com/Archives/1982/02/28/The-number-of
-women-attending-law-schools-has-more/6628383720400.

125  **On a touristy excursion:** Muriel Siebert and Aimee Lee Ball, *Changing the Rules: Adventures of a Wall Street Maverick* (New York: Free Press, 2002), p. 2.

127  **"I was certainly the only woman":** Siebert and Ball, p. 9.

128  **almost double the median income:** US Census Bureau, "Income of Families and Persons in the United States: 1958." Census.gov, October 8, 2021. https://www.census.gov
/library/publications/1960/demo/p60-033.html.

129  *That's take-a-vacation money:* Siebert and Ball, p. 13.

129  **French feminist and novelist:** George Sand, *Lire Gabriel.* Accessed January 14, 2022. http://textes.libres.free.fr/francais/george-sand_gabriel.htm.

129  **More than a century later:** Marilyn Loden, "100 Women: 'Why I Invented the Glass Ceiling Phrase.'" BBC News. BBC, December 13, 2017. https://www.bbc.com/news
/world-42026266.

129  **Loden's experiences mirrored:** Ibid.

129  **"What large firm":** Siebert and Ball, p. 29.

131  **"prospective petticoat invasion":** Sheri J. Caplan, *Petticoats and Pinstripes: Portraits of Women in Wall Street's History* (Santa Barbara, CA: Praeger, 2013).

131  **admitted to the London Stock Exchange:** "BBC On This Day | 26 | 1973: Stock Exchange Admits Women." BBC News. BBC, March 26, 1973. http://news.bbc.co.uk/onthisday
/hi/dates/stories/march/26/newsid_2531000/2531145.stm

131  **"Can I buy a seat":** Siebert and Ball, p. 31.

132  **"Holy shit, Mickie":** Siebert and Ball, p. 34.

132  **The last seat ever:** "NYSE Seat Sold for $3.5m." *The Times,* April 2, 2010. https://www
.thetimes.co.uk/article/nyse-seat-sold-for-dollar35m-f78bxrjkqoc.

133  **Three weeks after signing:** Siebert and Ball, p. 37.

134  **the need for a women's bathroom:** Joanna Scutts. "History of Women in Finance: How Muriel Siebert Opened Doors." *TIME,* April 19, 2016. https://time.com/4297571
/muriel-siebert-wall-street-history.

134  **use the bathroom:** "NYSE's 'Moving the Needle' Might Have to Start with 'Moving the Bathroom.'" *Forbes.* Forbes Magazine, August 3, 2012. https://www.forbes.com/sites
/goodmenproject/2012/08/02/266/?sh=39df9ee94c32.

134  **Women flocked to her:** Siebert and Ball, p. 41.

135  **"institutions of higher learning":** Siebert and Ball, p. 42.

136  **"Years later, I figured out":** Based on interviews with Neale Godfrey conducted throughout 2022.

138  **"do the woman a favor":** Judy Klemesrud, "Women's Bank Lures 350 Depositors," *New York Times*, October 17, 1975. https://www.nytimes.com/1975/10/17/archives/womens -bank-lures-350-depositors.html.

139  **It would also require her:** Siebert and Ball, p. 44.

139  **Siebert readily admitted:** Siebert and Ball, p. 78.

139  **two MCU employees:** Siebert and Ball, p. 79.

139  **take control of MCU:** Emanuel Perlmutter, "New York State Is Taking Over Municipal Credit Union in the City," *New York Times*, November 3, 1977. https://www.nytimes .com/1977/11/03/archives/new-york-state-is-taking-over-municipal-credit-union-in-the -city.html.

140  **defeated by a thirty-point margin:** Maurice Carroll, "Moynihan Wins Overwhelming Victory," *New York Times*, November 3, 1982. https://www.nytimes.com/1982/11/03 /nyregion/moynihan-wins-overwhelming-victory.html.

142  **Beyond giving different genders:** Based on conversations with Neale Godfrey through-out 2022.

142  **surveyed women working in the industry:** Daniel Thomas, "Women in Finance Say 'Mediocre' Male Managers Block Progress." Subscribe to read | Financial Times. *Financial Times*, June 16, 2021. https://www.ft.com/content/08ffibdo-2e2b-4d2o-bb9f -dfe8c5a9807b.

143  **sexual harassment was first defined:** "Document 34: EEOC Guidelines on Sexual Harassment, 45 Federal Register 74676 (10 November 1980), Codified in 29 C.F.R. §1604.11." Document 34: EEOC Guidelines on Sexual Harassment, 10 November 1980 | Alexander Street Documents. Accessed January 12, 2022. https://documents .alexanderstreet.com/d/1000674188.

143  **Feenstra of Louisiana:** *Kirchberg v. Feenstra*, 450 U.S. 455 (1981). Justia Law. Accessed June 4, 2023. https://supreme.justia.com/cases/federal/us/450/455.

144  **a landmark civil rights case:** *Obergefell v. Hodges*. Legal Information Institute. Legal Information Institute. Accessed January 19, 2022. https://www.law.cornell.edu /supremecourt/text/14-556.

145  **a book that appeared in 1994:** *The Beardstown Ladies' Common-Sense Investment Guide: How We Beat the Stock Market—And How You Can Too* (New York: Hyperion, 1994).

145  **the erstwhile bank teller:** Mark Gongloff, "Where Are They Now: The Beard-stown Ladies," *Wall Street Journal*, May 1, 2006. https://www.wsj.com/articles /SB114596682916135186.

146  **the returns that looked too good:** "Beardstown Ladies Had the Wrong Results," *New York Times*, March 18, 1998. https://www.nytimes.com/1998/03/18/business /beardstown-ladies-had-the-wrong-results.html.

Chapter 7: Old Dreams, New Realities

147  **wage gap narrowed more:** "Earnings and the Gender Wage Gap," Status of Women in the States, March 4, 2015. https://statusofwomendata.org/earnings-and-the-gender -wage-gap.

147  **made great strides toward:** Leslie Lazin Novack and David R. Novack, "Being Female

Eighties and Nineties: Conflicts between New Opportunities and Traditional Expectations among White, Middle Class, Heterosexual College Women," *Sex Roles* 35, no. 1–2 (1996), pp. 57–77. https://doi.org/10.1007/bf01548175.

148 **"unwilling or psychologically unable":** Ibid.

148 **"caught in the middle":** Rosanna Hertz, *More Equal Than Others: Women and Men in Dual-Career Marriages* (Berkeley: California University Press, 1988).

148 **culturally iconic phrase:** Helen Gurley Brown, *Having It All* (New York: Simon & Schuster, 1982).

149 **from 1960 to 1983:** George Guilder, "Women in the Work Force," *The Atlantic.* Atlantic Media Company, September 1, 1986. https://www.theatlantic.com/magazine/archive /1986/09/women-in-the-work-force/304924.

150 **echoing Gurley Brown's sentiments:** Gloria Sorensen and Lois M. Verbrugge, "Women, Work, and Health," *Annual Review of Public Health* 8, no. 1 (1987), pp. 235–51. https:// doi.org/10.1146/annurev.pu.08.050187.001315.

150 **her pandemic existence:** Emma Jacobs and Laura Noonan, "Is the Coronavirus Crisis Taking Women Back to the 1950s?" *Financial Times,* June 13, 2020. https://www.ft.com /content/7e147d57-050e-405c-a334-75a5ea748e2a.

150 **dropped out of the workforce:** "Four Times More Women Than Men Dropped Out of the Labor Force in September," National Women's Law Center: Home. Accessed March 7, 2022. https://nwlc.org/wp-content/uploads/2020/10/september-jobs-fs1 .pdf.

151 **quit the U.S. workforce:** Ernie Tedeschi, "The Mystery of How Many Mothers Have Left Work Because of School Closings," *New York Times,* October 29, 2020. https://www .nytimes.com/2020/10/29/upshot/mothers-leaving-jobs-pandemic.html.

151 **"Far more mothers":** Claudia Goldin, "Understanding the Economic Impact of Covid-19 on Women." *Brookings,* Brookings, 31 Mar. 2022, https://www.brookings .edu/bpea-articles/understanding-the-economic-impact-of-covid-19-on-women/

151 **more vulnerable to burnout:** Nancy Beauregard et al., "Gendered Pathways to Burnout: Results from the Salveo Study," *Annals of Work Exposures and Health* 62, no. 4 (2018), pp. 426–37. https://doi.org/10.1093/annweh/wxx114.

151 **Patricia Cremer's daily routine:** Georgia Dullea, "When Parents Work on Different Shifts," *New York Times,* October 31, 1983. https://www.nytimes.com/1983/10/31/style /when-parents-work-on-different-shifts.html.

153 **answers started to resemble:** Claudia Goldin, "The Quiet Revolution That Transformed Women's Employment, Education, and Family," *American Economic Review* 96, no. 2 (2006), pp. 1–21. https://doi.org/10.1257/000282806777212350.

153 **average age of first-time motherhood:** "Mean Age of Mother, 1970–2000," Accessed February 25, 2022. https://www.cdc.gov/nchs/data/nvsr/nvsr51/nvsr51_01.pdf.

153 **loss of prestige:** Goldin.

154 **regarded as less valuable:** Ibid.

155 **"Women still marry up":** Josie Cox, "Women Still Sacrifice Personal Happiness for Professional Brilliance," *Quartz.* Accessed February 25, 2022. https://qz.com/1746173 /women-still-have-to-choose-between-personal-and-professional-success.

155 **no-fault divorce bill:** W. Bradford Wilcox, "The Evolution of Divorce," *National Affairs,* Fall 2009. Accessed February 24, 2022. https://nationalaffairs.com/publications /detail/the-evolution-of-divorce.

155 **the divorce rate doubled:** "The U.S. Divorce Rate Has Hit a 50-Year Low." Institute for Family Studies. Accessed February 25, 2022. https://ifstudies.org/blog/the-us,divorce -rate-has-hit-a-50-year-low.

157   **Garland's situation spiraled:** Tamar Lewin, "Maternity Leave: Is It Leave, Indeed?" *New York Times*, July 22, 1984. https://www.nytimes.com/1984/07/22/business/maternity-leave-is-it-leave-indeed.html.

157   **"does not compel employers":** Amy Wilentz, "Garland's Bouquet." *TIME* magazine. Time Inc., January 26, 1987. http://content.time.com/time/subscriber/article /0,33009,963321,00.html.

158   **"perhaps the most obvious way":** Teresa A. Mauldin, "Women Who Remain Above the Poverty Level in Divorce: Implications for Family Policy," *Family Relations* 39, no. 2 (1990), p. 141. https://doi.org/10.2307/585715.

158   **any child support at all:** "Income Security and Education National Snapshot." Accessed March 2, 2022. https://nwlc.org/wp-content/uploads/2016/09/Poverty-Snapshot -Factsheet-2016.pdf.

158   **"disparity hasn't changed much":** Nicholas H. Wolfinger, "The Changing Economics of Single Motherhood," *Pacific Standard*. Pacific Standard, January 8, 2015. https:// psmag.com/economics/changing-economics-single-motherhood-97360.

158   **originally a term of respect:** Z. Berend, "'The Best or None!' Spinsterhood in Nineteenth-Century New England," *Journal of Social History* 33, no. 4 (2000), pp. 935–57. https://doi.org/10.1353/jsh.2000.0056.

159   **"It was fashionable":** Janelle Nanos, "'Spinster' and the Stigma of Being Single," *Boston* magazine. Boston Magazine, January 10, 2012. https://www.bostonmagazine.com /news/2012/01/10/spinster-and-the-stigma-of-being-single.

159   **as paragons of the ideal housewife:** Courtney G. Joslin, "Marital Status Discrimination 2.0," *Boston University Law Review* 805 (September 30, 2015), UC Davis Legal Studies Research Paper No. 460.

159   **"aura of wisdom":** "Marriage in the '80s," *Chicago Tribune*, January 1, 1970. https:// www.chicagotribune.com/news/ct-xpm-1987-02-01-8701080643-story.html.

159   **"successfully performing femininity":** Shelley Budgeon, "The 'Problem' With Single Women," *Journal of Social and Personal Relationships* 33, no. 3 (2015), pp. 401–18. https://doi.org/10.1177/0265407515607647.

160   **pernicious attitude of prejudice:** Anne Byrne and Deborah Carr, "Caught in the Cultural Lag: The Stigma of Singlehood," *Psychological Inquiry* 16, no. 2/3 (2005), pp. 84–91. http://www.jstor.org/stable/20447267.

160   **For full-time single workers:** "Highlights of women's earnings in 2020," U.S. Bureau of Labor Statistics, September 1, 2021. https://www.bls.gov/opub/reports/womens -earnings/2020/home.htm.

160   **about 39 million people:** "More Than One-Third of Prime-Age Americans Have Never Married." Accessed March 9, 2022. https://ifstudies.org/ifs-admin/resources/final2 -ifs-single-americansbrief2020.pdf.

160   **Marital privileges pervade:** Christina Campbell and Lisa Arnold, "The High Price of Being Single in America," *The Atlantic*, January 14, 2013. https://www.theatlantic.com /sexes/archive/2013/01/the-high-price-of-being-single-in-america/267043.

161   **more than three decades:** Katherine Goldstein, "I Was a Sheryl Sandberg Superfan. Then Her 'Lean in' Advice Failed Me," *Vox* magazine, December 6, 2018. https://www .vox.com/first-person/2018/12/6/18128838/michelle-obama-lean-in-sheryl-sandberg.

162   **That critique was compounded:** Sheera Frenkel et al., "Delay, Deny and Deflect: How Facebook's Leaders Fought through Crisis," *New York Times*, November 14, 2018. https://www.nytimes.com/2018/11/14/technology/facebook-data-russia-election -racism.html?module=inline.

162   **"It's not always enough"**: Erin Durkin, "Michelle Obama on 'Leaning In': 'Sometimes That Shit Doesn't Work,'" *The Guardian*, Guardian News and Media, December 3, 2018. https://www.theguardian.com/us-news/2018/dec/03/michelle-obama-lean-in -sheryl-sandberg.

162   **"I nodded my head vigorously"**: Caitlin Gibson, "The End of Leaning In: How Sheryl Sandberg's Message of Empowerment Fully Unraveled," *Washington Post*, December 26, 2018. https://www.washingtonpost.com/lifestyle/style/the-end-of-lean-in-how -sheryl-sandbergs-message-of-empowerment-fully-unraveled/2018/12/19/9561eb06 -fe2e-11e8-862a-b6a6f3ce8199_story.html.

163   **"When you have someone"**: Ibid.

Chapter 8: A Bimbo or a Bitch

164   **marital rape had finally been outlawed**: "Domestic Violence and Sexual Assault Resources." Accessed April 19, 2022. http://www.ncdsv.org/NCDSV_DVSAresources _8-2016.pdf.

164   **not unanimously loved**: F. J. Frommer, "Justice Ginsburg Thought Roe Was the Wrong Case to Settle Abortion Issue," *Washington Post*. Retrieved May 13, 2022, from https:// www.washingtonpost.com/history/2022/05/06/ruth-bader-ginsburg-roe-wade.

165   **cofounder of and chief litigator**: "Supreme Court Justice Ruth Bader Ginsburg," Clinton Digital Library. Accessed June 6, 2022. https://clinton.presidentiallibraries.us/rbg -topical-guide.

165   **Twelve years after Sandra Day O'Connor**: Richard L. Berke, "Clinton Names Ruth Ginsburg, Advocate for Women, to Court," *New York Times*, June 15, 1993. https://www .nytimes.com/1993/06/15/us/supreme-court-overview-clinton-names-ruth-ginsburg -advocate-for-women-court.html.

165   **nominated by President Clinton**: Clay Chandler, "Blinder, Yellen Named by Clinton to Fed Board," *Washington Post*, April 23, 1994. https://www.washingtonpost .com/archive/business/1994/04/23/blinder-yellen-named-by-clinton-to-fed-board /86e0e452-6f71-45b5-a02b-b44ea9c9016a.

165   **astronaut Eileen Collins**: "Shuttle Loses Its Glass Ceiling with First Female Commander," *Los Angeles Times*, March 5, 1998. https://www.latimes.com/archives/la-xpm -1998-mar-05-mn-25833-story.html.

165   **more women entered political office**: Allison Yarrow, "How the '90s Hurt Gender Equality Progress," *TIME*, June 13, 2018. https://time.com/5310256/90s-gender -equality-progress.

166   **playwright Eve Ensler**: Charles Isherwood, "The Culture Project and Plays That Make a Difference," *New York Times*, September 3, 2006. https://www.nytimes.com/2006 /09/03/theater/03ishe.html.

166   **a shade above 71 percent**: Pay Equity Information. Accessed April 19, 2022. https:// www.pay-equity.org/info-time.html.

167   **On a sunny Friday**: "Statement on Signing the Family and Medical Leave Act of 1993," Statement on Signing the Family and Medical Leave Act of 1993 | The American Presidency Project, February 5, 1993. https://www.presidency.ucsb.edu/documents /statement-signing-the-family-and-medical-leave-act-1993.

168   **Some research indicates**: Peter Blair and Benjamin Posmanick, *Why Did Gender Wage Convergence in the United States Stall?* NBER Working Paper Series. 2023. https://doi .org/10.3386/w30821.

168 **women hired after:** Mallika Thomas, "The Impact of Mandated Maternity Leave Policies on the Gender Gap in Promotions," Social Science Research Network, *SSRN Electronic Journal*, 2020. https://doi.org/10.2139/ssrn.3729663.

169 **"expected return on investment":** Ibid.

169 **clock-stopping policies:** "Equal but Inequitable: Who Benefits from Gender-Neutral Tenure Clock Stopping Policies?" IZA. Accessed April 21, 2022. https://www.iza .org/publications/dp/9904/equal-but-inequitable-who-benefits-from-gender-neutral -tenure-clock-stopping-policies.

170 **One glaring example:** Linda Trimble, *Ms. Prime Minister: Gender, Media, and Leadership* (Toronto: University of Toronto Press, 2017).

170 **particularly critically assessed:** Alice H. Eagly, Mona G. Makhijani, and Bruce G. Klonsky, "Gender and the Evaluation of Leaders: A Meta-Analysis," *Psychological Bulletin* 111, no. 1 (1992), pp. 3–22. https://doi.org/10.1037/0033-2909.111.1.3.

171 **was hired to work for IBM:** Ann Hopkins, "Price Waterhouse v. Hopkins: A Personal Account of a Sexual Discrimination Plaintiff." Accessed April 29, 2022. https:// scholarlycommons.law.hofstra.edu/cgi/viewcontent.cgi?article=1024&context=hlelj.

172 **"miserable, depressed, furious":** Ibid.

173 **back to Washington:** Ibid.

173 **Five and a half years later:** Spencer Rich, "Out of Court Settlement," *Washington Post*, June 16, 1984. https://www.washingtonpost.com/archive/politics/1984/06/16/out-of -court-settlement/e87c7ea3-59e5-4567-ab60-bc373b064f8c.

174 **"an employer who objects":** *Price Waterhouse v. Hopkins*, 490 U.S. 228 (1989). Justia Law. Accessed May 4, 2022. https://supreme.justia.com/cases/federal/us/490/228.

174 **"a theory of sex discrimination":** Ilona M. Turner, "Sex Stereotyping Per Se: Transgender Employees and Title VII," *California Law Review* 95 (2007), p. 561.

176 **"either loved her fiercely":** Brooks Barnes, "Ann Hopkins, Who Struck an Early Blow to the Glass Ceiling, Dies at 74," *New York Times*, July 17, 2018. https://www.nytimes .com/2018/07/17/obituaries/ann-hopkins-winner-of-a-workplace-bias-fight-dies-at-74 .html.

176 **wore a suit and Ferragamo pumps:** Ibid.

176 **"put a crack in it":** Ibid.

176 **gender dysphoria:** "Gender Dysphoria Diagnosis," *Psychiatry.org*. https://www .psychiatry.org/psychiatrists/diversity/education/transgender-and-gender -nonconforming-patients/gender-dysphoria-diagnosis.

176 **effeminate mannerisms:** *Jimmie L. Smith, Plaintiff-Appellant, v. City of Salem, Ohio, Thomas Eastek, Walter Greenamyer, Brooke Zellers, Larry D. Dejane, James A. Armeni, Joseph Julian, and Harry Dugan, Defendants-Appellees*, 369 F.3d 912 (6th Cir. 2004). Justia Law, https://law.justia.com/cases/federal/appellate-courts/F3/369/912/532333.

177 **"incredibly exciting":** Fred Barbash, "How a 1989 'Glass Ceiling' Ruling Led to the Government's Claim Against N.C.'s 'Bathroom Law,'" *Washington Post*, May 11, 2016, https://www.washingtonpost.com/news/morning-mix/wp/2016/05/11/how-a-1989 -glass-ceiling-case-unrelated-to-bathrooms-or-gender-identity-led-to-the-obama -administrations-case-against-n-c.

178 **trajectory of female corporate leaders:** Alessandra Stanley, "For Women, to Soar Is Rare, to Fall Is Human," *New York Times*, January 13, 2002. https://www.nytimes.com/2002 /01/13/business/for-women-to-soar-is-rare-to-fall-is-human.html.

178 **torrent of scrutiny:** Glenn Kessler, "Carly Fiorina's Misleading Claims about Her Business Record," *Washington Post*, May 8, 2015. https://www.washingtonpost.com/news

/fact-checker/wp/2015/05/08/carly-fiorinas-misleading-claims-about-her-business
-record.

179 **"particularly painful commentary"**: Carly Fiorina, *Tough Choices: A Memoir* (London: Nicholas Brealey, 2007).

179 **The article theorized**: Stanley.

179 **Investors said that Blanc**: "Shareholders Subjected the Female CEO of Insurance Giant Aviva to Multiple Sexist Comments at AGM That Left Board Chair 'Flabbergasted.'" Yahoo! Accessed May 26, 2022. https://www.yahoo.com/entertainment/shareholders -subjected-female-ceo-insurance-114931988.html.

179 **"hectoring is intentionally intimidating"**: Conversation with Allyson Zimmermann in May 2022.

180 **The pair found**: Michelle K. Ryan and Alexander S. Haslam, "The Glass Cliff: Exploring the Dynamics Surrounding the Appointment of Women to Precarious Leadership Positions," *Academy of Management Review* 32, no. 2 (2007), pp. 549–72. https://doi .org/10.5465/amr.2007.24351856.

180 **corroborating this theory**: Alison Cook and Christy Glass, "Above the Glass Ceiling: When Are Women and Racial/Ethnic Minorities Promoted to CEO?" *Strategic Management Journal* 35, no. 7 (2013), pp. 1080–89. https://doi.org/10.1002/smj.2161.

181 **faulty ignition switches**: "GM to Recall 1.5 Million Vehicles to Fix Electric Power Steering Issue." Reuters. Thomson Reuters, March 31, 2014. https://www.reuters.com /article/us-gm-recall-electric-power-steering-idUSBREA2U1ND20140331.

181 **weeks into Mary Barra's term**: "General Motors Announces 30th Recall of Year," CBS News. CBS Interactive, May 24, 2014. https://www.cbsnews.com/news/general -motors-announces-30th-recall-of-year/.

181 **teetering on the edge**: "Xerox CEO Anne Mulcahy Steps Down," CNNMoney. Cable News Network, May 22, 2009. https://money.cnn.com/2009/05/21/news/companies /xerox_ceo/.

181 **Bartz was pushed out**: Alexei Oreskovic and Edwin Chan, "Yahoo! CEO Bartz Fired over the Phone, Rocky Run Ends." Reuters. Thomson Reuters, September 7, 2011. https://www.reuters.com/article/us-yahoo-ceo/yahoo-ceo-bartz-fired-over-the-phone -rocky-run-ends-idUSTRE7857R320110907.

181 **"Tier 2 man"**: Stephen J. Dubner, "Extra: Carol Bartz Full Interview," Freakonomics, December 16, 2021. https://freakonomics.com/podcast/extra-carol-bartz-full -interview/.

182 **wake of the country's referendum**: Jena McGregor, "Congratulations, Theresa May. Now Mind That 'Glass Cliff,'" *Washington Post*, July 12, 2016. https://www.washingtonpost .com/news/on-leadership/wp/2016/07/12/congratulations-theresa-may-now-mind -that-glass-cliff.

182 **energy-supply crisis**: Elizabeth Piper, "UK's Truss Says She Will Resign as PM," Reuters. Thomson Reuters, October 20, 2022. https://www.reuters.com/world/uk /uks-truss-says-she-is-resigning-pm-2022-10-20.

182 **temporary caretaker administration**: Marine Strauss and Philip Blenkinsop, "Belgium Forms New Government After 16-Month Deadlock," Reuters. Thomson Reuters, September 30, 2020. https://www.reuters.com/article/uk-belgium-government -idUKKBN26L14L.

182 **most prominent women**: Arbora Johnson, "Biography: Janet Yellen," National Women's History Museum. Accessed June 4, 2023. https://www.womenshistory.org/education -resources/biographies/janet-yellen.

183 **only the second woman:** "Laura D. Tyson," Berkeley Haas, November 4, 2022. https://haas.berkeley.edu/faculty/tyson-laura.

183 **touted as a candidate for the job:** Louis Uchitelle, "An Appointment That Draws No Fire," *New York Times*, January 7, 1997. https://archive.nytimes.com/www.nytimes.com/library/politics/whouse/articles/010797yellen-profile.html.

183 **provoked a furor:** "President Summers's Remarks at the National Bureau of Economic Research, Jan. 14 2005: News: *The Harvard Crimson*." News | The Harvard Crimson, February 18, 2005. https://www.thecrimson.com/article/2005/2/18/full-transcript-president-summers-remarks-at.

183 **"extraordinarily fine economist":** Uchitelle, 1997.

185 **simply too short:** Philip Rucker et al., "Trump Slams Fed Chair, Questions Climate Change and Threatens to Cancel Putin Meeting in Wide-Ranging Interview with the Post," *Washington Post*, July 23, 2019. https://www.washingtonpost.com/politics/trump-slams-fed-chair-questions-climate-change-and-threatens-to-cancel-putin-meeting-in-wide-ranging-interview-with-the-post/2018/11/27/4362fae8-f26c-11e8-aeea-b85fd44449f5_story.html.

185 **grasp of macroeconomic policy:** Bess Levin and Kenzie Bryant, "Janet Yellen: Trump Is an Even Bigger Idiot Than He Looks," *Vanity Fair*, February 25, 2019. https://www.vanityfair.com/news/2019/02/janet-yellen-donald-trump-interview.

186 **"most accomplished people":** Neil Irwin, "Janet Yellen Has Excelled at Big Jobs. This Will Be the Hardest One Yet," *New York Times*, November 24, 2020. https://www.nytimes.com/2020/11/24/upshot/janet-yellen-treasury-challenges.html.

186 **On her first day:** "Day One Message to Staff from Secretary of the United States Department of the Treasury Janet L. Yellen," U.S. Department of the Treasury, January 26, 2021. https://home.treasury.gov/news/press-releases/jy0003.

186 **debates are futile:** Michelle K. Ryan et al., "Getting on Top of the Glass Cliff: Reviewing a Decade of Evidence, Explanations, and Impact," *The Leadership Quarterly* 27, no. 3 (2016), pp. 446–55. https://doi.org/10.1016/j.leaqua.2015.10.008.

187 **has enough gravitas:** Paul Krugman, "Sex, Money and Gravitas," *New York Times*, August 2, 2013. https://www.nytimes.com/2013/08/02/opinion/krugman-sex-money-and-gravitas.html.

188 **"pathetically adolescent":** Maureen Dowd, "Liberties; President Irresistible," *New York Times*, February 18, 1998. https://www.nytimes.com/1998/02/18/opinion/liberties-president-irresistible.html.

188 **Lewinsky's private life:** Alexandra Schwartz, "Monica Lewinsky and the Shame Game," *The New Yorker*, March 26, 2015. https://www.newyorker.com/culture/cultural-comment/monica-lewinsky-and-the-shame-game.

Chapter 9: Promises and Loopholes

191 **Ledbetter was born Lilly McDaniel:** Lilly M. Ledbetter and Lanier Scott Isom, *Grace and Grit: My Fight for Equal Pay and Fairness at Goodyear and Beyond* (New York: Three Rivers Press, 2012), p. 13.

191 **first laid eyes on Charles Ledbetter:** Ledbetter and Isom, p. 40.

193 **Late in 1968:** Ledbetter and Isom, pp. 52–53.

193 **Lilly filled out an application:** Ledbetter and Isom, p. 53.

194 **Early on, Ledbetter:** Ledbetter and Isom, p. 82.

195 **One day in May 1982:** Ledbetter and Isom, p. 85.

195 **Ledbetter felt compelled:** Lilly Ledbetter, "Lilly Ledbetter: My #MeToo Moment,"

*New York Times*, April 9, 2018. https://www.nytimes.com/2018/04/09/opinion/lilly-ledbetter-metoo-equal-pay.html.

196 **"a missionary in a strange land":** Ledbetter and Isom, p. 71.

197 **"I can put up with a lot":** Ledbetter and Isom, p. 91.

197 **"defined by fear":** Ledbetter and Isom, p. 104.

198 **deep reflection and self-confrontation:** Ledbetter and Isom, p. 121.

199 **handed in her retirement notice:** Ledbetter and Isom, p. 161.

200 **at home:** Ledbetter and Isom, p. 173.

200 **entire pot of coffee:** Ledbetter and Isom, p. 177.

201 **During the course of questioning:** *Ledbetter v. Goodyear Tire & Rubber Co.* Supreme Court of the United States. Accessed June 5, 2023. https://www.scotusblog.com/archives/LedbetterJoinAppendix.pdf.

202 **"been more shocked":** Ledbetter and Scott Isom, p. 200.

203 **Ledbetter pondered Justice Ruth Bader Ginsburg:** Ledbetter and Isom, p. 208.

203 **Goldfarb was at Disney World:** Based on conversations with Jon Goldfarb conducted in June 2022.

204 **One such case was:** *Ledbetter v. Goodyear Tire & Rubber Co., Inc.* Supreme Court of the united States. Accessed June 17, 2022. https://www.supremecourt.gov/opinions/06pdf/05-380.pdf.

204 **Ginsburg was joined:** *Ledbetter v. Goodyear Tire & Rubber Co.* Legal Information Institute. Legal Information Institute, May 29, 2007. https://www.law.cornell.edu/supct/html/05-1074.ZD.html.

206 **"subject to that discriminatory decision":** "House Dems Say Time Limit on Pay Discrimination Lawsuits Should Be Changed," Law.com, June 13, 2007. https://www.law.com/almID/920605483539/?slreturn=20220522111449.

206 **growing army of supporters:** "Lilly Ledbetter DNC Speech (Text, Video)." POLITICO. Accessed June 4, 2023. https://www.politico.com/story/2012/09/lilly-ledbetter-dnc-speech-text-080704.

206 **Charles's condition continued to deteriorate:** Ledbetter and Isom, p. 227.

207 **Perhaps sensing the overwhelming mix:** Ledbetter and Isom, p. 233.

207 **In January 2009:** S.181 - 111th congress (2009–2010): Lilly Ledbetter Fair Pay Act of . . . Accessed June 5, 2023. https://www.congress.gov/bill/111th/senate-bill/181.

208 **Signing the bill:** "Remarks by the President upon Signing the Lilly Ledbetter Bill." National Archives and Records Administration. Accessed June 4, 2023. https://obamawhitehouse.archives.gov/realitycheck/the-press-office/remarks-president-upon-signing-lilly-ledbetter-bill.

209 **declining share of workers:** "On the Books, Off the Record: Examining the Effectiveness of Pay Secrecy Laws in the U.S." Accessed June 17, 2022. https://www.iwpr.org/wp-content/uploads/2021/01/Pay-Secrecy-Policy-Brief-v4.pdf.

209 **Congress passed the NLRA in 1935:** "National Labor Relations Act." National Labor Relations Act, National Labor Relations Board. Accessed June 17, 2022. https://www.nlrb.gov/guidance/key-reference-materials/national-labor-relations-act.

209 **credited the Obama presidency:** Derek Thompson, "Thanks, Obama," *The Atlantic.* Atlantic Media Company, September 26, 2016. https://www.theatlantic.com/business/archive/2016/09/obamas-war-on-inequality/501620.

210 **failed to gain traction:** Jennifer Bendery, "Senate GOP Blocks Paycheck Fairness Act," HuffPost. HuffPost, February 14, 2013. https://www.huffpost.com/entry/paycheck-fairness-act-senate-vote_n_1571413.

210 **"provide adequate protections":** Ibid.

211   **"100 Days, 100 Ways":** Sunny Frothingham and Shilpa Phadke, "100 Days, 100 Ways the Trump Administration Is Harming Women and Families." Center for American Progress, August 15, 2017. https://www.americanprogress.org/article/100-days-100 -ways-trump-administration-harming-women-families.

211   **easier to identify:** Daniel Wiessner, "White House Blocks Obama-Era Rule Expanding Pay Data from Companies." Reuters. Thomson Reuters, August 30, 2017. https:// www.reuters.com/article/us-trump-paydata/white-house-blocks-obama-era-rule -expanding-pay-data-from-companies-idUSKCN1BA21Y.

211   **Trump nominated Eric Dreiband:** "Statement of Eric S. Dreiband." Accessed June 27, 2022. https://www.help.senate.gov/imo/media/doc/dreiband.pdf.

211   **defended Bloomberg LP:** "Bloomberg Wins Dismissal in Well-Publicized Pregnancy Discrimination Case Brought by EEOC." Jones Day. Accessed June 27, 2022. https:// www.jonesday.com/en/practices/experience/2009/08/bloomberg-wins-dismissal-in -well-publicized-pregnancy-discrimination-case-brought-by-eeoc.

212   **most affected by the Trump:** Ruth Dawson, "Trump Administration's Domestic Gag Rule Has Slashed the Title X Network's Capacity by Half." Guttmacher Institute, June 16, 2021. https://www.guttmacher.org/article/2020/02/trump-administrations -domestic-gag-rule-has-slashed-title-x-networks-capacity-half.

213   **chipped away at the foundations:** Aaron Blake, "Analysis | 21 Times Donald Trump Has Assured Us He Respects Women," *Washington Post*, November 25, 2021. https:// www.washingtonpost.com/news/the-fix/wp/2017/03/08/21-times-donald-trump-has -assured-us-he-respects-women.

213   **A decade and a half:** Based on conversations with Jon Goldfarb conducted in June 2022.

214   **ask about salary history:** James Bessen, Erich Denk, and Chen Men, *Perpetuating Wage Inequality: Evidence from Salary History Bans*, June 2020. https://doi.org/10.21203/rs .3.rs-2829726/v1.

Chapter 10: Cassandra and the Crash

215   **Something was bothering:** "Transcript: Holding Megabanks Accountable: A Review of Global Systemically Important Banks 10 Years after the Financial Crisis." House Committee on Financial Services, n.d. https://www.congress.gov/event/116th-congress /house-event/LC64813/text?s=1&r=5.

216   **In 2012, Lauren Rivera:** Lauren Rivera, "Hiring as Cultural Matching," *American Sociological Review* 77, no. 6 (2012), pp. 999–1022. https://doi.org/10.1177 /0003122412463213.

216   **When Rivera was a teenager:** Lauren Rivera, "'Cultural Capital': Its Influence in Education & the Workplace," Kellogg School of Management, October 25, 2022. https:// www.kellogg.northwestern.edu/news/blog/2022/10/25/cultural-capital-influence -education-workplace.aspx.

217   **"critical gate-keeping moments":** Lauren Rivera, "Hirable like Me," Kellogg Insight, May 10, 2019. https://insight.kellogg.northwestern.edu/article/hirable_like_me.

218   **"an outstanding CEO":** "Citi CEO Michael Corbat Announces Plans to Retire in February 2021, Board of Directors Selects Jane Fraser to Succeed Corbat as CEO." Citi. Accessed June 4, 2023. https://www.citigroup.com/global/news/press-release /2020/citi-ceo-michael-corbat-announces-plans-to-retire-in-february-2021-board-of -directors-selects-jane-fraser-to-succeed-corbat-as-ceo.

219   **Born grew up in California:** Rick Schmitt, "Prophet and Loss," *Stanford* magazine, March/April 2009. https://stanfordmag.org/contents/prophet-and-loss.

219 **"doing a terrible thing":** Sean Groom, "Legends in the Law: Brooksley Born, Washington Lawyer, 2003." Archived: https://archive.ph/20130414152307/http://www.dcbar.org/for _lawyers/resources/publications/washington_lawyer/october_2003/legends.cfm

219 **managed to convince:** Bethany McLean and Joseph Nocera, *All the Devils Are Here: The Hidden History of the Financial Crisis* (London: Portfolio, 2011).

219 **previously worked in government:** "Carolyn Agger (LL.B. 1938)." Yale Law Women. Accessed July 27, 2022. https://ylw.yale.edu/portraits-project/carolyn-agger-ll-b-1938.

220 **the NWLC spun off:** Schmitt.

221 **advise the president:** Sean Groom, "Legends in the Law: Brooksley Born, Washington Lawyer, 2003." Archived: https://archive.ph/20130414152307/http://www.dcbar.org /for_lawyers/resources/publications/washington_lawyer/october_2003/legends.cfm

221 **extremely prestigious accolade:** Awards & Recognition, Women's Bar Association, February 27, 2023. https://wbadc.org/about/awards-recognition.

221 **"Indisputably, she was qualified":** Schmitt.

222 **within a whisker:** Brett D. Fromson, "Bankers Trust, Gibson Settle Derivatives Suit," *Washington Post*, November 24, 1994. https://www.washingtonpost.com/archive /business/1994/11/24/bankers-trust-gibson-settle-derivatives-suit/80983166-42dd -4b7d-a796-2886b6a8a757.

222 **The memory of that:** McLean and Nocera, 2011.

223 **Rubin wasn't exactly delighted:** Michael Hirsh, *Capital Offense: How Washington's Wise Men Turned America's Future over to Wall Street* (Hoboken, NJ: Wiley, 2010), p. 1.

223 **invited Born to lunch:** Manuel Roig-Franzia, "Brooksley Born Warned about the Risks of Derivatives," *Seattle Times*. The Seattle Times Company, May 30, 2009. https://www .seattletimes.com/business/brooksley-born-warned-about-the-risks-of-derivatives.

223 **staffers under Greenspan:** Hirsh, 2010, p. 1

224 **"wizard of monetary policy":** Linton Weeks and John M. Berry, "The Shy Wizard of Money," *Washington Post*, March 24, 1997. https://www.washingtonpost.com/wp-srv /business/longterm/fed/greenspan/profile.htm.

224 **"Committee to Save the World":** Joshua Cooper Ramo, "The Three Marketeers," *TIME*. Time Inc., February 15, 1999. https://content.time.com/time/subscriber/article /0,33009,990206,00.html.

224 **the CFTC started preparing:** Clayton S. Rose and David Lane, "Lessons Learned? Brooksley Born & the OTC Derivatives Market (A)." Harvard Business School Case 311-044, November 2010.

225 **didn't even have jurisdiction:** Ibid.

225 **Rubin was incensed:** Maryann Haggerty, "Lessons Learned: Brooksley Born," *Journal of Financial Crises*: Vol. 4 (2022), Iss. 2, pp. 2027–30. https://elischolar.library.yale.edu /journal-of-financial-crises/vol4/iss2/91.

226 **"if there was a moment":** McLean and Nocera, 2011.

226 **not be seeking reappointment:** Chairperson Brooksley Born Announces Her Intention Not to Seek Reappointment to a Second Term, January 19, 1999. https://www.cftc.gov /sites/default/files/opa/press99/opa4231-99.htm.

227 **Michael Greenberger stated:** "Stanford Rock Center." Resource Library: Financial Crisis Inquiry Commission. Accessed August 3, 2022. https://fcic-static.law.stanford .edu/cdn_media/fcic-testimony.

227 **"I made a mistake":** Andrew Clark and Jill Treanor, "Greenspan - I Was Wrong about the Economy. Sort Of," *The Guardian*. Guardian News and Media, October 23, 2008. https://www.theguardian.com/business/2008/oct/24/economics-creditcrunch -federal-reserve-greenspan.

227    **In a 2009 *Frontline* episode:** *Frontline*, PBS. Public Broadcasting Service, October 20, 2009. https://www.pbs.org/video/frontline-the-warning.

228    **faced lower and less-frequent fines:** Scott Berinato, "Banks with More Women on Their Boards Commit Less Fraud," *Harvard Business Review*, April 13, 2021. https://hbr.org/2021/05/banks-with-more-women-on-their-boards-commit-less-fraud.

228    **"As I have said many times":** Christine Lagarde, "Ten Years after Lehman—Lessons Learned and Challenges Ahead," IMFBlog, September 5, 2018. https://blogs.imf.org/2018/09/05/ten-years-after-lehman-lessons-learned-and-challenges-ahead.

229    **white single male borrowers:** Elvin Wyly and C.S. Ponder, "Gender, Age, and Race in Subprime America," *Housing Policy Debate* 21, no. 4 (2011), pp. 529–64. https://doi.org/10.1080/10511482.2011.615850.

229    **female-headed households:** Melanie G. Long, "2008 Financial Crisis Still Seems Like Only Yesterday for Single Women," The Conversation, July 12, 2022. https://theconversation.com/2008-financial-crisis-still-seems-like-only-yesterday-for-single-women-93900.

229    **more pronounced in industries:** "Job Growth in the Great Recession Has Not Been Equal between Men and Women," Economic Policy Institute. Accessed August 4, 2022. https://www.epi.org/blog/job-growth-great-recession-equal-men-women.

230    **named Thasunda Brown Duckett:** Justin Baer, "TIAA Names JP Morgan's Thasunda Brown Duckett as CEO," *Wall Street Journal*, Dow Jones & Company, February 26, 2021. https://www.wsj.com/articles/tiaa-names-jpmorgans-thasunda-brown-duckett-as-ceo-11614267131.

231    **willing to forgo compensation:** Josie Cox, "The Face of Wall Street Is Changing but Gender Inequality Runs Deep," *Forbes Magazine*, May 28, 2021. https://www.forbes.com/sites/josiecox/2021/05/27/the-face-of-wall-street-is-changing-but-gender-inequality-runs-deep.

231    **"You're doing three jobs":** Jessica Hamlin, "The Pandemic Caused a 'Major Step Back' for Women in Financial Services," *Institutional Investor*, May 17, 2021. https://www.institutionalinvestor.com/article/b1rqd8w8wb3qrd/The-Pandemic-Caused-a-Major-Step-Back-for-Women-in-Financial-Services.

231    **approximately equivalent to:** Anu Madgavkar, Kweilin Ellingrud, and Mekala Krishnan, "The Economic Benefits of Gender Parity." McKinsey & Company. McKinsey & Company, March 7, 2016. https://www.mckinsey.com/mgi/overview/in-the-news/the-economic-benefits-of-gender-parity.

231    **equal pay in America:** Elizabeth Schulze, "Closing the Gender Pay Gap Could Have Big Economic Benefits," CNBC. CNBC, March 8, 2018. https://www.cnbc.com/2018/03/08/closing-the-gender-pay-gap-could-have-big-economic-benefits.html.

231    **women repay loans more:** "Professor Muhammad Yunus—Women at the Centre of Our Economic Activity." UN Women. Accessed August 5, 2022. https://beijing20.unwomen.org/en/news-and-events/stories/2014/10/oped-muhammad-yunus.

232    **cash tended to be spent:** Viviana A. Zelizer, "The Gender of Money," *Wall Street Journal*. Dow Jones & Company, January 27, 2011. https://www.wsj.com/articles/BL-IMB-1033.

232    **"caused not just by low incomes":** Nicholas Kristof and Sheryl WuDunn, "The Women's Crusade," *New York Times*, August 17, 2009. https://www.nytimes.com/2009/08/23/magazine/23Women-t.html?partner=rss&emc=rss.

232    **"when it comes to gender":** Based on conversations with Viviana Zelizer conducted in September 2022.

## Chapter 11: The Cost of Silence

233    **Look no further than Bernie Madoff:** Sarah Lynch, "Bernie Madoff, Disgraced Ponzi Schemer, Dies at 82." Reuters. Thomson Reuters, April 14, 2021. https://www.reuters.com/world/us/federal-bureau-prisons-says-ponzi-schemer-bernard-madoff-has-passed-away-2021-04-14.

233    **"Power disinhibits us":** Adam Grant, "Perspective | Power Doesn't Corrupt. It Just Exposes Who Leaders Really Are," *Washington Post*, February 23, 2019. https://www.washingtonpost.com/business/economy/power-doesnt-corrupt-it-just-exposes-who-leaders-really-are/2019/02/22/f5680116-3600-11e9-854a-7a14d7fec96a_story.html.

234    **Morgan Stanley and Merrill Lynch:** "Morgan Stanley Settles Sex Bias Lawsuit," NBCNews.com. NBCUniversal News Group, July 12, 2004. https://www.nbcnews.com/id/wbna5424478; Patrick McGeehan, "Merrill Lynch Settles Sex-Bias Suit, Creates System to Resolve Complaints," *Wall Street Journal*, Dow Jones & Company, May 5, 1998. https://www.wsj.com/articles/SB894325481931103500.

234    **one branch office of Smith Barney:** Susan Antilla, *Tales from the Boom-Boom Room: Women vs Wall Street* (Melbourne: Scribe Publications, 2002).

234    **ended up paying 150 million dollars:** Susan Antilla, "Decades after 'Boom-Boom Room' Suit, Bias Persists for Women," *New York Times*, May 22, 2016. https://www.nytimes.com/2016/05/23/business/dealbook/decades-after-boom-boom-room-suit-bias-persists-for-women.html.

234    **in the face of the toxic masculinity:** Jamie Fiore Higgins, *Bully Market: My Story of Money and Misogyny at Goldman Sachs* (New York: Simon & Schuster, 2022).

235    **most dramatic economic downturn:** Edmund L. Andrews and Jackie Calmes, "Fed Cuts Key Rate to a Record Low," *New York Times*, December 16, 2008. https://www.nytimes.com/2008/12/17/business/17fed.html.

235    **deploy any and all resources:** Stephen Moore, "Channeling Jimmy Carter," *Wall Street Journal*. Dow Jones & Company, December 20, 2008. https://www.wsj.com/articles/SB122972769811422699.

236    **as the technology ecosystem bulged:** Andrew Bary, "Big 5 Tech Stocks Now Account for 23% of the S&P 500," *Barron's*, July 26, 2021. https://www.barrons.com/articles/big-tech-stocks-sp-500-51627312933.

236    **"Silicon Valley has":** Sheelah Kolhatkar, "The Disrupters," *The New Yorker*, November 13, 2017. https://www.newyorker.com/magazine/2017/11/20/the-tech-industrys-gender-discrimination-problem.

236    **NDAs first got a lease on life:** Michelle Dean, "Contracts of Silence," *Columbia Journalism Review*, 2018. https://www.cjr.org/special_report/nda-agreement.php.

237    **Global networks of abuse:** Zelda Perkins, "An NDA from Harvey Weinstein Cost Me My Career—at Last, Banning Them Feels within Reach," *The Guardian*. Guardian News and Media, December 15, 2022. https://www.theguardian.com/commentisfree/2022/dec/15/nda-harvey-weinstein-confidentiality-clause-abuse.

237    **The R&B singer R. Kelly:** Elizabeth Wagmeister, "R. Kelly Silenced Aaliyah and Her Family with Non-Disclosure Agreement after Marriage Annulment, Docuseries Reveals," *Chicago Tribune*, January 4, 2023. https://www.chicagotribune.com/entertainment/ct-ent-r-kelly-docuseries-lifetime-20230104-tpsjrj6yevfijnky7dwzbxpcq4-story.html.

237    **Donald Trump was known:** Michael Kranish, "Trump Long Has Relied on Nondisclosure Deals to Prevent Criticism. That Strategy May Be Unraveling," *Washington Post*,

August 7, 2020. https://www.washingtonpost.com/politics/trump-nda-jessica-denson
-lawsuit/2020/08/06/202fed1c-d5ad-11ea-b9b2-1ea733b97910_story.html.

238 **cosponsored by Ifeoma Ozoma:** "California Companies Can No Longer Silence Work-ers in Victory for Tech Activists," *The Guardian*. Guardian News and Media, October 8, 2021. https://www.theguardian.com/technology/2021/oct/08/california-companies -can-no-longer-silence-workers-in-victory-for-tech-activists.

238 **"The purpose wasn't just":** Faith Karimi, "This Former Tech Worker Is Helping Change Laws for People Who Get Laid off," CNN, December 6, 2022. https://www .cnn.com/2022/12/06/business/ifeoma-ozoma-risk-takers-cec/index.html.

238 **Pinterest hired external counsel:** "Statement by the Board of Directors." Pinterest Newsroom, June 29, 2020. https://newsroom.pinterest.com/en/post/statement-by-the -board-of-directors.

238 **concluded that they:** Chauncey Alcorn, "Pinterest Hires Lawyers to Examine Its Work-place Culture after Accusations of Racism," CNN, June 29, 2020. https://www.cnn .com/2020/06/29/business/pinterest-lawyers-workplace-culture-racism.

239 **Her efforts culminated:** Bill Text - SB-331 Settlement and nondisparagement agree-ments. Accessed March 10, 2023. https://leginfo.legislature.ca.gov/faces/billNavClient .xhtml?bill_id=202120220SB331.

239 **"It is unconscionable":** Lauren Giella, "California Workers Can Call Out Boss's Bad Behavior without Losing Pay," *Newsweek*. Newsweek, October 8, 2021. https://www .newsweek.com/california-workers-can-call-out-bosss-bad-behavior-without-fear -losing-pay-benefits-1637167.

239 **"So much more work":** Based on conversations with Ifeoma Ozoma in March 2023.

240 **"Networks of complicity metastasized":** Peggy Cunningham et al., "Networks of Complic-ity: Social Networks and Sex Harassment," *Equality, Diversity and Inclusion: An Interna-tional Journal* 40, no. 4 (2019), pp. 392–409. https://doi.org/10.1108/edi-04-2019-0117.

240 **"Leaders must proactively work":** Peggy Cunningham and Minette Drumwright, "Banning Non-Disclosure Agreements Isn't Enough to Stop Unethical Workplace Leader Behaviour," The Conversation, July 18, 2022. https://theconversation.com /banning-non-disclosure-agreements-isnt-enough-to-stop-unethical-workplace-leader -behaviour-173574.

241 **A significant proportion:** "The Elephant in the Valley." The Elephant in the Valley. Accessed August 9, 2022. https://www.elephantinthevalley.com.

241 **speak candidly about her experience:** Ellen Pao, *Reset: My Fight for Inclusion and Lasting Change* (New York: Random House, 2017).

241 **Neither side commented:** Kurt Orzeck, "Ex-Facebook Employee Drops Suit Alleging Gender, Race Bias." Law360. Accessed September 9, 2022. https://www.law360.com /articles/712826/ex-facebook-employee-drops-suit-alleging-gender-race-bias.

242 **so few women employees:** Andrea Peterson, "The Network Effect at the Center of the Twitter Gender Discrimination Lawsuit," *Washington Post*, December 6, 2021. https:// www.washingtonpost.com/news/the-switch/wp/2015/03/23/the-network-effect-at-the -center-of-the-twitter-gender-discrimination-lawsuit.

242 **ultimately denied class action:** Joel Rosenblatt, Joel and Steve Stroth, "Former Twitter Engineer Loses Appeal of Rejected Group-Bias Law," *Bloomberg Law*, December 4, 2019. https://news.bloomberglaw.com/tech-and-telecom-law/former-twitter-engineer -loses-appeal-of-rejected-group-bias-law.

242 **The pace of major lawsuits:** "Uber Agrees to Settle California Discrimination Lawsuit for $10 Million," Reuters. Thomson Reuters, March 28, 2018. https://www.reuters.com /article/us-uber-lawsuit-idUSKBN1H40A7.

242 **Pinterest agreed to pay:** Erin Griffith, "Pinterest Settles Gender Discrimination Suit for $22.5 Million," *New York Times*, December 14, 2020. https://www.nytimes.com/2020 /12/14/technology/pinterest-gender-discrimination-lawsuit.html.

242 **consistently paying women less than men:** Nicholas Gordon, "Google to Pay $118m to Settle Lawsuit Alleging Gender Pay Bias," *Fortune*. Fortune, June 13, 2022. https:// fortune.com/2022/06/13/google-gender-class-action-lawsuit-hiring-levels-pay-equity -settlement.

242 **generated revenue of about 257 billion dollars:** "Alphabet Announces Fourth Quarter and Fiscal Year 2021 Results." Accessed September 23, 2022. https://abc.xyz/investor /static/pdf/2021Q4_alphabet_earnings_release.pdf?cache=d72fc76.

242 **The steep rise in the number:** Jessi Hempel, "The Pao Effect Is What Happens after Lean in | Backchannel." Wired. Conde Nast, September 20, 2017. https://www.wired .com/story/the-pao-effect-is-what-happens-after-lean-in.

243 **a vanishingly small minority:** "The Vile Experiences of Women in Tech," *The Economist*. The Economist Newspaper. Accessed September 9, 2022. https://www.economist .com/open-future/2019/05/03/the-vile-experiences-of-women-in-tech.

243 **"the countless times":** Liza Mundy, "Why Is Silicon Valley So Awful to Women?" *The Atlantic*, June 3, 2019. https://www.theatlantic.com/magazine/archive/2017/04/why -is-silicon-valley-so-awful-to-women/517788.

244 **being an early buyer of equity:** Jonathan Moules, "The Other Gender Gap: Equity and Equality in Silicon Valley," *Financial Times*. Financial Times, January 21, 2020. https:// www.ft.com/content/54734b3e-339e-11ea-a329-0bcf87a328f2.

244 **6 percent of all founder equity:** Josh Constine, "The Gap Table: Women Own Just 9% of Startup Equity," *TechCrunch*, September 18, 2018. https://techcrunch.com/2018/09 /18/the-gap-table/.

245 **received seven times more funding:** "Male and Female Entrepreneurs Get Asked Different Questions by VCs—and It Affects How Much Funding They Get," *Harvard Business Review*, June 27, 2017. https://hbr.org/2017/06/male-and-female-entrepreneurs -get-asked-different-questions-by-vcs-and-it-affects-how-much-funding-they-get.

245 **Despite that sizable jump:** "An Exceptional Year for Female Founders Still Means a Sliver of VC Funding," PitchBook. Accessed September 13, 2022. https://pitchbook .com/news/articles/female-founders-dashboard-2021-vc-funding-wrap-up.

Chapter 12: The American Fever Dream

249 **thousands of gender discrimination claims:** "Charge Statistics (Charges Filed with EEOC) FY 1997 through FY 2021." US EEOC. Accessed September 28, 2022. https:// www.eeoc.gov/statistics/charge-statistics-charges-filed-eeoc-fy-1997-through-fy-2021.

249 **lamented that the board opportunities:** Edith Cooper, "I Was Told I Have Career Advantages 'as a Black Woman.' Here's How I Replied," *New York Times*, November 2, 2021. https://www.nytimes.com/2021/11/02/opinion/culture/board-diversity-black-women .html.

250 **while sexual harassment:** Tracy Certo, "Lenore Blum Shocked the Community with Her Sudden Resignation from CMU. Here She Tells Us Why," NEXTpittsburgh, September 7, 2018. https://nextpittsburgh.com/features/lenore-blum-speaks-out-about -sexism-in-the-workplace.

250 **"The emotional tax":** "Emotional Tax and Work Teams: A View from 5 Countries," Catalyst, November 9, 2022. https://www.catalyst.org/reports/emotional-tax-teams.

251 **Nordell simulated ten years:** Jessica Nordell and Yaryna Serkez, "This Is How Everyday

Sexism Could Stop You from Getting That Promotion," *New York Times*, October 14, 2021. https://www.nytimes.com/interactive/2021/10/14/opinion/gender-bias.html.

252 **"The positive effects"**: Frank Dobbin and Alexandra Kalev, "Why Diversity Programs Fail," *Harvard Business Review*, March 29, 2023. https://hbr.org/2016/07/why-diversity -programs-fail.

254 **menopause symptoms significantly impact:** Effects of menopause are devastating for both women and employers according to new research from Lisa Health, October 17, 2022. https://www.prnewswire.com/news-releases/effects-of-menopause-are -devastating-for-both-women-and-employers-according-to-new-research-from-lisa -health-301649055.html.

255 **reason they abandon:** Mahalia Mayne, "One in 10 Women Have Quit Their Job Because of Menopause Symptoms, Survey Reveals," *People Management*, May 5, 2022. https:// www.peoplemanagement.co.uk/article/1754967/one-10-women-quit-job-menopause -symptoms-survey-reveals.

255 **"As a female CEO"**: Terry Weber, "Why Companies Need to Acknowledge Menopause in the Workplace." Accessed October 25, 2022. https://www.fastcompany.com /90792094/the-unspoken-reason-women-leave-the-workforce.

255 **One relatively small study:** Mindy S. Christianson et al., "Menopause Education: Needs Assessment of American Obstetrics and Gynecology Residents," *Menopause* 20, no. 11 (2013), pp. 1120–25. https://doi.org/10.1097/gme.0b013e31828ced7f.

255 **more than a third:** Amy L. Abel and Diane Lim, "Why Retaining Older Women in the Workforce Will Help the U.S. Economy." Knowledge at Wharton, June 6, 2018. https:// knowledge.wharton.upenn.edu/article/retaining-older-women-workforce-will-help-u-s -economy.

256 **the social stigma surrounding:** Isabel de Salis, "The Menopause: Dreaded, Derided and Seldom Discussed," The Conversation, October 18, 2017. https://theconversation .com/the-menopause-dreaded-derided-and-seldom-discussed-85281.

256 **"We've prayed about this"**: Julia Shapero, "Republicans, Anti-Abortion Groups Celebrate Supreme Court Overturning Roe v. Wade," Axios, June 24, 2022. https://www .axios.com/2022/06/24/republicans-celebrate-supreme-court-roe-wade.

257 **undermines the Supreme Court's legitimacy:** "Opinions." Supreme Court of the United States. Accessed September 28, 2022. https://www.supremecourt.gov/opinions /opinions.aspx.

257 **likely to increase for all women:** Stanford University, "Using Economics to Understand the Wide-Reaching Impacts of Overturning Roe v. Wade," *Stanford News*, July 18, 2022. https://news.stanford.edu/2022/07/18/using-economics-understand-wide-reaching -impacts-overturning-roe-v-wade.

258 **"15,000 dollars a year for an infant"**: Cody Mello-Klein, "Overturning Roe v. Wade Will Put Even More of an Economic Burden on Women, Northeastern Economist Says," News @ Northeastern, June 27, 2022. https://news.northeastern.edu/2022/06/27/roe -v-wade-economic-impact-women.

259 **In the first year alone:** "Supreme Court of the United States - Center for Reproductive Rights." Brief of Amici Curiae Economists in Support Of Respondents, September 20, 2021. https://reproductiverights.org/wp-content/uploads/2021/09/Economists -Amicus-Brief.pdf.

259 **ignited a pro-choice movement:** Rebecca Kelliher, "What the U.S. Can Learn from Ireland's Win on Abortion," *Slate* magazine, September 16, 2022. https://slate.com /news-and-politics/2022/09/ireland-abortion-lessons-for-america.html.

259 **many women have come forward:** Elizabeth Cohen and John Bonifield, "Texas Woman

Almost Dies Because She Couldn't Get an Abortion." CNN, November 17, 2022. https://www.cnn.com/2022/11/16/health/abortion-texas-sepsis/index.html.

259 **The root cause:** Alisha Haridasani Gupta, "Child Care in Crisis: Can Biden's Plan Save It?" *New York Times*, April 1, 2021. https://www.nytimes.com/2021/03/31/us/child-care -centers-crisis.html.

259 **The most obvious illustration:** Jack Rosenthal, "President Vetoes Child Care Plan as Irresponsible," *New York Times*, December 10, 1971. https://www.nytimes.com/1971 /12/10/archives/president-vetoes-child-care-plan-as-irresponsible-he-terms-bill.html.

260 **At the time of her writing:** Gupta, 2021.

261 **toddler childcare desert:** "Costly and Unavailable: America Lacks Sufficient Child Care Supply for Infants and Toddlers," Center for American Progress, August 4, 2020. https://www.americanprogress.org/article/costly-unavailable-america-lacks-sufficient -child-care-supply-infants-toddlers.

261 **One study in 2019:** "Sweden - Leavenetwork.org." Accessed October 27, 2022. https:// www.leavenetwork.org/fileadmin/user_upload/k_leavenetwork/annual_reviews/2019 /Sweden_2019_0824.pdf.

261 **a leader among advanced economies:** OECD. LFS by sex and age - indicators. Accessed October 27, 2022. https://stats.oecd.org/Index.aspx?DataSetCode=lfs_sexage_i_r.

261 **because of the systems:** "Employed and Unemployed Full- and Part-Time Workers by Age, Sex, Race, and Hispanic or Latino Ethnicity." U.S. Bureau of Labor Statistics. U.S. Bureau of Labor Statistics, January 20, 2022. https://www.bls.gov/cps/cpsaat08 .htm.

262 **doesn't guarantee maternity leave:** Kevin Shafer, "Why Canadian Dads Are More Involved in Raising Their Kids than American Fathers," The Conversation, September 15, 2022. https://theconversation.com/why-canadian-dads-are-more-involved-in -raising-their-kids-than-american-fathers-162977.

262 **"could reverse the trend":** "FRBSF Economic Letter - Federal Reserve Bank of San Francisco." Why Aren't U.S. Workers Working? November 13, 2018. https://www.frbsf .org/economic-research/wp-content/uploads/sites/4/el2018-24.pdf.

263 **inequality in unpaid care work:** Gaëlle Ferrant, Luca Maria Pesando, and Keiko Nowacka, "Unpaid Care Work: The Missing Link in the Analysis of Gender Gaps in Labour Outcomes," OECD, December 2014. https://www.oecd.org/dev/development -gender/Unpaid_care_work.pdf.

263 **At minimum wage levels:** Ayelet Sheffey, "Unpaid Care-Economy Work Amounts to $11 Trillion per Year, Bofa Estimates," *Business Insider*, May 12, 2021. https:// www.businessinsider.com/care-economy-unpaid-work-minimum-wage-jobs-labor -infrastructure-bofa-2021-5.

264 **"one crisis away from":** Devi Jags, "A Peek Inside Her Agenda: Eve Rodsky," Her Agenda, May 26, 2022. https://heragenda.com/p/eve-rodsky.

265 **Evidence of the disparity:** Asaf Levanon, Paula England, and Paul Allison, "Occupational Feminization and Pay: Assessing Causal Dynamics Using 1950–2000 U.S. Census Data." *Social Forces* 88, no. 2 (2009), pp. 865–91. https://doi.org/10.1353/sof .0.0264.

265 **As a result of:** Based on an interview with Eve Rodsky conducted in November 2022.

Chapter 13: Hope, or Something Like It

266 **On Sunday, May 31:** Ej Dickson, "How Nothing and Everything Has Changed in the 10 Years since George Tiller's Murder," *Rolling Stone*, May 31, 2019. https://www

.rollingstone.com/culture/culture-features/george-tiller-death-abortion-10-year
-anniversary-842786.

266  **The man who fired:** "Scott Roeder's Hard 50 Sentence Overturned," KMUW, October 27, 2014. https://www.kmuw.org/crime-and-courts/2014-10-24/scott-roeders-hard
-50-sentence-overturned.

266  **Tiller had been in the crosshairs:** Jennifer Donnally, "The Untold History Behind the 1991 Summer of Mercy," Kansas Historical Society, Winter 2016. https://www.kshs
.org/p/kansas-history-winter-2016-2017/19900.

267  **As reporters for the:** Judy Thomas and Katie Bernard, "'Summer of Mercy': How Protests Changed Abortion Rights and Politics in Kansas Forever," AOL, July 28, 2022. https://www.aol.com/summer-mercy-protests-changed-abortion-100000985.html.

267  **By the mid-1990s:** Ibid.

267  **"We were in a social protest":** Ibid.

268  **"Ashley All had other plans":** Based on conversations with Ashley All in May and June 2023.

268  **The task at hand:** Ibid.

269  **"This vote makes clear":** "Statement by President Joe Biden on Defeat of Kansas Ballot Measure Threatening Women's Right to Abortion," The White House, August 3, 2022. https://www.whitehouse.gov/briefing-room/statements-releases/2022/08/02
/statement-by-president-joe-biden-on-defeat-of-kansas-ballot-measure-threatening
-womens-right-to-abortion.

269  **"huge and decisive":** Dylan Lysen, Laura Ziegler, and Blaise Mesa, "Voters in Kansas Decide to Keep Abortion Legal in the State, Rejecting an Amendment." NPR, August 3, 2022. https://www.npr.org/sections/2022-live-primary-election-race-results/2022/08
/02/1115317596/kansas-voters-abortion-legal-reject-constitutional-amendment

270  **"They might move away":** EJ Dickson, 2019.

270  **In May 2023:** Laurie McGinley and Rachel Roubein, "FDA Advisers Back Making Birth Control Pill Available over the Counter," *Washington Post*, May 10, 2023. https://www
.washingtonpost.com/health/2023/05/10/birth-control-pill-over-the-counter-fda.

271  **Other commentators noted that:** Pam Belluck, "F.D.A. Advisers Say Benefits of Over-the-Counter Birth Control Pill Outweigh Risks," *New York Times*, May 10, 2023. https://www.nytimes.com/2023/05/10/health/fda-otc-birth-control-pill.html.

271  **America has been a laggard:** "OTC Access World Map," Free The Pill. Accessed May 23, 2023. https://freethepill.org/otc-access-world-map.

271  **One 2011 survey:** Daniel Grossman et al., "Interest in Over-the-Counter Access to Oral Contraceptives among Women in the United States," Contraception, October 2013. https://www.ncbi.nlm.nih.gov/pmc/articles/PMC3769514

272  **"Abortion bans are affecting":** William Lutz, "For the Class of 2023 in the Northeast, State Abortion Laws Are a Key Factor in College Decisions, According to a New Institute forWomen's Policy Research (IWPR) Poll," IWPR, May 10, 2023. https://iwpr.org
/iwpr-issues/reproductive-health/for-the-class-of-2023-in-the-northeast-state-abortion
-laws-are-a-key-factor-in-college-decisions-according-to-a-new-institute-for-womens
-policy-research-iwpr-poll.

272  **Previous research done:** Jeff Hayes and Elyse Shaw, "As States Eye Texas-Style Abortion Bans, Economic Costs to Bottom Line and Women Are High," IWPR, September 13, 2021. https://iwpr.org/iwpr-issues/reproductive-health/costs-of-restrictions-state-fact
-sheets.

272  **a survey of more than 14,000 individuals:** Josie Cox, "The Trust Crisis Facing Women

Leaders," BBC *Worklife*, November 30, 2022. https://www.bbc.com/worklife/article/20221129-the-trust-crisis-facing-women-leaders.

273 **more women than ever before are now:** Janakee Chavda, "In a Growing Share of U.S. Marriages, Husbands and Wives Earn about the Same," Pew Research Center's Social & Demographic Trends Project, Pew Research Center, April 14, 2023. https://www.pewresearch.org/social-trends/2023/04/13/in-a-growing-share-of-u-s-marriages-husbands-and-wives-earn-about-the-same.

274 **inherent distrust of women:** Mary Ann Sieghart, *The Authority Gap* (London: Penguin Random House UK, 2021), p. 51.

274 **"women are belittled":** Stephanie Merritt, "*The Authority Gap* by Mary Ann Sieghart Review—Mocked, Patronised and Still Paid Less than Men," *Guardian*, Guardian News and Media, July 5, 2021. https://www.theguardian.com/books/2021/jul/05/the-authority-gap-by-mary-ann-sieghart-review-why-women-are-still-taken-less-seriously-than-men-and-what-we-can-do-about-it.

274 **discredits the popular narrative:** Benjamin Artz et al., "Do Women Ask?" *Industrial Relations: A Journal of Economy and Society* 57, no. 4 (2018), pp. 611–36. https://doi.org/10.1111/irel.12214.

275 **Stanford neuroscientist Ben Barres:** Tara Bahrampour, "Crossing the Divide," *Washington Post*, July 20, 2018. https://www.washingtonpost.com/news/local/wp/2018/07/20/feature/crossing-the-divide-do-men-really-have-it-easier-these-transgender-guys-found-the-truth-was-more-complex.

276 **The settlement deal:** Goldman Gender Case, May 8, 2023. https://goldmangendercase.com/press-release-may-8-2023.

276 **But outside commentators:** Michael J. De La Merced, "Goldman Sachs to Pay $215 Million to Settle Gender Bias Suit," *New York Times*, May 9, 2023. https://www.nytimes.com/2023/05/09/business/dealbook/goldman-sachs-discrimination-lawsuit.html.

277 **previous year pocketed:** Lananh Nguyen, "Goldman Sachs Slashes CEO Solomon's Pay 29% to $25 Million," Reuters, January 27, 2023. https://www.reuters.com/business/finance/goldman-sachs-slashes-ceo-david-solomons-pay-by-29-25-million-2023-01-27.

277 **Just one day after:** Shayna Jacobs et al.,"Jury in Civil Trial Finds Trump Sexually Abused, Defamed E. Jean Carroll," Washington Post, May 10, 2023. https://www.washingtonpost.com/national-security/2023/05/09/e-jean-carroll-trump-jury.

278 **Ketanji Brown Jackson replaced:** Rose Horowitch, "Ketanji Brown Jackson Sworn in as First Black Woman on U.S. Supreme Court," Reuters, June 30, 2022. https://www.reuters.com/world/us/ketanji-brown-jackson-be-sworn-first-black-woman-us-supreme-court-2022-06-30.

278 **second woman ever:** "Claudine Gay Makes History as First Black Harvard President," *The Harvard Crimson*, December 16, 2022. https://www.thecrimson.com/article/2022/12/16/claudine-gay-makes-historic-first-again.

279 **more than 10 percent:** Emma Hinchliffe, "Women Run More than 10% of Fortune 500 Companies for the First Time," *Fortune*, January 12, 2023. https://fortune.com/2023/01/12/fortune-500-companies-ceos-women-10-percent.

279 **expanding employees' rights:** H.R.2617 - 117th Congress (2021–2022), p. Consolidated Appropriations Act . . . Accessed June 6, 2023. https://www.congress.gov/bill/117th-congress/house-bill/2617.

279 **Congress had already included:** Alisha Haridasani Gupta and Catherine Pearson, "A New Breast Pumping Law Has Gone into Effect. Here's What It Means," *New York*

*Times*, May 3, 2023. https://www.nytimes.com/2023/05/03/well/family/pump-act
-breastfeeding.html.

280   **in the gaming industry:** Keza MacDonald, "Is the Video Games Industry Finally Reck-
oning with Sexism?" *The Guardian*, July 22, 2020. https://www.theguardian.com
/games/2020/jul/22/is-the-video-games-industry-finally-reckoning-with-sexism.

280   **to make progress:** Amy Diehl and Leanne M. Dzubinski, *Glass Walls: Shattering the
Six Gender Bias Barriers Still Holding Women Back at Work* (Lanham, MD: Rowman &
Littlefield, 2023), p. 6.

## Epilogue

285   **"really, really smart":** Lin Bian et al., "Gender Stereotypes about Intellectual Ability Emerge Early and Influence Children's Interests," *Science* 355, no. 6323 (2017),
pp. 389–91. https://doi.org/10.1126/science.aah6524.

285   **never underestimate our power:** Hillary Paul Halpern and Maureen Perry-Jenkins,
"Parents' Gender Ideology and Gendered Behavior as Predictors of Children's Gender-
Role Attitudes: A Longitudinal Exploration." *Sex Roles* 74, no. 11–12 (2015), pp. 527–42.
https://doi.org/10.1007/s11199-015-0539-0.